# The Expositor's Bible
## The Book of Daniel
### By Frederic William Farrar, D.D., F.R.S.
#### Edited by Anthony Uyl

Woodstock, Ontario, 2017

*The Expositor's Bible: The Book of Daniel*
# The Expositor's Bible: The Book of Daniel
**By Frederic William Farrar, D.D., F.R.S. (1831-1903)**
Late Felllow of Trinity College, Cambridge; Archdeacon of Westminster
Originally Edited by Sir William Robertson Nicoll (1851-1923)
**This edition edited by Anthony Uyl**

Originally Printed in 1895
London, Hodder and Stoughton, 27 Paternoster Row
MDCCCXCV

The text of The Expositor's Bible: The Book of Daniel is all in the Public Domain. This edition is published by Devoted Publishing a division of 2165467 Ontario Inc.

**What kind of philosophies do you have?
Let us know!**

Contact us at: devotedpub@hotmail.com
Visit our shop on Facebook: @DevotedPublishing
**Published in Woodstock, Ontario, Canada 2017.**

For bulk educational rates, please contact us at the above email address.

ISBN: 978-1-77356-021-2

# Table of Contents

AUTHORITIES CONSULTED ..................................................................................... 5
    Footnote: ............................................................................................................................ 7
PART I - INTRODUCTION ............................................................................................. 8
    CHAPTER I - THE HISTORIC EXISTENCE OF THE PROPHET DANIEL ................. 8
        Footnotes: ........................................................................................................................ 10
    CHAPTER II - GENERAL SURVEY OF THE BOOK ..................................................... 12
        Footnotes: ........................................................................................................................ 18
    CHAPTER III - PECULIARITIES OF THE HISTORIC SECTION ................................ 21
        Footnotes: ........................................................................................................................ 27
    CHAPTER IV - GENERAL STRUCTURE OF THE BOOK ............................................ 29
        Footnotes: ........................................................................................................................ 30
    CHAPTER V - THE THEOLOGY OF THE BOOK OF DANIEL ................................... 31
        Footnotes: ........................................................................................................................ 31
    CHAPTER VI - PECULIARITIES OF THE APOCALYPTIC AND PROPHETIC SECTION OF THE BOOK ............................................................................................. 33
        Footnotes: ........................................................................................................................ 35
    CHAPTER VII - INTERNAL EVIDENCE ...................................................................... 36
        Footnotes: ........................................................................................................................ 38
    CHAPTER VIII - EVIDENCE IN FAVOUR OF THE GENUINENESS UNCERTAIN AND INADEQUATE .................................................................................... 40
        Footnotes: ........................................................................................................................ 42
    CHAPTER IX - EXTERNAL EVIDENCE AND RECEPTION INTO THE CANON ..... 44
        Footnotes: ........................................................................................................................ 47
    CHAPTER X - SUMMARY AND CONCLUSION ......................................................... 49
        Footnotes: ........................................................................................................................ 50
PART II - COMMENTARY ON THE HISTORIC SECTION .................................... 52
    CHAPTER I - THE PRELUDE ........................................................................................ 52
        Footnotes: ........................................................................................................................ 56
    CHAPTER II - THE DREAM-IMAGE OF RUINED EMPIRES ..................................... 59
        Footnotes: ........................................................................................................................ 65
    CHAPTER III - THE IDOL OF GOLD, AND THE FAITHFUL THREE ....................... 68
        Footnotes: ........................................................................................................................ 72
    CHAPTER IV - THE BABYLONIAN CEDAR, AND THE STRICKEN DESPOT ........ 75
        Footnotes: ........................................................................................................................ 80
    CHAPTER V - THE FIERY INSCRIPTION ................................................................... 82
        Footnotes: ........................................................................................................................ 85
    CHAPTER VI - STOPPING THE MOUTHS OF LIONS ................................................ 88
        Footnotes: ........................................................................................................................ 91
PART III - THE PROPHETIC SECTION OF THE BOOK ........................................ 93
    CHAPTER I - VISION OF THE FOUR WILD BEASTS ............................................... 93

Footnotes: ...................................................................................................................................97
CHAPTER II - THE RAM AND THE HE-GOAT ....................................................................100
   Footnotes: .................................................................................................................................103
CHAPTER III - THE SEVENTY WEEKS .................................................................................106
   Footnotes: .................................................................................................................................111
CHAPTER IV - INTRODUCTION TO THE CONCLUDING VISION ....................................115
   Footnotes: .................................................................................................................................116
CHAPTER V - AN ENIGMATIC PROPHECY PASSING INTO DETAILS OF THE REIGN OF ANTIOCHUS EPIPHANES ..........................................................................................................118
   Footnotes: .................................................................................................................................123
CHAPTER VI - THE EPILOGUE ...............................................................................................125
   Footnotes: .................................................................................................................................128

# AUTHORITIES CONSULTED

## COMMENTARIES AND TREATISES

The chief Rabbinic Commentaries were those of Rashi ( 1105); Abn Ezra ( 1167); Kimchi ( 1240); Abrabanel ( 1507). [1]

The chief Patristic Commentary is that by St. Jerome. Fragments are preserved of other Commentaries by Origen, Hippolytus, Ephræm Syrus, Julius Africanus, Theodoret, Athanasius, Basil, Eusebius, Polychronius, etc. (Mai, Script. Vet. Nov. Coll., i.).

The Scholastic Commentary attributed to St. Thomas Aquinas is spurious.

The chief Commentaries of the Reformation period are those by:--

Luther, Auslegung d. Proph. Dan., 1530-46 (Opp. Germ., vi., ed. Walch.)

OEcolampadius, In Dan. libri duo. Basle, 1530.

Melancthon, Comm. in Dan. Wittenburg, 1543.

Calvin, Prælect. in Dan. Geneva, 1563.

Modern Commentaries are numerous; among them we may mention those by:--

Newton, Observations upon the Prophecies. London, 1733.

Bertholdt, Daniel. Erlangen, 1806-8.

Rosenmüller, Scholia. 1832.

Hävernick. 1832 and 1838.

Hengstenberg. 1831.

There are Commentaries by Von Lengerke, 1835; Maurer, 1838; Hitzig, 1850; Ewald, 1867; Kliefoth, 1868; Keil, 1869; Kranichfeld, 1868; Kamphausen, 1868; Meinhold (Kurzgefasster Kommentar), 1889; Auberlen, 1857; Archdeacon Rose and Prof. J. M. Fuller (Speaker's Commentary), 1876; Rev. H. J. Deane (Bishop Ellicott's Commentary), 1884; Zöckler (Lange's Bibelwerk), 1889; A. A. Bevan (Cambridge), 1893; Meinhold, Beiträge, 1888.

The latest Commentary which has appeared is that by Hauptpastor Behrmann, in the Handkommentar z. Alten Testament. Göttingen, 1894.

Discussions in the various Introductions (Einleitungen, etc.) by Bleek, De Wette, Keil, Stähelin, Reuss, Cornely, Dr. S. Davidson, Kleinert, Cornill, König, etc.

## LIVES OF DANIEL

Pseudo-Epiphanius, Opera, ii. 243.

H. J. Deane, Daniel (Men of the Bible). 1892.

## THERE ARE ARTICLES ON DANIEL IN

Winer's Realwörterbuch, Second Edition.

Delitzsch, in Herzog's Real-Encyclopädie.

Graf, in Schenkel's Bibel-Lexicon, i. 564.

Bishop Westcott, in Dr. W. Smith's Bible Dictionary, New Edition. 1893.

Hamburger, Real-Encyclopädie, ii., s.v. "Geheimlehre," p. 265; s.vv. "Daniel," pp. 223-225; and Heiliges Schriftthum.

## TREATISES

Russel Martineau, Theological Review. 1865.

Prof. Margoliouth, The Expositor. April 1890.

Prof. J. M. Fuller, The Expositor, Third Series, vols. i., ii.

T. K. Cheyne, Encyclopædia Britannica, vi. 803.

Prof. Sayce, The Higher Criticism and the Monuments. 1894.

Prof. S. R. Driver, Introduction to the Literature of the Old Testament, pp. 458-483. 1891.

Prof. S. Leathes, in Book by Book, pp. 241-251.

C. von Orelli, Alttestamentliche Weissagung, p. 454. Wien, 1882.

Meinhold, Die Geschichtlichen Hagiographen (Strack and Zöckler, Kurzgefasster Kommentar, 1889).
Meinhold, Erklärung des Buches Daniels. 1889.

## TREATISES OR DISCUSSIONS BY

Dr. Pusey, Daniel the Prophet. 1864.
T. R. Birks, The Later Visions of Daniel. 1846.
Ellicott, Horæ Apocalypticæ. 1844.
Tregelles, Remarks on the Prophetic Visions of Daniel. 1852.
Hilgenfeld, Die Propheten Ezra u. Daniel. 1863.
Baxmann, Stud. u. Krit., iii. 489 ff. 1863.
Desprez, Daniel. 1865.
Hofmann, Weissagung und Erfüllung, i. 276-316.
Kuenen, Prophets and Prophecy in Israel, E. Tr. 1877.
Ewald, Die Propheten des Alten Bundes, iii. 298. 1868.
Hilgenfeld, Die jüdische Apokalyptic. 1857.
Lenormant, La Divination chez les Chaldeans. 1875.
Fabre d'Envieu, Le livre du Prophète Daniel. 1888.
Hebbelyuck, De auctoritate libr. Danielis. 1887.
Köhler, Bibl. Geschichte. 1893.

## INSCRIPTIONS AND MONUMENTS

Babylonian, Persian, and Median inscriptions bearing on the Book of Daniel are given by:--
Schrader, Keilinschriften und d. A. T., E. Tr., 1885-88; and in Records of the Past. See too Corpus Inscriptionum Semiticarum.
Sayce, The Higher Criticism, pp. 497-537.
These inscriptions have been referred to also by Cornill, Nestle, Nöldeke, Lagarde, etc.

## HISTORIES AND OTHER BOOKS

Sketches and fragments of many ancient historians:--
Josephus, Antiquitates Judaicæ, ll. x., xi., xii.
The Books of Maccabees.
Prideaux, Connection of the Old and New Testaments, ed. Oxford. 1828.
Ewald, Gesch. des Volkes Israel. 1843-50.
Grätz, Gesch. der Juden, Second Edition. 1863.
Jost, Gesch. d. Judenthums und seinen Sekten, i. 90-116. Leipzig, 1857.
Herzfeld, Gesch. des Volkes Israel, ii. 416. 1863.
Van Oort, Bible for Young People, E. Tr. 1877.
Kittel, Gesch. d. Hebräer, ii. 1892.
Schürer, Gesch. d. jüdischen Volkes. Leipzig, 1890.
Jahn, Hebrew Commonwealth, E. Tr. 1828.
Droysen, Gesch. d. Hellenismus, ii. 211.
E. Meyer, Gesch. d. Alterthums, i.

## SPECIAL TREATISES

Delitzsch, Messianische Weissagangen. Leipzig, 1890.
Riehm, Die Messianische Weissagung. Gotha, 1875.
Knabenbauer, Comment in Daniel. prophet., Lament., et Baruch. 1891.
Kuenen, Religion of Israel, E. Tr. 1874.
Bludau, De Alex. interpe. Danielis indole. 1891.
Nöldeke, D. Alttest. Literatur. 1868.
Fraidl, Exegese d. 70 Wochen Daniels. 1883.
Menken, Die Monarchienbild. 1887.
Kamphausen, Das Buch Daniel in die neuere Geschichtsforschung. Leipzig, 1893.
Lennep, De Zeventig Jaarweken van Daniel. Utrecht, 1888.
Dr. M. Joël, Notizen zum Buche Daniel. Breslau, 1873.
Derenbourg, Les Mots grecs dans le Livre biblique de Daniel. Mélanges Graux, 1888.
Cornill, Die Siebzig Jahrwochen Daniels. 1889.
Wolf, Die Siebzig Wochen Daniels. 1859.
Sanday, Inspiration (Bampton Lectures). 1894.

Sayce, Hibbert Lectures. 1887.
Roszmann, Die Makkabeische Erhebung.
J. F. Hoffmann, Antiochus IV. (Epiphanes). 1873.
Speaker's Commentary on Tobit, 1, 2 Maccabees, etc. 1888.

## *Footnote:*

1. The Commentary which passes as that of Saadia the Gaon is said to be spurious. His genuine Commentary only exists in manuscript.

# PART I - INTRODUCTION

*Ego men oun peri touton hos heuron kai anegnon, houtos egrapsa; ei de tis allos doxazein boulesetai peri auton anenkleton echeto ten eterognomosunen.*--Josephus, Antt., X. ii. 7.

## CHAPTER I - THE HISTORIC EXISTENCE OF THE PROPHET DANIEL

*"Trothe is the hiest thinge a man may kepe."*--Chaucer.

We propose in the following pages to examine the Book of the Prophet Daniel by the same general methods which have been adopted in other volumes of the Expositor's Bible. It may well happen that the conclusions adopted as regards its origin and its place in the Sacred Volume will not command the assent of all our readers. On the other hand, we may feel a reasonable confidence that, even if some are unable to accept the views at which we have arrived, and which we have here endeavoured to present with fairness, they will still read them with interest, as opinions which have been calmly and conscientiously formed, and to which the writer has been led by strong conviction.

All Christians will acknowledge the sacred and imperious duty of sacrificing every other consideration to the unbiassed acceptance of that which we regard as truth. Further than this our readers will find much to elucidate the Book of Daniel chapter by chapter, apart from any questions which affect its authorship or age.

But I should like to say on the threshold that, though I am compelled to regard the Book of Daniel as a work which, in its present form, first saw the light in the days of Antiochus Epiphanes, and though I believe that its six magnificent opening chapters were never meant to be regarded in any other light than that of moral and religious Haggadoth, yet no words of mine can exaggerate the value which I attach to this part of our Canonical Scriptures. The Book, as we shall see, has exercised a powerful influence over Christian conduct and Christian thought. Its right to a place in the Canon is undisputed and indisputable, and there is scarcely a single book of the Old Testament which can be made more richly "profitable for teaching, for reproof, for correction, for instruction in righteousness, that the man of God may be complete, completely furnished unto every good work." Such religious lessons are eminently suitable for the aims of the Expositor's Bible. They are not in the slightest degree impaired by those results of archæological discovery and "criticism" which are now almost universally accepted by the scholars of the Continent, and by many of our chief English critics. Finally unfavourable to the authenticity, they are yet in no way derogatory to the preciousness of this Old Testament Apocalypse.

\*\*\*

The first question which we must consider is, "What is known about the Prophet Daniel?"

I. If we accept as historical the particulars narrated of him in this Book, it is clear that few Jews have ever risen to so splendid an eminence. Under four powerful kings and conquerors, of three different nationalities and dynasties, he held a position of high authority among the haughtiest aristocracies of the ancient world. At a very early age he was not only a satrap, but the Prince and Prime Minister over all the satraps in Babylonia and Persia; not only a Magian, but the Head Magian, and Chief Governor over all the wise men of Babylon. Not even Joseph, as the chief ruler over all the house of Pharaoh, had anything like the extensive sway exercised by the Daniel of this Book. He was placed by Nebuchadrezzar "over the whole province of Babylon"; [2] under Darius he was President of the Board of Three to "whom all the satraps" sent their accounts; [3] and he was continued in office and prosperity under Cyrus the Persian. [4]

II. It is natural, then, that we should turn to the monuments and inscriptions of the Babylonian, Persian, and Median Empires to see if any mention can be found of so prominent a ruler. But hitherto neither has his name been discovered, nor the faintest trace of his existence.

III. If we next search other non-Biblical sources of information, we find much respecting him in the Apocrypha--"The Song of the Three Children," "The Story of Susanna," and "Bel and the Dragon." But these additions to the Canonical Books are avowedly valueless for any historic purpose. They are romances, in which the vehicle of fiction is used, in a manner which at all times was popular in Jewish literature, to teach lessons of faith and conduct by the example of eminent sages or saints. [5] The few other fictitious fragments preserved by Fabricius have not the smallest importance. [6] Josephus, beyond mentioning that Daniel and his three companions were of the family of King Zedekiah, [7] adds nothing appreciable to our information. He narrates the story of the Book, and in doing so adopts a somewhat apologetic tone, as though he specially declined to vouch for its historic exactness. For he says: "Let no one blame me for writing down everything of this nature, as I find it in our ancient books: for as to that matter, I have plainly assured those that think me defective in any such point, or complain of my management, and have told them, in the beginning of this history, that I intended to do no more than to translate the Hebrew books into the Greek language, and promised them to explain these facts, without adding anything to them of my own, or taking anything away from them." [8]

IV. In the Talmud, again, we find nothing historical. Daniel is always mentioned as a champion against idolatry, and his wisdom is so highly esteemed, that, "if all the wise men of the heathen," we are told, "were on one side, and Daniel on the other, Daniel would still prevail." [9] He is spoken of as an example of God's protection of the innocent, and his three daily prayers are taken as our rule of life. [10] To him are applied the verses of Lam. iii. 55-57: "I called upon Thy name, O Lord, out of the lowest pit.... Thou drewest near in the day that I called: Thou saidst, Fear not. O Lord, Thou hast pleaded the causes of my soul; Thou hast redeemed my life." We are assured that he was of Davidic descent; obtained permission for the return of the exiles; survived till the rebuilding of the Temple; lived to a great age, and finally died in Palestine. [11] Rav even went so far as to say, "If there be any like the Messiah among the living, it is our Rabbi the Holy: if among the dead, it is Daniel." [12] In the Avoth of Rabbi Nathan it is stated that Daniel exercised himself in benevolence by endowing brides, following funerals, and giving alms. One of the Apocryphal legends respecting him has been widely spread. It tells us that, when he was a second time cast into the den of lions under Cyrus, and was fasting from lack of food, the Prophet Habakkuk was taken by a hair of his head and carried by the angel of the Lord to Babylon, to give to Daniel the dinner which he had prepared for his reapers. [13] It is with reference to this Haggada that in the catacombs Daniel is represented in the lions' den standing naked between two lions--an emblem of the soul between sin and death--and that a youth with a pot of food is by his side.

There is a Persian apocalypse of Daniel translated by Merx (Archiv, i. 387), and there are a few worthless Mohammedan legends about him which are given in D'Herbelot's Bibliothèque orientale. They only serve to show how widely extended was the reputation which became the nucleus of strange and miraculous stories. As in the case of Pythagoras and Empedocles, they indicate the deep reverence which the ideal of his character inspired. They are as the fantastic clouds which gather about the loftiest mountain peaks. In later days he seems to have been comparatively forgotten. [14]

These references would not, however, suffice to prove Daniel's historical existence. They might merely result from the literal acceptance of the story narrated in the Book. From the name "Daniel," which is by no means a common one, and means "Judge of God," nothing can be learnt. It is only found in three other instances. [15]

Turning to the Old Testament itself, we have reason for surprise both in its allusions and its silences. One only of the sacred writers refers to Daniel, and that is Ezekiel. In one passage (xxviii. 3) the Prince of Tyrus is apostrophised in the words, "Behold, thou art wiser than Daniel; there is no secret that they can hide from thee." In the other (xiv. 14, 20) the word of the Lord declares to the guilty city, that "though these three men, Noah, Daniel, and Job, were in it, they should deliver but their own souls by their righteousness"; "they shall deliver neither son nor daughter." [16]

The last words may be regarded as a general allusion, and therefore we may pass over the circumstance that Daniel--who was undoubtedly a eunuch in the palace of Babylon, and who is often pointed to as a fulfilment of the stern prophecy of Isaiah to Hezekiah [17] --could never have had either son or daughter.

But in other respects the allusion is surprising.

i. It was very unusual among the Jews to elevate their contemporaries to such a height of exaltation, and it is indeed startling that Ezekiel should thus place his youthful contemporary on such a pinnacle as to unite his name to those of Noah the antediluvian patriarch and the mysterious man of Uz.

ii. We might, with Theodoret, Jerome, and Kimchi, account for the mention of Daniel's name at all in this connection by the peculiar circumstances of his life; [18] but there is little probability in the suggestions of bewildered commentators as to the reason why his name should be placed between those of Noah and Job. It is difficult, with Hävernick, to recognise any climax in the order; [19] nor can it be regarded as quite satisfactory to say, with Delitzsch, that the collocation is due to the fact that "as Noah was a righteous man of the old world, and Job of the ideal world, Daniel represented immediately the contemporaneous world." [20] If Job was a purely ideal instance of exemplary goodness, why may not Daniel have been the same?

To some critics the allusion has appeared so strange that they have referred it to an imaginary Daniel who had lived at the Court of Nineveh during the Assyrian exile;[21] or to some mythic hero who belonged to ancient days--perhaps, like Melchizedek, a contemporary of the ruin of the cities of the Plain.[22] Ewald tries to urge something for the former conjecture; yet neither for it nor for the latter is there any tittle of real evidence.[23] This, however, would not be decisive against the hypothesis, since in 1 Kings iv. 31 we have references to men of pre-eminent wisdom respecting whom no breath of tradition has come down to us.[24]

iii. But if we accept the Book of Daniel as literal history, the allusion of Ezekiel becomes still more difficult to explain; for Daniel must have been not only a contemporary of the prophet of the Exile, but a very youthful one. We are told--a difficulty to which we shall subsequently allude--that Daniel was taken captive in the third year of Jehoiakim (Dan. i. 1), about the year b.c. 606. Ignatius says that he was twelve years old when he foiled the elders; and the narrative shows that he could not have been much older when taken captive.[25] If Ezekiel's prophecy was uttered b.c. 584, Daniel at that time could only have been twenty-two: if it was uttered as late as b.c. 572,[26] Daniel would still have been only thirty-four, and therefore little more than a youth in Jewish eyes. It is undoubtedly surprising that among Orientals, who regard age as the chief passport to wisdom, a living youth should be thus canonised between the Patriarch of the Deluge and the Prince of Uz.

iv. Admitting that this pinnacle of eminence may have been due to the peculiar splendour of Daniel's career, it becomes the less easy to account for the total silence respecting him in the other books of the Old Testament--in the Prophets who were contemporaneous with the Exile and its close, like Haggai, Zechariah, and Malachi; and in the Books of Ezra and Nehemiah, which give us the details of the Return. No post-exilic prophets seem to know anything of the Book of Daniel.[27] Their expectations of Israel's future are very different from his.[28] The silence of Ezra is specially astonishing. It has often been conjectured that it was Daniel who showed to Cyrus the prophecies of Isaiah.[29] Certainly it is stated that he held the very highest position in the Court of the Persian King; yet neither does Ezra mention his existence, nor does Nehemiah--himself a high functionary in the Court of Artaxerxes--refer to his illustrious predecessor. Daniel outlived the first return of the exiles under Zerubbabel, and he did not avail himself of this opportunity to revisit the land and desolate sanctuary of his fathers which he loved so well.[30] We might have assumed that patriotism so burning as his would not have preferred to stay at Babylon, or at Shushan, when the priests and princes of his people were returning to the Holy City. Others of great age faced the perils of the Restoration; and if he stayed behind to be of greater use to his countrymen, we cannot account for the fact that he is not distantly alluded to in the record which tells how "the chief of the fathers, with all those whose spirit God had raised, rose up to go to build the House of the Lord which is in Jerusalem."[31] That the difficulty was felt is shown by the Mohammedan legend that Daniel did return with Ezra,[32] and that he received the office of Governor of Syria, from which country he went back to Susa, where his tomb is still yearly visited by crowds of adoring pilgrims.

v. If we turn to the New Testament, the name of Daniel only occurs in the reference to "the abomination of desolation, spoken of by Daniel the prophet."[33] The Book of Revelation does not name him, but is profoundly influenced by the Book of Daniel both in its form and in the symbols which it adopts.[34]

vi. In the Apocrypha Daniel is passed over in complete silence among the lists of Hebrew heroes enumerated by Jesus the son of Sirach. We are even told that "neither was there a man born like unto Joseph, a leader of his brethren, a stay of the people" (Ecclus. xlix. 15). This is the more singular because not only are the achievements of Daniel under four heathen potentates greater than those of Joseph under one Pharaoh, but also several of the stories of Daniel at once remind us of the story of Joseph, and even appear to have been written with silent reference to the youthful Hebrew and his fortunes as an Egyptian slave who was elevated to be governor of the land of his exile.

## Footnotes:

2. Dan. ii. 48.

3. Dan. v. 29, vi. 2.

4. Dan. vi. 28. There is a Daniel of the sons of Ithamar in Ezra viii. 2, and among those who sealed the covenant in Neh. x. 6.

5. For a full account of the Agada (also called Agadtha and Haggada), I must refer the reader to Hamburger's Real-Encyklopädie für Bibel und Talmud, ii. 19-27, 921-934. The first two forms of the words are Aramaic; the third was a Hebrew form in use among the Jews in Babylonia. The word is derived from ngd, "to say" or "explain." Halacha was the rule of religious praxis, a sort of Directorium Judaicum: Haggada was the result of free religious reflection. See further Strack, Einl. in den Thalmud, iv. 122.

6. Fabricius, Cod. Pseudepigr. Vet. Test., i. 1124.

7. Jos., Antt., X. xi. 7. But Pseudo-Epiphanius (De Vit. Dan., x.) says: Gegone ton exochon tes basilikes huperesias. So too the Midrash on Ruth, 7.
8. Jos., Antt., X. x. 6.
9. Yoma, f. 77.
10. Berachôth, f. 31.
11. Sanhedrin, f. 93. Midrash Rabba on Ruth, 7, etc., quoted by Hamburger, Real-Encyclopädie, i. 225.
12. Kiddushin, f. 72, 6; Hershon, Genesis acc. to the Talmud, p. 471.
13. Bel and the Dragon, 33-39. It seems to be an old Midrashic legend. It is quoted by Dorotheus and Pseudo-Epiphanius, and referred to by some of the Fathers. Eusebius supposes another Habakkuk and another Daniel; but "anachronisms, literary extravagances, or legendary character are obvious on the face of such narratives. Such faults as these, though valid against any pretensions to the rank of authentic history, do not render the stories less effective as pieces of Haggadic satire, or less interesting as preserving vestiges of a cycle of popular legends relating to Daniel" (Rev. C. J. Ball, Speaker's Commentary, on Apocrypha, ii. 350).
14. Höttinger, Hist. Orientalis, p. 92.
15. Ezra viii. 2; Neh. x. 6. In 1 Chron. iii. 1 Daniel is an alternative name for David's son Chileab-- perhaps a clerical error. If so, the names Daniel, Mishael, Azariah, and Hananiah are only found in the two post-exilic books, whence Kamphausen supposes them to have been borrowed by the writer.
16. No valid arguments can be adduced in favour of Winckler's suggestion that Ezek. xxviii. 1-10, xiv. 14-20, are late interpolations. In these passages the name is spelt dn'l; not, as in our Book, dny'l.
17. Isa. xxxix. 7.
18. See Rosenmüller, Scholia, ad loc.
19. Ezek., p. 207.
20. Herzog, R. E., s.v.
21. Ewald, Proph. d. Alt. Bund., ii. 560; De Wette, Einleit., § 253.
22. So Von Lengerke, Dan., xciii. ff.; Hitzig, Dan., viii.
23. He is followed by Bunsen, Gott in der Gesch., i. 514.
24. Reuss, Heil. Schrift., p. 570.
25. Ignat., Ad Magnes, 3 (Long Revision: see Lightfoot, ii., § ii., p. 749). So too in Ps. Mar. ad Ignat., 3. Lightfoot thinks that this is a transference from Solomon (l.c., p. 727).
26. See Ezek. xxix. 17.
27. See Zech. ii. 6-10; Ezek. xxxvii. 9, etc.
28. See Hag. ii. 6-9, 20-23; Zech. ii. 5-17, iii. 8-10; Mal. iii. 1.
29. Ezra (i. 1) does not mention the striking prophecies of the later Isaiah (xliv. 28, xlv. 1), but refers to Jeremiah only (xxv. 12, xxix. 10).
30. Dan. x. 1-18, vi. 10.
31. Ezra i. 5.
32. D'Herbelot, l.c.
33. Matt. xxiv. 15; Mark xiii. 14. There can be of course no certainty that the "spoken of by Daniel the prophet" is not the comment of the Evangelist.
34. See Elliott, Horæ Apocalypticæ, passim.

# CHAPTER II - GENERAL SURVEY OF THE BOOK

*1. The Language*

Unable to learn anything further respecting the professed author of the Book of Daniel, we now turn to the Book itself. In this section I shall merely give a general sketch of its main external phenomena, and shall chiefly pass in review those characteristics which, though they have been used as arguments respecting the age in which it originated, are not absolutely irreconcilable with the supposition of any date between the termination of the Exile (b.c. 536) and the death of Antiochus Epiphanes (b.c. 164).

I. First we notice the fact that there is an interchange of the first and third person. In chapters i.-vi. Daniel is mainly spoken of in the third person: in chapters vii.-xii. he speaks mainly in the first.

Kranichfeld tries to account for this by the supposition that in chapters i.-vi. we practically have extracts from Daniel's diaries, [35] whereas in the remainder of the Book he describes his own visions. The point cannot be much insisted upon, but the mention of his own high praises (e.g., in such passages as vi. 4) is perhaps hardly what we should have expected.

II. Next we observe that the Book of Daniel, like the Book of Ezra [36] is written partly in the sacred Hebrew, partly in the vernacular Aramaic, which is often, but erroneously, called Chaldee. [37]

The first section (i. 1-ii. 4a) is in Hebrew. The language changes to Aramaic after the words, "Then spake the Chaldeans to the king in Syriac" (ii. 4a); [38] and this is continued to vii. 28. The eighth chapter begins with the words, "In the third year of the reign of King Belshazzar a vision appeared unto me, even unto me Daniel"; and here the Hebrew is resumed, and is continued till the end of the Book.

The question at once arises why the two languages were used in the same Book.

It is easy to understand that, during the course of the seventy years' Exile, many of the Jews became practically bilingual, and would be able to write with equal facility in one language or in the other.

This circumstance, then, has no bearing on the date of the Book. Down to the Maccabean age some books continued to be written in Hebrew. These books must have found readers. Hence the knowledge of Hebrew cannot have died away so completely as has been supposed. The notion that after the return from the Exile Hebrew was at once superseded by Aramaic is untenable. Hebrew long continued to be the language normally spoken at Jerusalem (Neh. xiii. 24), and the Jews did not bring back Aramaic with them to Palestine, but found it there. [39]

But it is not clear why the linguistic divisions in the Book were adopted. Auberlen says that, after the introduction, the section ii. 4a-vii. 28 was written in Chaldee, because it describes the development of the power of the world from a world-historic point of view; and that the remainder of the Book was written in Hebrew, because it deals with the development of the world-powers in their relation to Israel the people of God. [40] There is very little to be said in favour of a structure so little obvious and so highly artificial. A simpler solution of the difficulty would be that which accounts for the use of Chaldee by saying that it was adopted in those parts which involved the introduction of Aramaic documents. This, however, would not account for its use in chap. vii., which is a chapter of visions in which Hebrew might have been naturally expected as the vehicle of prophecy. Strack and Meinhold think that the Aramaic and Hebrew parts are of different origin. König supposes that the Aramaic sections were meant to indicate special reference to the Syrians and Antiochus. [41] Some critics have thought it possible that the Aramaic sections were once written in Hebrew. That the text of Daniel has not been very carefully kept becomes clear from the liberties to which it was subjected by the Septuagint translators. If the Hebrew of Jer. x. 11 (a verse which only exists in Aramaic) has been lost, it is not inconceivable that the same may have happened to the Hebrew of a section of Daniel. [42]

The Talmud throws no light on the question. It only says that--

i. "The men of the Great Synagogue wrote" [43] --by which is perhaps meant that they "edited"--"the Book of Ezekiel, the Twelve Minor Prophets, the Book of Daniel, and the Book of Ezra"; [44] and that--

ii. "The Chaldee passages in the Book of Ezra and the Book of Daniel defile the hands." [45]

The first of these two passages is merely an assertion that the preservation, the arrangement, and the admission into the Canon of the books mentioned was due to the body of scribes and priests--a very shadowy and unhistorical body--known as the Great Synagogue. [46]

The second passage sounds startling, but is nothing more than an authoritative declaration that the Chaldee sections of Daniel and Ezra are still parts of Holy Scripture, though not written in the sacred language.

It is a standing rule of the Talmudists that All Holy Scripture defiles the hands--even the long-disputed Books of Ecclesiastes and Canticles. [47] Lest any should misdoubt the sacredness of the Chaldee sections, they are expressly included in the rule. It seems to have originated thus: The eatables of the heave offerings were kept in close proximity to the scroll of the Law, for both were considered equally sacred. If a mouse or rat happened to nibble either, the offerings and the books became defiled, and therefore defiled the hands that touched them. [48] To guard against this hypothetical defilement it was decided that all handling of the Scriptures should be followed by ceremonial ablutions. To say that the Chaldee chapters "defile the hands" is the Rabbinic way of declaring their Canonicity.

Perhaps nothing certain can be inferred from the philological examination either of the Hebrew or of the Chaldee portions of the Book; but they seem to indicate a date not earlier than the age of Alexander (b.c. 333). On this part of the subject there has been a great deal of rash and incompetent assertion. It involves delicate problems on which an independent and a valuable opinion can only be offered by the merest handful of living scholars, and respecting which even these scholars sometimes disagree. In deciding upon such points ordinary students can only weigh the authority and the arguments of specialists who have devoted a minute and lifelong study to the grammar and history of the Semitic languages.

I know no higher contemporary authorities on the date of Hebrew writings than the late veteran scholar F. Delitzsch and Professor Driver.

1. Nothing was more beautiful and remarkable in Professor Delitzsch than the open-minded candour which compelled him to the last to advance with advancing thought; to admit all fresh elements of evidence; to continue his education as a Biblical inquirer to the latest days of his life; and without hesitation to correct, modify, or even reverse his previous conclusions in accordance with the results of deeper study and fresh discoveries. He wrote the article on Daniel in Herzog's Real-Encyclopädie, and in the first edition of that work maintained its genuineness; but in the later editions (iii. 470) his views approximate more and more to those of the Higher Criticism. Of the Hebrew of Daniel he says that "it attaches itself here and there to Ezekiel, and also to Habakkuk; in general character it resembles the Hebrew of the Chronicler who wrote shortly before the beginning of the Greek period (b.c. 332), and as compared either with the ancient Hebrew, or with the Hebrew of the Mishnah is full of singularities and harshnesses of style." [49]

So far, then, it is clear that, if the Hebrew mainly resembles that of b.c. 332, it is hardly likely that it should have been written before b.c. 536.

Professor Driver says, "The Hebrew of Daniel in all distinctive features resembles, not the Hebrew of Ezekiel, or even of Haggai and Zechariah, but that of the age subsequent to Nehemiah"--whose age forms the great turning-point in Hebrew style.

He proceeds to give a list of linguistic peculiarities in support of this view, and other specimens of sentences constructed, not in the style of classical Hebrew, but in "the later uncouth style" of the Book of Chronicles. He points out in a note that it is no explanation of these peculiarities to argue that, during his long exile, Daniel may have partially forgotten the language of his youth; "for this would not account for the resemblance of the new and decadent idioms to those which appeared in Palestine independently two hundred and fifty years afterwards." [50] Behrmann, in the latest commentary on Daniel, mentions, in proof of the late character of the Hebrew: (1) the introduction of Persian words which could not have been used in Babylonian before the conquest of Cyrus (as in i. 3, 5, xi. 45, etc.); (2) many Aramaic or Aramaising words, expressions, and grammatical forms (as in i. 5, 10, 12, 16, viii. 18, 22, x. 17, 21, etc.); (3) neglect of strict accuracy in the use of the Hebrew tenses (as in viii. 14, ix. 3 f., xi. 4 f., etc.); (4) the borrowing of archaic expressions from ancient sources (as in viii. 26, ix. 2, xi. 10, 40, etc.); (5) the use of technical terms and periphrases common in Jewish apocalypses (xi. 6, 13, 35, 40, etc.). [51]

2. These views of the character of the Hebrew agree with those of previous scholars. Bertholdt and Kirms declare that its character differs toto genere from what might have been expected had the Book been genuine. Gesenius says that the language is even more corrupt than that of Ezra, Nehemiah, and Malachi. Professor Driver says the Persian words presuppose a period after the Persian Empire had been well established; the Greek words demand, the Hebrew supports, and the Aramaic permits a date after the conquest of Palestine by Alexander the Great. De Wette and Ewald have pointed out the lack of the old passionate spontaneity of early prophecy; the absence of the numerous and profound paronomasiæ, or plays on words, which characterised the burning oratory of the prophets; and the peculiarities of the style--which is sometimes obscure and careless, sometimes pompous, iterative, and artificial. [52]

3. It is noteworthy that in this Book the name of the great Babylonian conqueror, with whom, in the narrative part, Daniel is thrown into such close connexion, is invariably written in the absolutely erroneous form which his name assumed in later centuries--Nebuchadnezzar. A contemporary, familiar with the Babylonian language, could not have been ignorant of the fact that the only correct form of the name is Nebuchadrezzar--i.e., Nebu-kudurri-utsur, "Nebo protect the throne." [53]

4. But the erroneous form Neduchadnezzar is not the only one which entirely militates against the notion of a contemporary writer. There seem to be other mistakes about Babylonian matters into which a person in Daniel's position could not have fallen. Thus the name Belteshazzar seems to be connected in the writer's mind with Bel, the favourite deity of Nebuchadrezzar; but it can only mean Balatu-utsur, "his life protect," which looks like a mutilation. Abed-nego is an astonishingly corrupt form for Abed-nabu, "the servant of Nebo." Hammelzar, Shadrach, Meshach, Ashpenaz, are declared by Assyriologists to be "out of keeping with Babylonian science." In ii. 48 signîn means a civil ruler;--does not imply Archimagus, as the context seems to require, but, according to Lenormant, a high civil officer.

5. The Aramaic of Daniel closely resembles that of Ezra. Nöldeke calls it a Palestinian or Western Aramaic dialect, later than that of the Book of Ezra. [54] It is of earlier type than that of the Targums of Jonathan and Onkelos; but that fact has very little bearing on the date of the Book, because the differences are slight, and the resemblances manifold, and the Targums did not appear till after the Christian Era, nor assume their present shape perhaps before the fourth century. Further, "recently discovered inscriptions have shown that many of the forms in which the Aramaic of Daniel differs from that of the Targums were actually in use in neighbouring countries down to the first century a.d." [55]

6. Two further philological considerations bear on the age of the Book.

i. One of these is the existence of no less than fifteen Persian words (according to Nöldeke and others), especially in the Aramaic part. These words, which would not be surprising after the complete establishment of the Persian Empire, are surprising in passages which describe Babylonian institutions before the conquest of Cyrus. [56] Various attempts have been made to account for this phenomenon. Professor Fuller attempts to show, but with little success, that some of them may be Semitic. [57] Others argue that they are amply accounted for by the Persian trade which, as may be seen from the Records of the Past, [58] existed between Persia and Babylonia as early as the days of Belshazzar. To this it is replied that some of the words are not of a kind which one nation would at once borrow from another, [59] and that "no Persian words have hitherto been found in Assyrian or Babylonian inscriptions prior to the conquest of Babylon by Cyrus, except the name of the god Mithra."

ii. But the linguistic evidence unfavourable to the genuineness of the Book of Daniel is far stronger than this, in the startling fact that it contains at least three Greek words. After giving the fullest consideration to all that has been urged in refutation of the conclusion, this circumstance has always been to me a strong confirmation of the view that the Book of Daniel in its present form is not older than the days of Antiochus Epiphanes.

Those three Greek words occur in the list of musical instruments mentioned in iii. 5, 7, 10, 15. They are: qytrm, kitharos, kitharis, "harp"; phsntryn, psanterîn, psalterion, "psaltery"; [60] svmphny', sumpOnyah, sumphonia, A.V. "dulcimer," but perhaps "bagpipes." [61]

Be it remembered that these musical instruments are described as having (b.c. 550). Now, this is the date at which Pisistratus was tyrant at Athens, in the days of Pythagoras and Polycrates, before Athens became a fixed democracy. It is just conceivable that in those days the Babylonians might have borrowed from Greece the word kitharis. [62] It is, indeed, supremely unlikely, because the harp had been known in the East from the earliest days; and it is at least as probable that Greece, which at this time was only beginning to sit as a learner at the feet of the immemorial East, borrowed the idea of the instrument from Asia. Let it, however, be admitted that such words as yayîn, "wine" (oinos), lappid, "a torch" (lampas), and a few others, may indicate some early intercourse between Greece and the East, and that some commercial relations of a rudimentary kind were existent even in prehistoric days. [63]

But what are we to say of the two other words? Both are derivatives. Psalterion does not occur in Greek before Aristotle (d. 322); nor sumphonia before Plato (d. 347). In relation to music, and probably as the name of a musical instrument, sumphonia is first used by Polybius (xxvi. 10, § 5, xxxi. 4, § 8), and in express connexion with the festivities of the very king with whom the apocalyptic section of Daniel is mainly occupied--Antiochus Epiphanes. [64] The attempts of Professor Fuller and others to derive these words from Semitic roots are a desperate resource, and cannot win the assent of a single trained philologist. "These words," says Professor Driver, "could not have been used in the Book of Daniel, unless it had been written after the dissemination of Greek influence in Asia through the conquest of Alexander the Great." [65]

## 2. The Unity of the Book

The Unity of the Book of Daniel is now generally admitted. No one thought of questioning it in days before the dawn of criticism, but in 1772 Eichhorn and Corrodi doubted the genuineness of the Book. J. D. Michaelis endeavoured to prove that it was "a collection of fugitive pieces," consisting of six historic pictures, followed by four prophetic visions. [66] Bertholdt, followed the erroneous tendency of criticism which found a foremost exponent in Ewald, and imagined the possibility of detecting the work of many different hands. He divided the Book into fragments by nine different authors. [67]

Zöckler, in Lange's Bibelwerk, persuaded himself that the old "orthodox" views of Hengstenberg and Auberlen were right; but he could only do this by sacrificing the authenticity of parts of the Book, and assuming more than one redaction. Thus he supposes that xi. 5-39 are an interpolation by a writer in the days of Antiochus Epiphanes. Similarly, Lenormant admits interpolations in the first half of the Book. But to concede this is practically to give up the Book of Daniel as it now stands.

The unity of the Book of Daniel is still admitted or assumed by most critics. [68] It has only been recently questioned in two directions.

Meinhold thinks that the Aramaic and historic sections are older than the rest of the Book, and were written about b.c. 300 to convert the Gentiles to monotheism. [69] He argues that the apocalyptic section was written later, and was subsequently incorporated with the Book. A somewhat similar view is held by Zöckler, [70] and some have thought that Daniel could never have written of himself in such highly favourable terms as, e.g., in Dan. vi. 4. [71] The first chapter, which is essential as an introduction to the Book, and the seventh, which is apocalyptic, and is yet in Aramaic, create objections to the acceptance of this theory. Further, it is impossible not to observe a certain unity of style and parallelism of treatment between the two parts. Thus, if the prophetic section is mainly devoted to Antiochus Epiphanes, the historic section seems to have an allusive bearing on his impious madness. In ii. 10, 11, and vi. 8, we have descriptions of daring Pagan edicts, which might be intended to furnish a contrast with the attempts of Antiochus to suppress the worship of God. The feast of Belshazzar may well be a "reference to the Syrian despot's revelries at Daphne." Again, in ii. 43--where the mixture of iron and clay is explained by "they shall mingle themselves with the seed of men"--it seems far from improbable that there is a reference to the unhappy intermarriages of Ptolemies and Seleucidæ. Berenice, daughter of Ptolemy II. (Philadelphus), married Antiochus II. (Theos), and this is alluded to in the vision of xi. 6. Cleopatra, daughter of Antiochus III. (the Great), married Ptolemy V. (Epiphanes), which is alluded to in xi. 17. [72] The style seems to be stamped throughout with the characteristics of an individual mind, and the most cursory glance suffices to show that the historic and prophetic parts are united by many points of connexion and resemblance. Meinhold is quite unsuccessful in the attempt to prove a sharp contrast of views between the sections. The interchange of persons--the third person being mainly used in the first seven chapters, and the first person in the last five--may be partly due to the final editor; but in any case it may easily be paralleled, and is found in other writers, as in Isaiah (vii. 3, xx. 2) and the Book of Enoch (xii.).

But it may be said in general that the authenticity of the Book is now rarely defended by any competent critic, except at the cost of abandoning certain sections of it as interpolated additions; and as Mr. Bevan somewhat caustically remarks, "the defenders of Daniel have, during the last few years, been employed chiefly in cutting Daniel to pieces." [73]

## 3. The General Tone of the Book

The general tone of the Book marks a new era in the education and progress of the Jews. The lessons of the Exile uplifted them from a too narrow and absorbing particularism to a wider interest in the destinies of humanity. They were led to recognise that God "has made of one every nation of men for to dwell on all the face of the earth, having determined their appointed seasons, and the bounds of their habitation; that they should seek God, if haply they might feel after Him, and find Him, though He is not far from each one of us." [74] The standpoint of the Book of Daniel is larger and more cosmopolitan in this respect than that of earlier prophecy. Israel had begun to mingle more closely with other nations, and to be a sharer in their destinies. Politically the Hebrew race no longer formed a small though independent kingdom, but was reduced to the position of an entirely insignificant sub-province in a mighty empire. The Messiah is no longer the Son of David, but the Son of Man; no longer only the King of Israel, but of the world. Mankind--not only the seed of Jacob--fills the field of prophetic vision. Amid widening horizons of thought the Jews turned their eyes upon a great past, rich in events, and crowded with the figures of heroes, saints, and sages. At the same time the world seemed to be growing old, and its ever-deepening wickedness seemed to call for some final judgment. We begin to trace in the Hebrew writings the colossal conceptions, the monstrous imagery, the daring conjectures, the more complex religious ideas, of an exotic fancy. [75]

"The giant forms of Empires on their way
To ruin, dim and vast,"

begin to fling their weird and sombre shadows over the page of sacred history and prophetic anticipation.

## 4. The Style of the Book

The style of the Book of Daniel is new, and has very marked characteristics, indicating its late position in the Canon. It is rhetorical rather than poetic. "Totum Danielis librum," says Lowth, "e poetarum censu excludo." [76] How widely does the style differ from the rapt passion and glowing picturesqueness of Isaiah, from the elegiac tenderness of Jeremiah, from the lyrical sweetness of many of the Psalms! How very little does it correspond to the three great requirements of poetry, that it should be, as Milton so finely said, "simple, sensuous, passionate"! A certain artificiality of diction, a sounding oratorical stateliness, enhanced by dignified periphrases and leisurely repetitions, must strike the most casual reader; and this is sometimes carried so far as to make the movement of the narrative heavy and pompous. [77] This peculiarity is not found to the same extent in any other book of the Old Testament Canon, but it recurs in the Jewish writings of a later age. From the apocryphal books, for instance, the poetical element is with trifling exceptions, such as the Song of the Three Children, entirely absent, while the taste for rhetorical ornamentation, set speeches, and dignified elaborateness is found in many of them.

This evanescence of the poetic and impassioned element separates Daniel from the Prophets, and marks the place of the Book among the Hagiographa, where it was placed by the Jews themselves. In all the great Hebrew seers we find something of the ecstatic transport, the fire shut up within the bones and breaking forth from the volcanic heart, the burning lips touched by the hands of seraphim with a living coal from off the altar. The word for prophet (nabî, Vates) implies an inspired singer rather than a soothsayer or seer (roeh, chozeh). It is applied to Deborah and Miriam [78] because they poured forth from exultant hearts the pæan of victory. Hence arose the close connexion between music and poetry.[79] Elisha required the presence of a minstrel to soothe the agitation of a heart thrown into tumult by the near presence of a revealing Power. [80] Just as the Greek word mantis, from mainomai, implies a sort of madness, and recalls the foaming lip and streaming hair of the spirit-dilated messenger, so the Hebrew verb naba meant, not only to proclaim God's oracles, but to be inspired by His possession as with a Divine frenzy. [81] "Madman" seemed a natural term to apply to the messenger of Elisha. [82] It is easy therefore to see why the Book of Daniel was not placed among the prophetic rolls. This vera passio, this ecstatic elevation of thought and feeling, are wholly wanting in this earliest attempt at a philosophy of history. We trace in it none of that "blasting with excess of light," none of that shuddering sense of being uplifted out of self, which marks the higher and earlier forms of prophetic inspiration. Daniel is addressed through the less exalted medium of visions, and in his visions there is less of "the faculty Divine." The instinct--if instinct it were and not knowledge of the real origin of the Book--which led the "Men of the Great Synagogue" to place this Book among the Ketubhîm, not among the Prophets, was wise and sure. [83]

## 5. The Standpoint of the Author

*"In Daniel öffnet sich eine ganz neue Welt."*--Eichhorn, Einleit., iv. 472.

The author of the Book of Daniel seems naturally to place himself on a level lower than that of the prophets who had gone before him. He does not count himself among the prophets; on the contrary, he puts them far higher than himself, and refers to them as though they belonged to the dim and distant past (ix. 2, 6). In his prayer of penitence he confesses, "Neither have we hearkened unto thy servants the prophets, which spake in Thy Name to our kings, our princes, and our fathers"; "Neither have we obeyed the voice of the Lord our God, to walk in His laws, which He set before us by His servants the prophets." Not once does he use the mighty formula "Thus saith Jehovah"--not once does he assume, in the prophecies, a tone of high personal authority. He shares the view of the Maccabean age that prophecy is dead. [84]

In Dan. ix. 2 we find yet another decisive indication of the late age of this writing. He tells us that he "understood by books" (more correctly, as in the A.V., "by the books" [85]) "the number of the years whereof the word of the Lord came to Jeremiah the prophet." The writer here represents himself as a humble student of previous prophets, and this necessarily marks a position of less freshness and independence. "To the old prophets," says Bishop Westcott, "Daniel stands in some sense as a commentator." No doubt the possession of those living oracles was an immense blessing, a rich inheritance; but it involved a danger. Truths established by writings and traditions, safe-guarded by schools and institutions, are too apt to come to men only as a power from without, and less as "a hidden and inly burning flame." [86]

By "the books" can hardly be meant anything but some approach to a definite Canon. If so, the Book of Daniel in its present form can only have been written subsequently to the days of Ezra. "The account which assigns a collection of books to Nehemiah (2 Macc. ii. 13)," says Bishop Westcott, "is in itself a confirmation of the general truth of the gradual formation of the Canon during the Persian period. The various classes of books were completed in succession; and this view harmonises with what must have been the natural development of the Jewish faith after the Return. The persecution of Antiochus (b.c. 168) was for the Old Testament what the persecution of Diocletian was for the New--the final crisis which stamped the sacred writings with their peculiar character. The king sought out the

Books of the Law (1 Macc. i. 56) and burnt them; and the possession of a 'Book of the Covenant' was a capital crime. According to the common tradition, the proscription of the Law led to the public use of the writings of the prophets." [87]

\*\*\*

The whole method of Daniel differs even from that of the later and inferior prophets of the Exile--Haggai, Malachi, and the second Zechariah. The Book is rather an apocalypse than a prophecy: "the eye and not the ear is the organ to which the chief appeal is made." Though symbolism in the form of visions is not unknown to Ezekiel and Zechariah, yet those prophets are far from being apocalyptic in character. On the other hand, the grotesque and gigantic emblems of Daniel--these animal combinations, these interventions of dazzling angels who float in the air or over the water, these descriptions of historical events under the veil of material types seen in dreams--are a frequent phenomenon in such late apocryphal writings as the Second Book of Esdras, the Book of Enoch, and the præ-Christian Sibylline oracles, in which talking lions and eagles, etc., are frequent. Indeed, this style of symbolism originated among the Jews from their contact with the graven mysteries and colossal images of Babylonian worship. The Babylonian Exile formed an epoch in the intellectual development of Israel fully as important as the sojourn in Egypt. It was a stage in their moral and religious education. It was the psychological preparation requisite for the moulding of the last phase of revelation--that apocalyptic form which succeeds to theophany and prophecy, and embodies the final results of national religious inspiration. That the apocalyptic method of dealing with history in a religious and an imaginative manner naturally arises towards the close of any great cycle of special revelation is illustrated by the flood of apocalypses which overflowed the early literature of the Christian Church. But the Jews clearly saw that, as a rule, an apocalypse is inherently inferior to a prophecy, even when it is made the vehicle of genuine prediction. In estimating the grades of inspiration the Jews placed highest the inward illumination of the Spirit, the Reason, and the Understanding; next to this they placed dreams and visions; and lowest of all they placed the accidental auguries derived from the Bath Qôl. An apocalypse may be of priceless value, like the Revelation of St. John; it may, like the Book of Daniel, abound in the noblest and most thrilling lessons; but in intrinsic dignity and worth it is always placed by the instinct and conscience of mankind on a lower grade than such outpourings of Divine teachings as breathe and burn through the pages of a David and an Isaiah.

*6. The Moral Element*

Lastly, among these salient phenomena of the Book of Daniel we are compelled to notice the absence of the predominantly moral element from its prophetic portion. The author does not write in the tone of a preacher of repentance, or of one whose immediate object it is to ameliorate the moral and spiritual condition of his people. His aims were different. [88] The older prophets were the ministers of dispensations between the Law and the Gospel. They were, in the beautiful language of Herder,--
"Die Saitenspiel in Gottes mächtigen Händen."
Doctrine, worship, and consolation were their proper sphere. They were "oratores Legis, advocati patriæ." In them prediction is wholly subordinate to moral warning and instruction. They denounce, they inspire: they smite to the dust with terrible invective; they uplift once more into glowing hope. The announcement of events yet future is the smallest part of the prophet's office, and rather its sign than its substance. The highest mission of an Amos or an Isaiah is not to be a prognosticator, but to be a religious teacher. He makes his appeals to the conscience, not to the imagination--to the spirit, not to the sense. He deals with eternal principles, and is almost wholly indifferent to chronological verifications. To awaken the death-like slumber of sin, to fan the dying embers of faithfulness, to smite down the selfish oppressions of wealth and power, to startle the sensual apathy of greed, were the ordinary and the noblest aims of the greater and the minor prophets. It was their task far rather to forth-tell than to foretell; and if they announce, in general outline and uncertain perspective, things which shall be hereafter, it is only in subordination to high ethical purposes, or profound spiritual lessons. So it is also in the Revelation of St. John. But in the "prophetic" part of Daniel it is difficult for the keenest imagination to discern any deep moral, or any special doctrinal significance, in all the details of the obscure wars and petty diplomacy of the kings of the North and South.

In point of fact the Book of Daniel, even as an apocalypse, suffers severely by comparison with that latest canonical Apocalypse of the Beloved Disciple which it largely influenced. It is strange that Luther, who spoke so slightingly of the Revelation of St. John, should have placed the Book of Daniel so high in his estimation. It is indeed a noble book, full of glorious lessons. Yet surely it has but little of the sublime and mysterious beauty, little of the heart-shaking pathos, little of the tender sweetness of consolatory power, which fill the closing book of the New Testament. Its imagery is far less exalted, its hope of immortality far less distinct and unquenchable. Yet the Book of Daniel, while it is one of the earliest, still remains one of the greatest specimens of this form of sacred literature. It inaugurated the new epoch of "apocalyptic" which in later days was usually pseudepigraphic, and sheltered itself under the names of Enoch, Noah, Moses, Ezra, and even the heathen Sibyls. These apocalypses are of very unequal value. "Some," as Kuenen says, "stand comparatively high; others are far below mediocrity." But the genus to which they belong has its own peculiar defect. They are works of art: they are not spontaneous; they smell of the lamp. A fruitless and an unpractical peering into the future was encouraged by these writings, and became predominant in some Jewish circles. But the Book of Daniel is incomparably superior in every possible respect to Baruch, or the Book of Enoch, or the Second Book of Esdras; and if we place it for a moment by the side of such books as those contained in the Codex Pseudepigraphus of Fabricius, its high worth and Canonical authority are vindicated with extraordinary force. How lofty and enduring are the lessons to be learnt alike from its historic and predictive sections we shall have abundant opportunities of seeing in the following pages. So far from undervaluing its teaching, I have always been strongly drawn to this Book of Scripture. It has never made the least difference in my reverent acceptance of it that I have, for many years, been convinced that it cannot be regarded as literal history or ancient prediction. Reading it as one of the noblest specimens of the Jewish Haggada or moral Ethopoeia, I find it full of instruction in righteousness, and rich in examples of life. That Daniel was a real person, that he lived in the days of the Exile, and that his life was distinguished by the splendour of its faithfulness I hold to be entirely possible. When we regard the stories here related of him as moral legends, possibly based on a groundwork of real tradition, we read the Book with a full sense of its value, and feel the power of the lessons which it was designed to teach, without being perplexed by its apparent improbabilities, or worried by its immense historic and other difficulties.

The Book is in all respects unique, a writing sui generis; for the many imitations to which it led are but imitations. But, as the Jewish writer Dr. Joël truly says, the unveiling of the secret as to the real lateness of its date and origin, so far from causing any loss in its beauty and interest, enhance both in a remarkable degree. It is thus seen to be the work of a brave and gifted anonymous author about b.c. 167, who brought his piety and his patriotism to bear on the troubled fortunes of his people at an epoch in which such piety and patriotism were of priceless value. We have in its later sections no voice of enigmatic prediction, foretelling the minutest complications of a distant secular future, but mainly the review of contemporary events by a wise and an earnest writer whose faith and hope remained unquenchable in the deepest night of persecution and apostasy. [89] Many passages of the Book are dark, and will remain dark, owing partly perhaps to corruptions and uncertainties of the text, and partly to imitation of a style which had become archaic, as well as to the peculiarities of the apocalyptic form. But the general idea of the Book has now been thoroughly elucidated, and the interpretation of it in the following pages is accepted by the great majority of earnest and faithful students of the Scriptures.

## *Footnotes:*

35. Kranichfeld, Das Buch Daniel, p. 4.
36. See Ezra iv. 7, vi. 18, vii. 12-26.
37. "The term 'Chaldee' for the Aramaic of either the Bible or the Targums is a misnomer, the use of which is only a source of confusion" (Driver, p. 471). A single verse of Jeremiah (x. 11) is in Aramaic: "Thus shall ye say unto them, The gods who made not heaven and earth shall perish from the earth and from under heaven." Perhaps Jeremiah gave the verse "to the Jews as an answer to the heathen among whom they were" (Pusey, p. 11).
38. 'rmyt; LXX., Suristi--i.e., in Aramaic. The word may be a gloss, as it is in Ezra iv. 7 (Lenormant). See, however, Kamphausen, p. 14. We cannot here enter into minor points, such as that in ii.-vi. we have 'lv for "see," and in vii. 2, 3, 'rv; which Meinhold takes to prove that the historic section is earlier than the prophetic.
39. Driver, p. 471; Nöldeke, Enc. Brit., xxi. 647; Wright, Grammar, p. 16. Ad. Merx has a treatise on Cur in lib. Dan. juxta Hebr. Aramaica sit adhibita dialectus, 1865; but his solution, "Scriptorem omnia quæ rudioribus vulgi ingeniis apta viderentur Aramaice præposuisse" is wholly untenable.
40. Auberlen, Dan., pp. 28, 29 (E. Tr.).
41. Einleit., § 383.
42. Cheyne, Enc. Brit., s.v. "Daniel."
43. ktvv. See 2 Esdras xiv. 22-48: "In forty days they wrote two hundred and four books."
44. Baba-Bathra, f. 15, 6: comp. Sanhedrin, f. 83, 6.
45. Yaddayim, iv.; Mish., 5.
46. See Rau, De Synag. Magna., ii. 66 ff.; Kuenen, Over de Mannen der Groote Synagoge, 1876; Ewald, Hist. of Israel, v. 168-170 (E. Tr.); Westcott, s.v. "Canon" (Smith's Dict., i. 500).
47. Yaddayim, iii.; Mish., 5; Hershon, Treasures of the Talmud, pp. 41-43.
48. Hershon (l.c.) refers to Shabbath, f. 14, 1.
49. Herzog, l.c.; so too König, Einleit., § 387: "Das Hebr. der B. Dan. ist nicht blos nachexilisch sondern auch nachchronistisch." He instances ribbo (Dan. xi. 12) for rebaba, "myriads" (Ezek. xvi. 7);

and tamîd, "the daily burnt offering" (Dan. viii. 11), as post-Biblical Hebrew for 'olath hatamîd (Neh. x. 34), etc. Margoliouth (Expositor, April 1890) thinks that the Hebrew proves a date before b.c. 168: on which view see Driver, p, 483.

50. Lit. of Old Test., pp. 473-476.

51. Das Buch Dan., iii.

52. See Glassius, Philol. Sacr., p. 931; Ewald, Die Proph. d. A. Bundes, i. 48; De Wette, Einleit., § 347.

53. Ezekiel always uses the correct form (xxvi. 7, xxix. 18, xxx. 10). Jeremiah uses the correct form except in passages which properly belong to the Book of Kings.

54. Nöldeke, Semit. Spr., p. 30; Driver, p. 472; König, p. 387.

55. Driver, p. 472, and the authorities there quoted; as against McGill and Pusey (Daniel, pp. 45 ff., 602 ff.). Dr. Pusey's is the fullest repertory of arguments in favour of the authenticity of Daniel, many of which have become more and more obviously untenable as criticism advances. But he and Keil add little or nothing to what had been ingeniously elaborated by Hengstenberg and Hävernick. For a sketch of the peculiarities in the Aramaic see Behrmann, Daniel, v.-x. Renan (Hist. Gén. des Langues Sém., p. 219) exaggerates when he says, "La langue des parties chaldénnes est beaucoup plus basse que celle des fragments chaldéens du Livre d'Esdras, et s'incline beaucoup vers la langue du Talmud."

56. Meinhold, Beiträge, pp. 30-32; Driver, p. 470.

57. Speaker's Commentary, vi. 246-250.

58. New Series, iii. 124.

59. E.g., hdm, "limb"; rz, "secret"; phtgm, "message." There are no Persian words in Ezekiel, Haggai, Zechariah, or Malachi; they are found in Ezra and Esther, which were written long after the establishment of the Persian Empire.

60. The change of n for l is not uncommon: comp. bention, phintatos, etc.

61. The word svk', Sab'ka, also bears a suspicious resemblance to sambuke, but Athenæus says (Deipnos., iv. 173) that the instrument was invented by the Syrians. Some have seen in karôz (iii. 4, "herald") the Greek kerux, and in hamnîk, "chain," the Greek maniakes: but these cannot be pressed.

62. It is true that there was some small intercourse between even the Assyrians and Ionians (Ja-am-na-a) as far back as the days of Sargon (b.c. 722-705); but not enough to account for such words.

63. Sayce, Contemp. Rev., December 1878.

64. Some argue that in this passage sumphonia means "a concert" (comp. Luke xv. 25); but Polybius mentions it with "a horn" (keration). Behrmann (p. ix) connects it with siphon, and makes it mean "a pipe."

65. Pusey says all he can on the other side (pp. 23-28), and has not changed the opinion of scholars (pp. 27-33). Fabre d'Envieu (i. 101) also desperately denies the existence of any Greek words. On the other side see Derenbourg, Les Mots grecs dans le Livre biblique de Daniel (Mélanges Graux, 1884).

66. Orient. u. Exeg. Bibliothek, 1772, p. 141. This view was revived by Lagarde in the Göttingen Gel. Anzeigen, 1891.

67. Daniel neu Übersetz. u. Erklärt., 1808; Köhler, Lehrbuch, ii. 577. The first who suspected the unity of the Book because of the two languages was Spinoza (Tract-historicopol, x. 130 ff.). Newton (Observations upon the Prophecies of Daniel and the Apocalypse, i. 10) and Beausobre (Remarques sur le Nouv. Test., i. 70) shared the doubt because of the use of the first person in the prophetic (Dan. vii.-xii.) and the third in the historic section (Dan. i.-vi.). Michaelis, Bertholdt, and Reuss considered that its origin was fragmentary; and Lagarde (who dated the seventh chapter a.d. 69) calls it "a bundle of flyleaves." Meinhold and Strack, like Eichhorn, regard the historic section as older than the prophetic; and Cornill thinks that the Book was put together in great haste. Similarly, Graf (Der Prophet Jeremia) regards the Aramaic verse, Jer. x. 11, as a marginal gloss. Lagarde argues, from the silence of Josephus about many points, that he could not have had the present Book of Daniel before him (e.g., Dan. vii. or ix.-xii.); but the argument is unsafe. Josephus seems to have understood the Fourth Empire to be the Roman, and did not venture to write of its destruction. For this reason he does not explain "the stone" of Dan. ii. 45.

68. By De Wette, Schrader, Hitzig, Ewald, Gesenius, Bleek, Delitzsch, Von Lengerke, Stähelin, Kamphausen, Wellhausen, etc. Reuss, however, says (Heil. Schrift., p. 575), "Man könnte auf die Vorstellung kommen das Buch habe mehr als einen Verfasser"; and König thinks that the original form of the book may have ended with chap. vii. (Einleit., § 384).

69. Beiträge, 1888. See too Kranichfeld, Das Buch Daniel, p. 4. The view is refuted by Budde, Theol. Lit. Zeitung, 1888, No. 26. The conjecture has often occurred to critics. Thus Sir Isaac Newton, believing that Daniel wrote the last six chapters, thought that the six first "are a collection of historical papers written by others" (Observations, i. 10).

70. Einleit., p. 6.

71. Other critics who incline to one or other modification of this view of the two Daniels are

*The Expositor's Bible: The Book of Daniel*
Tholuck, d. A.T. in N.T., 1872; C. v. Orelli, Alttest. Weissag., 1882; and Strack.

72. Hengstenberg also points to verbal resemblances between ii. 44 and vii. 14; iv. 5 and vii. 1; ii. 31 and vii. 2; ii. 38 and vii. 17, etc. (Genuineness of Daniel, E. Tr., pp. 186 ff.).

73. A Short Commentary, p. 8.

74. Acts xvii. 26, 27.

75. See Hitzig, p. xii; Auberlen, p. 41.

76. Reuss says too severely, "Die Schilderungen aller dieser Vorgänge machen keinen gewinnenden Eindruck.... Der Stil ist unbeholfen, die Figuren grotesk, die Farben grell." He admits, however, the suitableness of the Book for the Maccabean epoch, and the deep impression it made (Heil. Schrift. A. T., p. 571).

77. See iii. 2, 3, 5, 7; viii. 1, 10, 19; xi. 15, 22, 31, etc.

78. Exod. xv. 20; Judg. iv. 4.

79. 1 Sam. x. 5; 1 Chron. xxv. 1, 2, 3.

80. 2 Kings iii. 15.

81. Jer. xxix. 26; 1 Sam. xviii. 10, xix. 21-24.

82. 2 Kings ix. 11. See Expositor's Bible, Second Book of Kings, p. 113.

83. On this subject see Ewald, Proph. d. A. Bundes, i. 6; Novalis, Schriften, ii. 472; Herder, Geist der Ebr. Poesie, ii. 61; Knobel, Prophetismus, i. 103. Even the Latin poets were called prophetæ, "bards" (Varro, De Ling. Lat., vi. 3). Epimenides is called "a prophet" in Tit. i. 12. See Plato, Tim., 72, a.; Phædr., 262, d.; Pind., Fr., 118; and comp. Eph. iii. 5, iv. 11.

84. Dan. ix. 6, 10. So conscious was the Maccabean age of the absence of prophets, that, just as after the Captivity a question is postponed "till there should arise a priest with the Urim and Thummin," so Judas postponed the decision about the stones of the desecrated altar "until there should come a prophet to show what should be done with them" (1 Macc. iv. 45, 46, ix. 27, xiv. 41). Comp. Song of the Three Children, 15; Psalm lxxiv. 9; Sota, f. 48, 2. See infra, Introd., chap. viii.

85. Dan. ix. 2, hassepharîm, ta biblia.

86. Ewald, Proph. d. A. B., p. 10. Judas Maccabæus is also said to have "restored" (episunegage) the lost (diapeptokota) sacred writings (2 Macc. ii. 14).

87. Smith's Dict. of the Bible, i. 501. The daily lesson from the Prophets was called the Haphtarah (Hamburger, Real-Encycl., ii. 334).

88. On this subject see Kuenen, The Prophets, iii. 95 ff.; Davison, On Prophecy, pp. 34-67; Herder, Hebr. Poesie, ii. 64; De Wette, Christl. Sittenlehre, ii. 1.

89. Joël, Notizen, p. 7.

# CHAPTER III - PECULIARITIES OF THE HISTORIC SECTION

No one can have studied the Book of Daniel without seeing that, alike in the character of its miracles and the minuteness of its supposed predictions, it makes a more stupendous and a less substantiated claim upon our credence than any other book of the Bible, and a claim wholly different in character. It has over and over again been asserted by the uncharitableness of a merely traditional orthodoxy that inability to accept the historic verity and genuineness of the Book arises from secret faithlessness, and antagonism to the admission of the supernatural. No competent scholar will think it needful to refute such calumnies. It suffices us to know before God that we are actuated simply by the love of truth, by the abhorrence of anything which in us would be a pusillanimous spirit of falsity. We have too deep a belief in the God of the Amen, the God of eternal and essential verity, to offer to Him "the unclean sacrifice of a lie." An error is not sublimated into a truth even when that lie has acquired a quasi-consecration, from its supposed desirability for purposes of orthodox controversy, or from its innocent acceptance by generations of Jewish and Christian Churchmen through long ages of uncritical ignorance. Scholars, if they be Christians at all, can have no possible a-priori objection to belief in the supernatural. If they believe, for instance, in the Incarnation of our Lord and Saviour Jesus Christ, they believe in the most mysterious and unsurpassable of all miracles, and beside that miracle all minor questions of God's power or willingness to manifest His immediate intervention in the affairs of men sink at once into absolute insignificance.

But our belief in the Incarnation, and in the miracles of Christ, rests on evidence which, after repeated examination, is to us overwhelming. Apart from all questions of personal verification, or the Inward Witness of the Spirit, we can show that this evidence is supported, not only by the existing records, but by myriads of external and independent testimonies. The very same Spirit which makes men believe where the demonstration is decisive, compels them to refuse belief to the literal verity of unique miracles and unique predictions which come before them without any convincing evidence. The narratives and visions of this Book present difficulties on every page. They were in all probability never intended for anything but what they are--Haggadoth, which, like the parables of Christ, convey their own lessons without depending on the necessity for accordance with historic fact.

Had it been any part of the Divine will that we should accept these stories as pure history, and these visions as predictions of events which were not to take place till centuries afterwards, we should have been provided with some aids to such belief. On the contrary, in whatever light we examine the Book of Daniel, the evidence in its favour is weak, dubious, hypothetical, and a priori; while the evidence against it acquires increased intensity with every fresh aspect in which it is examined. The Book which would make the most extraordinary demands upon our credulity if it were meant for history, is the very Book of which the genuineness and authenticity are decisively discredited by every fresh discovery and by each new examination. There is scarcely one learned European scholar by whom they are maintained, except with such concessions to the Higher Criticism as practically involve the abandonment of all that is essential in the traditional theory.

And we have come to a time when it will not avail to take refuge in such transferences of the discussions in alteram materiam, and such purely vulgar appeals ad invidiam, as are involved in saying, "Then the Book must be a forgery," and "an imposture," and "a gross lie." To assert that "to give up the Book of Daniel is to betray the cause of Christianity," [90] is a coarse and dangerous misuse of the weapons of controversy. Such talk may still have been excusable even in the days of Dr. Pusey (with whom it was habitual); it is no longer excusable now. Now it can only prove the uncharitableness of the apologist, and the impotence of a defeated cause. Yet even this abandonment of the sphere of honourable argument is only one degree more painful than the tortuous subterfuges and wild assertions to which such apologists as Hengstenberg, Keil, and their followers were long compelled to have recourse. Anything can be proved about anything if we call to our aid indefinite suppositions of errors of transcription, interpolations, transpositions, extraordinary silences, still more extraordinary methods of presenting events, and (in general) the unconsciously disingenuous resourcefulness of traditional harmonics. To maintain that the Book of Daniel, as it now stands, was written by Daniel in the days of the Exile is to cherish a belief which can only, at the utmost, be extremely uncertain, and which must be maintained in defiance of masses of opposing evidence. There can be little intrinsic value in a determination to believe historical and literary assumptions which can no longer be maintained except by preferring the flimsiest hypotheses to the most certain facts.

My own conviction has long been that in these Haggadoth, in which Jewish literature delighted in the præ-Christian era, and which continued to be written even till the Middle Ages, there was not the least pretence or desire to deceive at all. I believe them to have been put forth as moral legends--as avowed fiction nobly used for the purposes of religious teaching and encouragement. In ages of ignorance, in which no such thing as literary criticism existed, a popular Haggada might soon come to be regarded as historical, just as the Homeric lays were among the Greeks, or just as Defoe's story of the Plague of London was taken for literal history by many readers even in the seventeenth century.

Ingenious attempts have been made to show that the author of this Book evinces an intimate familiarity with the circumstances of the Babylonian religion, society, and history. In many cases this is the reverse of the fact. The instances adduced in favour of any knowledge except of the most general description are entirely delusive. It is frivolous to maintain, with Lenormant, that an exceptional acquaintance with Babylonian custom was required to describe Nebuchadrezzar as consulting diviners for the interpretation of a dream! To say nothing of the fact that a similar custom has prevailed in all nations and all ages from the days of Samuel to those of Lobengula, the writer had the prototype of Pharaoh before him, and has evidently been influenced by the story of Joseph. [91] Again, so far from showing surprising acquaintance with the organisation of the caste of Babylonian diviners, the writer has made a mistake in their very name, as well as in the statement that a faithful Jew, like Daniel, was made the chief of their college! [92] Nor, again, was there anything so unusual in the presence of women at feasts--also recognised in the Haggada of Esther--as to render this a sign of extraordinary information. Once more, is it not futile to adduce the allusion to punishment by burning alive as a proof of insight into Babylonian peculiarities? This punishment had already been mentioned by Jeremiah in the case of Nebuchadrezzar. "Then shall be taken up a curse by all the captivity of Judah which are in Babylon, saying, The Lord make thee like Zedekiah and like Ahab" (two false prophets), "whom the King of Babylon roasted in the fire." [93] Moreover, it occurs in the Jewish traditions which described a miraculous escape of exactly the same character in the legend of Abraham. He, too, had been supernaturally rescued from the burning fiery furnace of Nimrod, to which he had been consigned because he refused to worship idols in Ur of the Chaldees. [94]

When the instances mainly relied upon prove to be so evidentially valueless, it would be waste of time to follow Professor Fuller through the less important and more imaginary proofs of accuracy which his industry has amassed. Meanwhile the feeblest reasoner will see that while a writer may easily be accurate in general facts, and even in details, respecting an age long previous to that in which he wrote, the existence of violent errors as to matters with which a contemporary must have been familiar at once refutes all pretence of historic authenticity in a book professing to have been written by an author in the days and country which he describes.

Now such mistakes there seem to be, and not a few of them, in the pages of the Book of Daniel. One or two of them can perhaps be explained away by processes which would amply suffice to show that "yes" means "no," or that "black" is a description of "white"; but each repetition of such processes leaves us more and more incredulous. If errors be treated as corruptions of the text, or as later interpolations, such arbitrary methods of treating the Book are practically an admission that, as it stands, it cannot be regarded as historical.

I. We are, for instance, met by what seems to be a remarkable error in the very first verse of the Book, which tells us that "In the third year of Jehoiakim, King of Judah, came Nebuchadnezzar"--as in later days he was incorrectly called--"King of Babylon, unto Jerusalem, and besieged it."

It is easy to trace whence the error sprang. Its source lies in a book which is the latest in the whole Canon, and in many details difficult to reconcile with the Book of Kings--a book of which the Hebrew resembles that of Daniel--the Book of Chronicles. In 2 Chron. xxxvi. 6 we are told that Nebuchadnezzar came up against Jehoiakim, and "bound him in fetters to carry him to Babylon"; and also--to which the author of Daniel directly refers--that he carried off some of the vessels of the House of God, to put them in the treasure-house of his god. In this passage it is not said that this occurred "in the third year of Jehoiakim," who reigned eleven years; but in 2 Kings xxiv. 1 we are told that "in his days Nebuchadnezzar came up, and Jehoiakim became his servant three years." The passage in Daniel looks like a confused reminiscence of the "three years" with "the third year of Jehoiakim." The elder and better authority (the Book of Kings) is silent about any deportation having taken place in the reign of Jehoiakim, and so is the contemporary Prophet Jeremiah. But in any case it seems impossible that it should have taken place so early as the third year of Jehoiakim, for at that time he was a simple vassal of the King of Egypt. If this deportation took place in the reign of Jehoiakim, it would certainly be singular that Jeremiah, in enumerating three others, in the seventh, eighteenth, and twenty-third year of Nebuchadrezzar, [95] should make no allusion to it. But it is hard to see how it could have taken place before Egypt had been defeated in the Battle of Carchemish, and that was not till b.c. 597, the fourth year of Jehoiakim. [96] Not only does Jeremiah make no mention of so remarkable a deportation as this, which as the earliest would have caused the deepest anguish, but, in the fourth year of Jehoiakim (Jer. xxxvi. 1), he writes a roll to threaten evils which are still future, and in the fifth year proclaims a fast in the hope that the imminent peril may even yet be averted (Jer. xxxvi. 6-10). It is only after the violent obstinacy of the king that the destructive advance of Nebuchadrezzar is finally prophesied (Jer. xxxvi. 29) as something which has not yet occurred. [97]

II. Nor are the names in this first chapter free from difficulty. Daniel is called Belteshazzar, and the remark of the King of Babylon--"whose name was Belteshazzar, according to the name of my god"--certainly suggests that the first syllable is (as the Massorets assume) connected with the god Bel. But the name has nothing to do with Bel. No contemporary could have fallen into such an error; [98] still less a king who spoke Babylonian. Shadrach may be Shudur-aku, "command of Aku," the moon-god; but Meshach is inexplicable; and Abed-nego is a strange corruption for the obvious and common Abed-nebo, "servant of Nebo." Such a corruption could hardly have arisen till Nebo was practically forgotten. And what is the meaning of "the Melzar" (Dan. i. 11)? The A.V. takes it to be a proper name; the R.V. renders it "the steward." But the title is unique and obscure. [99] Nor can anything be made of the name of Ashpenaz, the prince of the eunuchs, whom, in one manuscript, the LXX. call Abiesdri. [100]

III. Similar difficulties and uncertainties meet us at every step. Thus, in the second chapter (ii. 1), the dream of Nebuchadrezzar is fixed in the second year of his reign. This does not seem to be in accord with i. 3, 18, which says that Daniel and his three companions were kept under the care of the prince of the eunuchs for three years. Nothing, of course, is easier than to invent harmonistic hypotheses, such as that of Rashi, that "the second year of the reign of Nebuchadrezzar" has the wholly different meaning of "the second year after the destruction of the Temple"; or as that of Hengstenberg, followed by many modern apologists, that Nebuchadrezzar had previously been associated in the kingdom with Nabopolassar, and that this was the second year of his independent reign. Or, again, we may, with Ewald, read "the twelfth year." But by these methods we are not taking the Book as it stands, but are supposing it to be a network of textual corruptions and conjectural combinations.

IV. In ii. 2 the king summons four classes of hierophants to disclose his dream and its interpretation. They are the magicians (Chartummîm), the enchanters (Ashshaphîm), the sorcerers (Mechashsh'phîm), and the Chaldeans (Kasdîm). [101] The Chartummîm occur in Gen. xli. 8 (which seems to be in the writer's mind); and the Mechashsh'phîm occur in Exod. vii. 11, xxii. 18; but the mention of Kasdîm, "Chaldeans," is, so far as we know, an immense anachronism. In much later ages the name was used, as it was among the Roman writers, for wandering astrologers and quacks. [102] But this degenerate sense of the word was, so far as we can judge, wholly unknown to the age of Daniel. It never once occurs in this sense on any of the monuments. Unknown to the Assyrian-Babylonian language, and only acquired long after the end of the Babylonian Empire, such a usage of the word is, as Schrader says, "an indication of the post-exilic composition of the Book." [103] In the days of Daniel "Chaldeans" had no meaning resembling that of "magicians" or "astrologers." In every other writer of the Old Testament, and in all contemporary records, Kasdîm simply means the Chaldean nation, and never a learned caste. [104] This single circumstance has decisive weight in proving the late age of the Book of Daniel.

V. Again, we find in ii. 14, "Arioch, the chief of the executioners." Schrader precariously derives the name from Eri-aku, "servant of the moon-god"; but, however that may be, we already find the name as that of a king Ellasar in Gen. xiv. 1, and we find it again for a king of the Elymæans in Judith i. 6. In ver. 16 Daniel "went in and desired of the king" a little respite; but in ver. 25 Arioch tells the king, as though it were a sudden discovery of his own, "I have found a man of the captives of Judah, that will make known unto the king the interpretation." This was a surprising form of introduction, after we have been told that the king himself had, by personal examination, found that Daniel and his young companions were "ten times better than all the magicians and astrologers that were in all his realm." It seems, however, as if each of these chapters was intended to be recited as a separate Haggada.

VI. In ii. 46, after the interpretation of the dream, "the King Nebuchadnezzar fell upon his face, and worshipped Daniel, and commanded that they should offer an oblation and sweet odours unto him." This is another of the immense surprises of the Book. It is exactly the kind of incident in which the haughty theocratic sentiment of the Jews found delight, and we find a similar spirit in the many Talmudic inventions in which Roman emperors, or other potentates, are represented as paying extravagant adulation to Rabbinic sages. There is (as we shall see) a similar story narrated by Josephus of Alexander the Great prostrating himself before the high priest Jaddua, but it has long been relegated to the realm of fable as an outcome of Jewish self-esteem. [105] It is probably meant as a concrete illustration of the glowing promises of Isaiah, that "kings and queens shall bow down to thee with their faces towards the earth, and lick up the dust of thy feet"; [106] and "the sons of them that despised thee shall bow themselves down at the soles of thy feet." [107]

VII. We further ask in astonishment whether Daniel could have accepted without indignant protest the offering of "an oblation and sweet odours." To say that they were only offered to God in the person of Daniel is the idle pretence of all idolatry. They are expressly said to be offered "to Daniel." A Herod could accept blasphemous adulations; [108] but a Paul and a Barnabas deprecate such devotions with intense disapproval.[109]

VIII. In ii. 48 Nebuchadrezzar appoints Daniel, as a reward for his wisdom, to rule over the whole province of Babylon, and to be Rab-signîn, "chief ruler," and to be over all the wise men (Khakamim) of Babylon. Lenormant treats this statement as an interpolation, because he regards it as "evidently impossible." We know that in the Babylonian priesthood, and especially among the sacred caste, there was a passionate religious intolerance. It is inconceivable that they should have accepted as their religious superior a monotheist who was the avowed and uncompromising enemy to their whole system of idolatry. It is equally inconceivable that Daniel should have accepted the position of a hierophant in a polytheistic cult. In the next three chapters there is no allusion to Daniel's tenure of these strange and exalted offices, either civil or religious.[110]

IX. The third chapter contains another story, told in a style of wonderful stateliness and splendour, and full of glorious lessons; but here again we encounter linguistic and other difficulties. Thus in iii. 2, though "all the rulers of the provinces" and officers of all ranks are summoned to the dedication of Nebuchadrezzar's colossus, there is not an allusion to Daniel throughout the chapter. Four of the names of the officers in iii. 2, 3, appear, to our surprise, to be Persian;[111] and, of the six musical instruments, three--the lute, psaltery, and bagpipe[112] --have obvious Greek names, two of which (as already stated) are of late origin, while another, the sab'ka, resembles the Greek sambuke, but may have come to the Greeks from the Aramæans.[113] The incidents of the chapter are such as find no analogy throughout the Old or New Testament, but exactly resemble those of Jewish moralising fiction, of which they furnish the most perfect specimen. It is exactly the kind of concrete comment which a Jewish writer of piety and genius, for the encouragement of his afflicted people, might have based upon such a passage as Isa. xliii. 2, 3: "When thou walkest through the fire, thou shalt not be burned; neither shall the flame kindle upon thee. For I am the Lord thy God, the Holy One of Israel, thy Saviour." Nebuchadrezzar's decree, "That every people, nation, and language, which speak anything amiss against the God of Shadrach, Meshach, and Abed-nego, shall be cut in pieces, and their houses shall be made a dunghill," can only be paralleled out of the later Jewish literature.[114]

X. In chap. iv. we have another monotheistic decree of the King of Babylon, announcing to "all people, nations, and languages" what "the high God hath wrought towards me." It gives us a vision which recalls Ezek. xxxi. 3-18, and may possibly have been suggested by that fine chapter.[115] The language varies between the third and the first person. In iv. 13 Nebuchadrezzar speaks of "a watcher and a holy one." This is the first appearance in Jewish literature of the word 'ir, "watcher," which is so common in the Book of Enoch.[116] In ver. 26 the expression "after thou shalt have known that the heavens do rule" is one which has no analogue in the Old Testament, though exceedingly common in the superstitious periphrases of the later Jewish literature. As to the story of the strange lycanthropy with which Nebuchadrezzar was afflicted, though it receives nothing but the faintest shadow of support from any historic record, it may be based on some fact preserved by tradition. It is probably meant to reflect on the mad ways of Antiochus. The general phrase of Berossus, which tells us that Nebuchadrezzar "fell into a sickness and died,"[117] has been pressed into an historical verification of this narrative! But the phrase might have been equally well used in the most ordinary case,[118] which shows what fancies have been adduced to prove that we are here dealing with history. The fragment of Abydenus in his Assyriaca, preserved by Eusebius,[119] shows that there was some story about Nebuchadrezzar having uttered remarkable words upon his palace-roof. The announcement of a coming irrevocable calamity to the kingdom from a Persian mule, "the son of a Median woman," and the wish that "the alien conqueror" might be driven "through the desert where wild beasts seek their food, and birds fly hither and thither," has, however, very little to do with the story of Nebuchadrezzar's madness. Abydenus says that, "when he had thus prophesied, he suddenly vanished"; and he adds nothing about any restoration to health or to his kingdom. All that can be said is that there was current among the Babylonian Jews some popular legend of which the writer of the Book of Daniel availed himself for the purpose of his edifying Midrash.

XI. When we reach the fifth chapter, we are faced by a new king, Belshazzar, who is somewhat emphatically called the son of Nebuchadrezzar.[120]

History knows of no such king.[121] The prince of whom it does know was never king, and was a son, not of Nebuchadrezzar, but of the usurper Nabunaid; and between Nebuchadrezzar and Nabunaid there were three other kings.[122]

There was a Belshazzar--Bel-sar-utsur, "Bel protect the prince"--and we possess a clay cylinder of his father Nabunaid, the last king of Babylon, praying the moon-god that "my son, the offspring of my heart, might honour his godhead, and not give himself to sin."[123] But if we follow Herodotus, this Belshazzar never came to the throne; and according to Berossus he was conquered in Borsippa. Xenophon, indeed, speaks of "an impious king" as being slain in Babylon; but this is only in an avowed romance which has not the smallest historic validity.[124] Schrader conjectures that Nabunaid may have gone to take the field against Cyrus (who conquered and pardoned him, and allowed him to end his days as governor of Karamania), and that Belshazzar may have been killed in Babylon. These are mere hypotheses; as are those of Josephus, [125] who identifies Belshazzar with Nabunaid (whom he calls Naboandelon); and of Babelon, who tries to make him the same as Maruduk-shar-utsur (as though Bel was the same as Maruduk), which is impossible, as this king reigned before Nabunaid. No contemporary writer could have fallen into the error either of calling Belshazzar "king"; or of insisting on his being "the son" of Nebuchadrezzar; [126] or of representing him as Nebuchadrezzar's successor. Nebuchadrezzar was succeeded by--

Evil-merodach
circ. b.c.
561 (Avil-marduk). [127] Nergal-sharezer"
559 (Nergal-sar-utsur). Lakhabbashi-marudu"
555 (an infant). (Laborosoarchod) Nabunaid "
554.
Nabunaid reigned till about b.c. 538, when Babylon was taken by Cyrus.

The conduct of Belshazzar in the great feast of this chapter is probably meant as an allusive contrast to the revels and impieties of Antiochus Epiphanes, especially in his infamous festival at the grove of Daphne.

XII. "That night," we are told, "Belshazzar, the Chaldean king, was slain." It has always been supposed that this was an incident of the capture of Babylon by assault, in accordance with the story of Herodotus, repeated by so many subsequent writers. But on this point the inscriptions of Cyrus have revolutionised our knowledge. "There was no siege and capture of Babylon; the capital of the Babylonian Empire opened its gates to the general of Cyrus. Gobryas and his soldiers entered the city without fighting, and the daily services in the great temple of Bel-merodach suffered no interruption. Three months later Cyrus himself arrived, and made his peaceful entry into the new capital of his empire. We gather from the contract-tablets that even the ordinary business of the place had not been affected by the war. The siege and capture of Babylon by Cyrus is really a reflection into the past of the actual sieges undergone by the city in the reigns of Darius, son of Hystaspes and Xerxes. It is clear, then, that the editor of the fifth chapter of the Book of Daniel could have been as little a contemporary of the events he professes to record as Herodotus. For both alike, the true history of the Babylonian Empire has been overclouded and foreshortened by the lapse of time. The three kings who reigned between Nebuchadrezzar and Nabunaid have been forgotten, and the last king of the Babylonian Empire has become the son of its founder." [128]

Snatching at the merest straws, those who try to vindicate the accuracy of the writer--although he makes Belshazzar a king, which he never was; and the son of Nebuchadrezzar, which is not the case; or his grandson, of which there is no tittle of evidence; and his successor, whereas four kings intervened;--think that they improve the case by urging that Daniel was made "the third ruler in the kingdom"--Nabunaid being the first, and Belshazzar being the second! Unhappily for their very precarious hypothesis, the translation "third ruler" appears to be entirely untenable. It means "one of a board of three."

XIII. In the sixth chapter we are again met by difficulty after difficulty.

Who, for instance, was Darius the Mede? We are told (v. 30, 31) that, on the night of his impious banquet, "Belshazzar the king of the Chaldeans" was slain, "and Darius the Median took the kingdom, being about threescore and two years old." We are also told that Daniel "prospered in the reign of Darius, and in the reign of Cyrus the Persian" (vi. 28). But this Darius is not even noticed elsewhere. Cyrus was the conqueror of Babylon, and between b.c. 538-536 there is no room or possibility for a Median ruler.

The inference which we should naturally draw from these statements in the Book of Daniel, and which all readers have drawn, was that Babylon had been conquered by the Medes, and that only after the death of a Median king did Cyrus the Persian succeed.

But historic monuments and records entirely overthrow this supposition. Cyrus was the king of Babylon from the day that his troops entered it without a blow. He had conquered the Medes and suppressed their royalty. "The numerous contract-tables of the ordinary daily business transactions of Babylon, dated as they are month by month, and almost day by day from the reign of Nebuchadrezzar to that of Xerxes, prove that between Nabonidus and Cyrus there was no intermediate ruler." The contemporary scribes and merchants of Babylon knew nothing of any King Belshazzar, and they knew even less of any King Darius the Mede. No contemporary writer could possibly have fallen into such an error. [129]

And against this obvious conclusion, of what possible avail is it for Hengstenberg to quote a late Greek lexicographer (Harpocration, a.d. 170?), who says that the coin "a daric" was named after a Darius earlier than the father of Xerxes?--or for others to identify this shadowy Darius the Mede with Astyages? [130] --or with Cyaxares II. in the romance of Xenophon? [131] --or to say that Darius the Mede is

Gobryas (Ugbaru) of Gutium,[132] --a Persian, and not a king at all--who under no circumstances could have been called "the king" by a contemporary (vi. 12, ix. 1), and whom, apparently for three months only, Cyrus made governor of Babylon? How could a contemporary governor have appointed "one hundred and twenty princes which should be over the whole kingdom,"[133] when, even in the days of Darius Hystaspis, there were only twenty or twenty-three satrapies in the Persian Empire?[134] And how could a mere provincial viceroy be approached by "all the presidents of the kingdom, the governors, and the princes, the counsellors, and the captains," to pass a decree that any one who for thirty days offered any prayer to God or man, except to him, should be cast into the den of lions? The fact that such a decree could only be made by a king is emphasised in the narrative itself (vi. 12: comp. iii. 29). The supposed analogies offered by Professor Fuller and others in favour of a decree so absurdly impossible-- except in the admitted licence and for the high moral purpose of a Jewish Haggada--are to the last degree futile. In any ordinary criticism they would be set down as idle special pleading. Yet this is only one of a multitude of wildly improbable incidents, which, from misunderstanding of the writer's age and purpose, have been taken for sober history, though they receive from historical records and monuments no shadow of confirmation, and are in not a few instances directly opposed to all that we now know to be certain history. Even if it were conceivable that this hypothetic "Darius the Mede" was Gobryas, or Astyages, or Cyaxares, it is plain that the author of Daniel gives him a name and national designation which lead to mere confusion, and speaks of him in a way which would have been surely avoided by any contemporary.

"Darius the Mede," says Professor Sayce, "is in fact a reflection into the past of Darius the son of Hystaspes,[135] just as the siege and capture of Babylon by Cyrus are a reflection into the past of its siege and capture by the same prince. The name of Darius and the story of the slaughter of the Chaldean king go together. They are alike derived from the unwritten history which, in the East of to-day, is still made by the people, and which blends together in a single picture the manifold events and personages of the past. It is a history which has no perspective, though it is based on actual facts; the accurate combinations of the chronologer have no meaning for it, and the events of a century are crowded into a few years. This is the kind of history which the Jewish mind in the age of the Talmud loved to adapt to moral and religious purposes. This kind of history then becomes as it were a parable, and under the name of Haggada serves to illustrate that teaching of the law."[136]

The favourable view given of the character of the imaginary Darius the Mede, and his regard for Daniel, may have been a confusion with the Jewish reminiscences of Darius, son of Hystaspes, who permitted the rebuilding of the Temple under Zerubbabel.[137]

If we look for the source of the confusion, we see it perhaps in the prophecy of Isaiah (xiii. 17, xiv. 6-22), that the Medes should be the destroyers of Babylon; or in that of Jeremiah--a prophet of whom the author had made a special study (Dan. ix. 2)--to the same effect (Jer. li. 11-28); together with the tradition that a Darius--namely, the son of Hystaspes--had once conquered Babylon.

XIV. But to make confusion worse confounded, if these chapters were meant for history, the problematic "Darius the Mede" is in Dan. ix. 1 called "the son of Ahasuerus."

Now Ahasuerus (Achashverosh) is the same as Xerxes, and is the Persian name Khshyarsha; and Xerxes was the son, not the father, of Darius Hystaspis, who was a Persian, not a Mede. Before Darius Hystaspis could have been transformed into the son of his own son Xerxes, the reigns, not only of Darius, but also of Xerxes, must have long been past.

XV. There is yet another historic sign that this Book did not originate till the Persian Empire had long ceased to exist. In xi. 2 the writer only knows of four kings of Persia.[138] These are evidently Cyrus, Cambyses, Darius Hystaspis, and Xerxes--whom he describes as the richest of them. This king is destroyed by the kingdom of Grecia--an obvious confusion of popular tradition between the defeat inflicted on the Persians by the Republican Greeks in the days of Xerxes (b.c. 480), and the overthrow of the Persian kingdom under Darius Codomannus by Alexander the Great (b.c. 333).

***

These, then, are some of the apparent historic impossibilities by which we are confronted when we regard this Book as professed history. The doubts suggested by such seeming errors are not in the least removed by the acervation of endless conjectures. They are greatly increased by the fact that, so far from standing alone, they are intensified by other difficulties which arise under every fresh aspect under which the Book is studied. Behrmann, the latest editor, sums up his studies with the remark that "there is an almost universal agreement that the Book, in its present form and as a whole, had its origin in the Maccabean age; while there is a widening impression that in its purpose it is not an exclusive product of that period." No amount of casuistical ingenuity can long prevail to overthrow the spreading conviction that the views of Hengstenberg, Hävernick, Keil, Pusey, and their followers, have been refuted by the light of advancing knowledge--which is a light kindled for us by God Himself.

## Footnotes:

90. Thus Dr. Pusey says: "The Book of Daniel is especially fitted to be a battle-field between faith and unbelief. It admits of no half-measures. It is either Divine or an imposture. To write any book under the name of another, and to give it out to be his, is, in any case, a forgery dishonest in itself, and destructive of all trustworthiness. But the case of the Book of Daniel, if it were not his, would go far beyond even this. The writer, were he not Daniel, must have lied on a frightful scale. In a word, the whole Book would be one lie in the Name of God." Few would venture to use such language in these days. It is always a perilous style to adopt, but now it has become suicidal. It is founded on an immense and inexcusable anachronism. It avails itself of an utterly false misuse of the words "faith" and "unbelief," by which "faith" becomes a mere synonym for "that which I esteem orthodox," or that which has been the current opinion in ages of ignorance. Much truer faith may be shown by accepting arguments founded on unbiassed evidence than by rejecting them. And what can be more foolish than to base the great truths of the Christian religion on special pleadings which have now come to wear the aspect of ingenious sophistries, such as would not be allowed to have the smallest validity in any ordinary question of literary or historic evidence? Hengstenberg, like Pusey, says in his violent ecclesiastical tone of autocratic infallibility that the interpretation of the Book by most eminent modern critics "will remain false so long as the word of Christ is true--that is, for ever." This is to make "the word of Christ" the equivalent of a mere theological blindness and prejudice! Assertions which are utterly baseless can only be met by assertions based on science and the love of truth. Thus when Rupprecht says that "the modern criticism of the Book of Daniel is unchristian, immoral, and unscientific," we can only reply with disdain, Novimus istas lekuthous. In the present day they are mere bluster of impotent odium theologicum.
91. Gen. xli.
92. See Lenormant, La Divination, p. 219.
93. Jer. xxix. 22. The tenth verse of this very chapter is referred to in Dan. ix. 2. The custom continued in the East centuries afterwards. "And if it was known to a Roman writer (Quintus Curtius, v. 1) in the days of Vespasian, why" (Mr. Bevan pertinently asks) "should it not have been known to a Palestinian writer who lived centuries earlier?" (A. A. Bevan, Short Commentary, p. 22).
94. Avodah-Zarah, f. 3, 1; Sanhedrin, f. 93, 1; Pesachim, f. 118, 1; Eiruvin, f. 53, 1.
95. Jer. lii. 28-30. These were in the reign of Jehoiachin.
96. Jer. xlvi. 2: comp. Jer. xxv. The passage of Berossus, quoted in Jos., Antt. X. xi. 1, is not trustworthy, and does not remove the difficulty.
97. The attempts of Keil and Pusey to get over the difficulty, if they were valid, would reduce Scripture to a hopeless riddle. The reader will see all the latest efforts in this direction in the Speaker's Commentary and the work of Fabre d'Envieu. Even such "orthodox" writers as Dorner, Delitzsch, and Gess, not to mention hosts of other great critics, have long seen the desperate impossibility of these arguments.
98. Balatsu-utsur, "protect his life." The root balâtu, "life," is common in Assyrian names. The mistake comes from the wrong vocalisation adopted by the Massorets (Meinhold, Beiträge, p. 27).
99. Schrader dubiously connects it with matstsara, "guardian."
100. Lenormant, p. 182, regards it as a corruption of Ashbenazar, "the goddess has pruned the seed" (??); but assumed corruptions of the text are an uncertain expedient.
101. On these see Rob. Smith, Cambr. Journ. of Philol., No. 27, p. 125.
102. Juv., Sat., x. 96: "Cum grege Chaldæo"; Val. Max., iii. 1; Cic., De Div., i. 1, etc.
103. Keilinschr., p. 429; Meinhold, p. 28.
104. Isa. xxiii. 13; Jer. xxv. 12; Ezek. xii. 13; Hab. i. 6.
105. Jos., Antt., XI. viii. 5.
106. Isa. xlix. 23.
107. Isa. lx. 14.
108. Acts xii. 22, 23.
109. Acts xiv. 11, 12, xxviii. 6.
110. See Jer. xxxix. 3. And if he held this position, how could he be absent in chap. iii.?
111. Namely, the words for "satraps," "governors," "counsellors," and "judges," as well as the courtiers in iii. 24. Bleek thinks that to enhance the stateliness of the occasion the writer introduced as many official names as he knew.
112. Supra, p. 23.
113. Athen., Deipnos., iv. 175.
114. The Persian titles in iii. 24 alone suffice to indicate that this could not be Nebuchadrezzar's actual decree. See further, Meinhold, pp. 30, 31. We are evidently dealing with a writer who introduces many Persian words, with no consciousness that they could not have been used by Babylonian kings.
115. The writer of Daniel was evidently acquainted with the Book of Ezekiel. See Delitzsch in Herzog, s.v. "Daniel," and Driver, p. 476.

116. See iv. 16, 25-30.
117. Preserved by Jos.: comp. Ap., I. 20.
118. The phrase is common enough: e.g., in Jos., Antt., X. xi. 1 (comp. c. Ap., I. 19); and a similar phrase, empeson eis arrhostian, is used of Antiochus Epiphanes in 1 Macc. vi. 8.
119. Præp. Ev., ix. 41. Schrader (K. A. T., ii. 432) thinks that Berossus and the Book of Daniel may both point to the same tradition; but the Chaldee tradition quoted by the late writer Abydenus errs likewise in only recognising two Babylonish kings instead of four, exclusive of Belshazzar. See, too, Schrader, Jahrb. für Prot. Theol., 1881, p. 618.
120. Dan. v. 11. The emphasis seems to show that "son" is really meant--not grandson. This is a little strange, for Jeremiah (xxvii. 7) had said that the nations should serve Nebuchadrezzar, "and his son, and his son's son"; and in no case was Belshazzar Nebuchadrezzar's son's son, for his father Nabunaid was an usurping son of a Rab-mag.
121. Schrader, p. 434 ff.; and in Riehm, Handwörterb., ii. 163; Pinches, in Smith's Bibl. Dict., i. 388, 2nd edn. The contraction into Belshazzar from Bel-sar-utsur seems to show a late date.
122. That the author of Daniel should have fallen into these errors is the more remarkable because Evil-merodach is mentioned in 2 Kings xxv. 27; and Jeremiah in his round number of seventy years includes three generations (Jer. xxvii. 7). Herodotus and Abydenus made the same mistake. See Kamphausen, pp. 30, 31.
123. Herod., i. 191. See Rawlinson, Herod., i. 434.
124. Xen., Cyrop., VII. v. 3.
125. Antt., X. xi. 2. In c. Ap., I. 20, he calls him Nabonnedus.
126. This is now supposed to mean "grandson by marriage," by inventing the hypothesis that Nabunaid married a daughter of Nebuchadrezzar. But this does not accord with Dan. v. 2, 11, 22; and so in Baruch i. 11, 12.
127. 2 Kings xxv. 27.
128. Sayce, The Higher Criticism and the Monuments, p. 527.
129. I need not enter here upon the confusion of the Manda with the Medes, on which see Sayce, Higher Criticism and Monuments, p. 519 ff.
130. Winer, Realwörterb., s.v. "Darius."
131. So Bertholdt, Von Lengerke, Auberlen. It is decidedly rejected by Schrader (Riehm, Handwörterb., i. 259). Even Cicero said, "Cyrus ille a Xenophonte non ad historiæ fidem scriptus est" (Ad Quint. Fratr., Ep. i. 3). Niebuhr called the Cyropædia "einen elenden und läppischen Roman" (Alt. Gesch., i. 116). He classes it with Télémaque or Rasselas. Xenophon was probably the ultimate authority for the statement of Josephus (Antt., X. xi. 4), which has no weight. Herodotus and Ktesias know nothing of the existence of any Cyaxares II., nor does the Second Isaiah (xlv.), who evidently contemplates Cyrus as the conqueror and the first king of Babylon. Are we to set a professed romancer like Xenophon, and a late compiler like Josephus, against these authorities?
132. T. W. Pinches, in Smith's Bibl. Dict., i. 716, 2nd edn. Into this theory are pressed the general expressions that Darius "received the kingdom" and was "made king," which have not the least bearing on it. They may simply mean that he became king by conquest, and not in the ordinary course--so Rosenmüller, Hitzig, Von Lengerke, etc.; or perhaps the words show some sense of uncertainty as to the exact course of events. The sequence of Persian kings in Seder Olam, 28-30, and in Rashi on Dan. v. 1, ix. 1, is equally unhistorical.
133. This is supported by the remark that this three-months viceroy "appointed governors in Babylon"!
134. Herod., iii. 89; Records of the Past, viii. 88.
135. See, too, Meinhold (Beiträge, p. 46), who concludes his survey with the words, "Sprachliche wie sachliche Gründe machen es nicht nur wahrscheinlich sondern gewiss dass an danielsche Autorschaft von Dan. ii.-vi., überhanpt an die Entstehung zur Zeit der jüdischen Verbannung nicht zu denken ist." He adds that almost all scholars believe the chapters to be no older than the age of the Maccabees, and that even Kahnis (Dogmatik, i. 376) and Delitzsch (Herzog, s.v. "Dan.") give up their genuineness. He himself believes that these Aramaic chapters were incorporated by a later writer, who wrote the introduction.
136. Sayce. l.c., p. 529.
137. Kamphausen, p. 45.
138. Sayce, l.c. The author of the Book of Daniel seems only to have known of three kings of Persia after Cyrus (xi. 2). But five are mentioned in the Old Testament--Cyrus, Darius, Artaxerxes, Xerxes, and Darius III. (Codomannus, Neh. xii. 22). There were three Dariuses and three Artaxerxes, but he only knows one of each name (Kamphausen, p. 32). He might easily have overlooked the fact that the Darius of Neh. xii. 22 was a wholly different person from the Darius of Ezra vi. 1.

# CHAPTER IV - GENERAL STRUCTURE OF THE BOOK

In endeavouring to see the idea and construction of a book there is always much room for the play of subjective considerations. Meinhold has especially studied this subject, but we cannot be certain that his views are more than imaginative. He thinks that chap. ii., in which we are strongly reminded of the story of Joseph and of Pharaoh's dreams, is intended to set forth God as Omniscient, and chap. iii. as Omnipotent. To these conceptions is added in chap. iv. the insistence upon God's All-holiness. The fifth and sixth chapters form one conception. Since the death of Belshazzar is assigned to the night of his banquet no edict could be ascribed to him resembling those attributed to Nebuchadrezzar. The effect of Daniel's character and of the Divine protection accorded to him on the mind of Darius is expressed in the strong edict of the latter in vi. 26, 27. This is meant to illustrate that the All-wise, Almighty, All-holy God is the Only Living God. The consistent and homogeneous object of the whole historic section is to set forth the God of the Hebrews as exalting Himself in the midst of heathendom, and extorting submission by mighty portents from heathen potentates. In this the Book offers a general analogy to the section of the history of the Israelites in Egypt narrated in Exod. i. 12. The culmination of recognition as to the power of God is seen in the decree of Darius (vi. 26, 27), as compared with that of Nebuchadrezzar in iv. 33. According to this view, the meaning and essence of each separate chapter are given in its closing section, and there is artistic advance to the great climax, marked alike by the resemblances of these four paragraphs (ii. 47, iii. 28, 29, iv. 37, vi. 26, 27), and by their differences. To this main purpose all the other elements of these splendid pictures--the faithfulness of Hebrew worshippers, the abasement of blaspheming despots, the mission of Israel to the nations--are subordinated. The chief aim is to set forth the helpless humiliation of all false gods before the might of the God of Israel. It might be expressed in the words, "Of a truth, Lord, the kings of Assyria have laid waste all the nations, and cast their gods into the fire; for they were no gods, but the work of men's hands, wood and stone."

A closer glance at these chapters will show some grounds for these conclusions.

Thus, in the second chapter, the magicians and sorcerers repudiate all possibility of revealing the king's dream and its interpretation, because they are but men, and the gods have not their dwelling with mortal flesh (ii. 11); but Daniel can tell the dream because he stands near to his God, who, though He is in heaven, yet is All-wise, and revealeth secrets.

In the third chapter the destruction of the strongest soldiers of Nebuchadrezzar by fire, and the absolute deliverance of the three Jews whom they have flung into the furnace, convince Nebuchadrezzar that no god can deliver as the Almighty does, and that therefore it is blasphemy deserving of death to utter a word against Him.

In chap. iv. the supremacy of Daniel's wisdom as derived from God, the fulfilment of the threatened judgment, and the deliverance of the mighty King of Babylon from his degrading madness when he lifts up his eyes to heaven, convince Nebuchadrezzar still more deeply that God is not only a Great God, but that no other being, man or god, can even be compared to Him. He is the Only and the Eternal God, who "doeth according to His will in the army of heaven," as well as "among the inhabitants of the earth," and "none can stay His hand." This is the highest point of conviction. Nebuchadrezzar confesses that God is not only Primus inter pares, but the Irresistible God, and his own God. And after this, in the fifth chapter, Daniel can speak to Belshazzar of "the Lord of heaven" (v. 23); and as the king's Creator; and of the nothingness of gods of silver, and gold, and brass, and wood, and stone;--as though those truths had already been decisively proved. And this belief finds open expression in the decree of Darius (vi. 26, 27), which concludes the historic section.

It is another indication of this main purpose of these histories that the plural form of the Name of God--Elohîm--does not once occur in chaps. ii.-vi. It is used in i. 2, 9, 17; but not again till the ninth chapter, where it occurs twelve times; once in the tenth (x. 12); and twice of God in the eleventh chapter (xi. 32, 37). In the prophetic section (vii. 18, 22, 25, 27) we have "Most High" in the plural ('elionîn); [139] but with reference only to the One God (see vii. 25). But in all cases where the heathen are addressed this plural becomes the singular (ehlleh, 'lh), as throughout the first six chapters. This avoidance of so common a word as the plural Elohîm for God, because the plural form might conceivably have been misunderstood by the heathen, shows the elaborate construction of the Book.[140] God is called Eloah

Shamaîn, "God of heaven," in the second and third chapters; but in later chapters we have the common post-exilic phrase in the plural.[141]

In the fourth and fifth chapters we have God's Holiness first brought before us, chiefly on its avenging side; and it is not till we have witnessed the proof of His Unity, Wisdom, Omnipotence, and Justice, which it is the mission of Israel to make manifest among the heathen, that all is summed up in the edict of Darius to all people, nations, and languages.

The omission of any express recognition of God's tender compassion is due to the structure of these chapters; for it would hardly be possible for heathen potentates to recognise that attribute in the immediate presence of His judgments. It is somewhat remarkable that the name "Jehovah" is avoided.[142] As the Jews purposely pronounced it with wrong vowels, and the LXX. render it by kurios, the Samaritan by symh, and the Rabbis by "the Name," so we find in the Book of Daniel a similar avoidance of the awful Tetragrammaton.

## Footnotes:

139. Literally, as in margin, "most high things" or "places."
140. In iv. 5, 6; and elohîn means "gods" in the mouth of a heathen ("spirit of the holy gods").
141. Elohîn occurs repeatedly in chap. ix., and in x. 12, xi. 32, 37.
142. It only occurs in Dan. ix.

# CHAPTER V - THE THEOLOGY OF THE BOOK OF DANIEL

As regards the religious views of the Book of Daniel some of them at any rate are in full accordance with the belief in the late origin of the Book to which we are led by so many indications.[143]

I. Thus in Dan. xii. 2 (for we may here so far anticipate the examination of the second section of the Book) we meet, for the first time in Scripture, with a distinct recognition of the resurrection of the individual dead.[144] This, as all know, is a doctrine of which we only find the faintest indication in the earlier books of the Canon. Although the doctrine is still but dimly formulated, it is clearer in this respect than Isa. xxv. 8, xxvi. 19.

II. Still more remarkable is the special prominence of angels. It is not God who goes forth to war (Judg. v. 13, 23), or takes personal part in the deliverance or punishment of nations (Isa. v. 26, vii. 18). Throned in isolated and unapproachable transcendence, He uses the agency of intermediate beings (Dan. iv. 14).[145]

In full accordance with late developments of Jewish opinion angels are mentioned by special names, and appear as Princes and Protectors of special lands.[146] In no other book in the Old Testament have we any names given to angels, or any distinction between their dignities, or any trace of their being in mutual rivalry as Princes or Patrons of different nationalities. These remarkable features of angelology only occur in the later epoch, and in the apocalyptic literature to which this Book belongs. Thus they are found in the LXX. translations of Deut. xxxii. 8 and Isa. xxx. 4, and in such post-Maccabean books as those of Enoch and Esdras.[147]

III. Again, we have the fixed custom of three daily formal prayers, uttered towards the Kibleh of Jerusalem. This may, possibly, have begun during the Exile. It became a normal rule for later ages.[148] The Book, however, like that of Jonah, is, as a whole, remarkably free from any extravagant estimate of Levitical minutiæ.

IV. Once more, for the first time in Jewish story, we find extreme importance attached to the Levitical distinction of clean and unclean meats, which also comes into prominence in the age of the Maccabees, as it afterwards constituted a most prominent element in the ideal of Talmudic religionism.[149] Daniel and the Three Children are vegetarians, like the Pharisees after the destruction of the Second Temple, mentioned in Baba Bathra, f. 60, 2.

V. We have already noticed the avoidance of the sacred name "Jehovah" even in passages addressed to Jews (Dan. ii. 18), though we find "Jehovah" in 2 Chron. xxxvi. 7. Jehovah only occurs in reference to Jer. xxv. 8-11, and in the prayer of the ninth chapter, where we also find Adonai and Elohîm.

Periphrases for God, like "the Ancient of Days," become normal in Talmudic literature.

VI. Again, the doctrine of the Messiah, like these other doctrines, is, as Professor Driver says, "taught with greater distinctness and in a more developed form than elsewhere in the Old Testament, and with features approximating to, though not identical with, those met with in the earlier parts of the Book of Enoch (b.c. 100). In one or two instances these developments may have been partially moulded by foreign influences.[150] They undoubtedly mark a later phase of revelation than that which is set before us in other books of the Old Testament. And the conclusion indicated by these special features in the Book is confirmed by the general atmosphere which we breathe throughout it. The atmosphere and tone are not those of any other writings belonging to the Jews of the Exile; it is rather that of the Maccabean Chasidîm." How far the Messianic Bar Enosh (vii. 13) is meant to be a person will be considered in the comment on that passage.

We shall see in later pages that the supreme value and importance of the Book of Daniel, rightly understood, consists in this--that "it is the first attempt at a Philosophy, or rather at a Theology of History."[151] Its main object was to teach the crushed and afflicted to place unshaken confidence in God.

## Footnotes:

143. The description of God as "the Ancient of Days" with garments white as snow, and of His throne of flames on burning wheels, is found again in the Book of Enoch, written about b.c. 141 (Enoch

*The Expositor's Bible: The Book of Daniel*
xiv.).

144. See Dan. xii. 2. Comp. Jos., B. J., II. viii. 14; Enoch xxii. 13, lx. 1-5, etc.

145. Comp. Smend, Alttest. Relig. Gesch., p. 530. For references to angels in Old Testament see Job i. 6, xxxviii. 7; Jer. xxiii. 18; Psalm lxxxix. 7; Josh. v. 13-15; Zech. i. 12, iii. 1. See further Behrmann, Dan., p. xxiii.

146. Dan. iv. 14, ix. 21, x. 13, 20.

147. See Enoch lxxi. 17, lxviii. 10, and the six archangels Uriel, Raphael, Reguel, Michael, Saragael, and Gabriel in Enoch xx.-xxxvi. See Rosh Hashanah, f. 56, 1; Bereshîth Rabba, c. 48; Hamburger, i. 305-312.

148. Berachôth, f. 31; Dan. vi. 11. Comp. Psalm lv. 18; 1 Kings viii. 38-48.

149. 1 Macc. i. 62; Dan. i. 8; 2 Macc. v. 27, vi. 18-vii. 42.

150. Introd., p. 477. Comp. 2 Esdras xiii. 41-45, and passim; Enoch xl., xlv., xlvi., xlix., and passim; Hamburger, Real-Encycl., ii. 267 ff. With "the time of the end" and the numerical calculations comp. 2 Esdras vi. 6, 7.

151. Roszmann, Die Makkabäische Erhebung, p. 45. See Wellhausen, Die Pharis. u. d. Sadd., 77 ff.

# CHAPTER VI - PECULIARITIES OF THE APOCALYPTIC AND PROPHETIC SECTION OF THE BOOK

If we have found much to lead us to serious doubts as to the authenticity and genuineness--i.e., as to the literal historicity and the real author--of the Book of Daniel in its historic section, we shall find still more in the prophetic section. If the phenomena already passed in review are more than enough to indicate the impossibility that the Book could have been written by the historic Daniel, the phenomena now to be considered are such as have sufficed to convince the immense majority of learned critics that, in its present form, the Book did not appear before the days of Antiochus Epiphanes. [152] The probable date is b.c. 164. As in the Book of Enoch xc. 15, 16, it contains history written under the form of prophecy.

Leaving minuter examination to later chapters of commentary, we will now take a brief survey of this unique apocalypse.

I. As regards the style and method the only distant approach to it in the rest of the Old Testament is in a few visions of Ezekiel and Zechariah, which differ greatly from the clear, and so to speak classic, style of the older prophets. But in Daniel we find visions far more enigmatical, and far less full of passion and poetry. Indeed, as regards style and intellectual force, the splendid historic scenes of chaps. i.-vi. far surpass the visions of vii.-xii., some of which have been described as "composite logographs," in which the ideas are forcibly juxtaposed without care for any coherence in the symbols--as, for instance, when a horn speaks and has eyes. [153]

Chap. vii. contains a vision of four different wild beasts rising from the sea: a lion, with eagle-wings, which afterwards becomes semi-human; a bear, leaning on one side, and having three ribs in its mouth; a four-winged, four-headed panther; and a still more terrible creature, with iron teeth, brazen claws, and ten horns, among which rises a little horn, which destroyed three of the others--it has man's eyes and a mouth speaking proud things.

There follows an epiphany of the Ancient of Days, who destroys the little horn, but prolongs for a time the existence of the other wild beasts. Then comes One in human semblance, who is brought before the Ancient of Days, and is clothed by Him with universal and eternal power.

We shall see reasons for the view that the four beasts--in accordance with the interpretation of the vision given to Daniel himself--represent the Babylonian, the Median, the Persian, and the Greek empires, issuing in the separate kingdoms of Alexander's successors; and that the little horn is Antiochus Epiphanes, whose overthrow is to be followed immediately by the Messianic Kingdom. [154]

The vision of the eighth chapter mainly pursues the history of the fourth of these kingdoms. Daniel sees a ram standing eastward of the river-basin of the Ulai, having two horns, of which one is higher than the other. It butts westward, northward, and southward, and seemed irresistible, until a he-goat from the West, with one horn between its eyes, confronted it, and stamped it to pieces. After this its one horn broke into four towards the four winds of heaven, and one of them shot forth a puny horn, which grew great towards the South and East, and acted tyrannously against the Holy People, and spoke blasphemously against God. Daniel hears the holy ones declaring that its powers shall only last two thousand three hundred evening-mornings. An angel bids Gabriel to explain the vision to Daniel; and Gabriel tells the seer that the ram represents the Medo-Persian and the he-goat the Greek Kingdom. Its great horn is Alexander; the four horns are the kingdoms of his successors, the Diadochi; the little horn is a king bold of vision and versed in enigmas, whom all agree to be Antiochus Epiphanes.

In the ninth chapter we are told that Daniel has been meditating on the prophecy of Jeremiah that Jerusalem should be rebuilt after seventy years, and as the seventy years seem to be drawing to a close he humbles himself with prayer and fasting. But Gabriel comes flying to him at the time of the evening sacrifice, and explains to him that the seventy years is to mean seventy weeks of years--i.e., four hundred and ninety years, divided into three periods of 7 + 62 + 1. At the end of seven (i.e., forty-nine) years an anointed prince will order the restoration of Jerusalem. The city will continue, though in humiliation, for sixty-two (i.e., four hundred and thirty-four) years, when "an anointed" will be cut off, and a prince will destroy it. During half a week (i.e., for three and a half years) he will cause the sacrifice and oblation to cease; and he will make a covenant with many for one week, at the end of which he will be cut off.

Here, again, we shall have reason to see that the whole prophecy culminates in, and is mainly concerned with, Antiochus Epiphanes. In fact, it furnishes us with a sketch of his fortunes, which, in connexion with the eleventh chapter, tells us more about him than we learn from any extant history.

In the tenth chapter Daniel, after a fast of twenty-one days, sees a vision of Gabriel, who explains to him why his coming has been delayed, soothes his fears, touches his lips, and prepares him for the vision of chapter eleven. That chapter is mainly occupied with a singularly minute and circumstantial history of the murders, intrigues, wars, and intermarriages of the Lagidæ and Seleucidæ. So detailed is it that in some cases the history has to be reconstructed out of it. This sketch is followed by the doings and final overthrow of Antiochus Epiphanes.

The twelfth chapter is the picture of a resurrection, and of words of consolation and exhortation addressed to Daniel.

Such in briefest outline are the contents of these chapters, and their peculiarities are very marked. Until the reader has studied the more detailed explanation of the chapters separately, and especially of the eleventh, he will be unable to estimate the enormous force of the arguments adduced to prove the impossibility of such "prophecies" having emanated from Babylon and Susa about b.c. 536. Long before the astonishing enlargement of our critical knowledge which has been the work of the last generation-- nearly fifty years ago--the mere perusal of the Book as it stands produced on the manly and honest judgment of Dr. Arnold a strong impression of uncertainty. He said that the latter chapters of Daniel would, if genuine, be a clear exception to the canons of interpretation which he laid down in his Sermons on Prophecy, since "there can be no reasonable spiritual meaning made out of the kings of the North and South." "But," he adds, "I have long thought that the greater part of the Book of Daniel is most certainly a very late work of the time of the Maccabees; and the pretended prophecies about the kings of Grecia and Persia, and of the North and South, are mere history, like the poetical prophecies in Virgil and elsewhere. In fact, you can trace distinctly the date when it was written, because the events up to that date are given with historical minuteness, totally unlike the character of real prophecy; and beyond that date all is imaginary." [155]

The Book is the earliest specimen of its kind known to us. It inaugurated a new and important branch of Jewish literature, which influenced many subsequent writers. An apocalypse, so far as its literary form is concerned, "claims throughout to be a supernatural revelation given to mankind by the mouth of those men in whose names the various writings appear." An apocalypse--such, for instance, as the Books of Enoch, the Assumption of Moses, Baruch, 1, 2 Esdras, and the Sibylline Oracles--is characterised by its enigmatic form, which shrouds its meaning in parables and symbols. It indicates persons without naming them, and shadows forth historic events under animal forms, or as operations of Nature. Even the explanations which follow, as in this Book, are still mysterious and indirect.

II. In the next place an apocalypse is literary, not oral. Schürer, who classes Daniel among the oldest and most original of pseudepigraphic prophecies, etc., rightly says that "the old prophets in their teachings and exhortations addressed themselves directly to the people first and foremost through their oral utterances; and then, but only as subordinate to these, by written discourses as well. But now, when men felt themselves at any time compelled by their religious enthusiasm to influence their contemporaries, instead of directly addressing them in person like the prophets of old, they did so by a writing purporting to be the work of some one or other of the great names of the past, in the hope that in this way the effect would be all the surer and all the more powerful." [156] The Daniel of this Book represents himself, not as a prophet, but as a humble student of the prophets. He no longer claims, as Isaiah did, to speak in the Name of God Himself with a "Thus saith Jehovah."

III. Thirdly, it is impossible not to notice that Daniel differs from all other prophecies by its all-but-total indifference to the circumstances and surroundings in the midst of which the prediction is supposed to have originated. The Daniel of Babylon and Susa is represented as the writer; yet his whole interest is concentrated, not in the events which immediately interest the Jews of Babylon in the days of Cyrus, or of Jerusalem under Zerubbabel, but deals with a number of predictions which revolve almost exclusively about the reign of a very inferior king four centuries afterwards. And with this king the predictions abruptly stop short, and are followed by the very general promise of an immediate Messianic age.

We may notice further the constant use of round and cyclic numbers, such as three and its compounds (i. 5, iii. 1, vi. 7, 10, vii. 5, 8); four (ii., vii. 6, and viii. 8, xi. 12); seven and its compounds (iii. 19, iv. 16, 23, ix. 24, etc.). The apocalyptic symbols of Bears, Lions, Eagles, Horns, Wings, etc., abound in the contemporary and later Books of Enoch, Baruch, 4 Esdras, the Assumption of Moses, and the Sibyllines, as well as in the early Christian apocalypses, like that of Peter. The authors of the Sibyllines (b.c. 140) were acquainted with Daniel; the Book of Enoch breathes exactly the same spirit with this Book, in the transcendentalism which avoids the name Jehovah (vii. 13; Enoch xlvi. 1, xlvii. 3), in the number of angels (vii. 10; Enoch xl. 1, lx. 2), their names, the title of "watchers" given to them, and their guardianship of men (Enoch xx. 5). The Judgment and the Books (vii. 9, 10, xii. 1) occur again in Enoch xlvii. 3, lxxxi. 1, as in the Book of Jubilees, and the Testament of the Twelve Patriarchs. [157]

## Footnotes:

152. Among these critics are Delitzsch, Riehm, Ewald, Bunsen, Hilgenfeld, Cornill, Lücke, Strack, Schürer, Kuenen, Meinhold, Orelli, Joël, Reuss, König, Kamphausen, Cheyne, Driver, Briggs, Bevan, Behrmann, etc.

153. Renan, History of Israel, iv. 354. He adds, "L'essence du genre c'est le pseudonyme, ou si l'on veut l'apocryphisme" (p. 356).

154. Lagarde, Gott. Gel. Anzieg., 1891, pp. 497-520, stands almost, if not quite, alone in arguing that Dan. vii. was not written till a.d. 69, and that the "little horn" is meant for Vespasian. The relation of the fourth empire of Dan. vii. to the iron part of the image in Dan. ii. refutes this view: both can only refer to the Greek Empire. Josephus (Antt., X. xi. 7) does not refer to Dan. vii.; but neither does he to ix.-xii., for reasons already mentioned. See Cornill, Einleit., p. 262.

155. Stanley, Life of Arnold, p. 505.

156. Schürer, Hist. of the Jew. People, iii. 24 (E. Tr.).

157. On the close resemblance between Daniel and other apocryphal books see Behrmann, Dan., pp. 37-39; Dillmann, Das Buch Henoch. For its relation to the Book of Baruch see Schrader, Keilinschriften, 435 f. Philo does not allude to Daniel.

# CHAPTER VII - INTERNAL EVIDENCE

I. Other prophets start from the ground of the present, and to exigencies of the present their prophecies were primarily directed. It is true that their lofty moral teaching, their rapt poetry, their impassioned feeling, had its inestimable value for all ages. But these elements scarcely exist in the Book of Daniel. Almost the whole of its prophecies bear on one short particular period nearly four hundred years after the supposed epoch of their delivery. What, then, is the phenomenon they present? Whereas other prophets, by studying the problems of the present in the light flung upon them by the past, are enabled, by combining the present with the past, to gain, with the aid of God's Holy Spirit, a vivid glimpse of the immediate future, for the instruction of the living generation, the reputed author of Daniel passes over the immediate future with a few words, and spends the main part of his revelations on a triad of years separated by centuries from contemporary history. Occupied as this description is with the wars and negotiations of empires which were yet unborn, it can have had little practical significance for Daniel's fellow-exiles. Nor could these "predictions" have been to prove the possibility of supernatural foreknowledge, [158] since, even after their supposed fulfilment, the interpretation of them is open to the greatest difficulties and the gravest doubts. If to a Babylonian exile was vouchsafed a gift of prevision so minute and so marvellous as enabled him to describe the intermarriages of Ptolemies and Seleucidæ four centuries later, surely the gift must have been granted for some decisive end. But these predictions are precisely the ones which seem to have the smallest significance. We must say, with Semler, that no such benefit seems likely to result from this predetermination of comparatively unimportant minutiæ as God must surely intend when He makes use of means of a very extraordinary character. It might perhaps be said that the Book was written, four hundred years before the crisis occurred, to console the Jews under their brief period of persecution by the Seleucidæ. It would be indeed extraordinary that so curious, distant, and roundabout a method should have been adopted for an end which, in accordance with the entire economy of God's dealings with men in revelation, could have been so much more easily and so much more effectually accomplished in simpler ways. Further, unless we accept an isolated allusion to Daniel in the imaginary speech of the dying Mattathias, there is no trace whatever that the Book had the smallest influence in inspiring the Jews in that terrible epoch. And the reference of Mattathias, if it was ever made at all, may be to old tradition, and does not allude to the prophecies about Antiochus and his fate.

But, as Hengstenberg, the chief supporter of the authenticity of the Book of Daniel, well observes,[159] "Prophecy can never entirely separate itself from the ground of the present, to influence which is always its more immediate object, and to which therefore it must constantly construct a bridge.[160] On this also rests all certainty of exposition as to the future. And that the means should be provided for such a certainty is a necessary consequence of the Divine nature of prophecy. A truly Divine prophecy cannot possibly swim in the air; nor can the Church be left to mere guesses in the exposition of Scripture which has been given to her as a light amid the darkness."

II. And as it does not start from the ground of the present, so too the Book of Daniel reverses the method of prophecy with reference to the future.

For the genuine predictions of Scripture advance by slow and gradual degrees from the uncertain and the general to the definite and the special. Prophecy marches with history, and takes a step forward at each new period.[161] So far as we know there is not a single instance in which any prophet alludes to, much less dwells upon, any kingdom which had not then risen above the political horizon.[162]

In Daniel the case is reversed: the only kingdom which was looming into sight is dismissed with a few words, and the kingdom most dwelt upon is the most distant and quite the most insignificant of all, of the very existence of which neither Daniel nor his contemporaries had even remotely heard.[163]

III. Then again, although the prophets, with their divinely illuminated souls, reached far beyond intellectual sagacity and political foresight, yet their hints about the future never distantly approach to detailed history like that of Daniel. They do indeed so far lift the veil of the Unseen as to shadow forth the outline of the near future, but they do this only on general terms and on general principles.[164] Their object, as I have repeatedly observed, was mainly moral, and it was also confessedly conditional, even when no hint is given of the implied condition.[165] Nothing is more certain than the wisdom and beneficence of that Divine provision which has hidden the future from men's eyes, and even taught us to regard all prying into its minute events as vulgar and sinful.[166] Stargazing and monthly prognostication were rather the characteristics of false religion and unhallowed divinations than of faithful and holy souls. Nitzsch [167] most justly lays it down as an essential condition of prophecy that it should not disturb man's relation to history. Anything like detailed description of the future would intolerably perplex and confuse our sense of human free-will. It would drive us to the inevitable conclusion that men are but puppets moved irresponsibly by the hand of inevitable fate. Not one such prophecy, unless this be one, occurs anywhere in the Bible. We do not think that (apart from Messianic prophecies) a single instance can be given in which any prophet distinctly and minutely predicts a future series of events of which the fulfilment was not near at hand. In the few cases when some event, already imminent, is predicted apparently with some detail, it is not certain whether some touches--names, for instance--may not have been added by editors living subsequently to the occurrence of the event. [168] That there has been at all times a gift of prescience, whereby the Spirit of God, "entering into holy souls, has made them sons of God and prophets," is indisputable. It is in virtue of this high foreknowledge[169] that the voice of the Hebrew Sibyl has

> "Rolled sounding onwards through a thousand years
> Her deep prophetic bodiments."

Even Demosthenes, by virtue of a statesman's thoughtful experience, can describe it as his office and duty "to see events in their beginnings, to discern their purport and tendencies from the first, and to forewarn his countrymen accordingly." Yet the power of Demosthenes was as nothing compared with that of an Isaiah or a Nahum; and we may safely say that the writings alike of the Greek orator and the Hebrew prophets would have been comparatively valueless had they merely contained anticipations of future history, instead of dealing with truths whose value is equal for all ages--truths and principles which give clearness to the past, security to the present, and guidance to the future. Had it been the function of prophecy to remove the veil of obscurity which God in His wisdom has hung over the destinies of men and kingdoms, it would never have attained, as it has done, to the love and reverence of mankind.

IV. Another unique and abnormal feature is found in the close and accurate chronological calculations in which the Book of Daniel abounds. We shall see later on that the dates of the Maccabean reconsecration of the Temple and the ruin of Antiochus Epiphanes are indicated almost to the day. The numbers of prophecy are in all other cases symbolical and general. They are intentional compounds of seven--the sum of three and four, which are the numbers that mystically shadow forth God and the world--a number which even Cicero calls "rerum omnium fere modus"; and of ten, the number of the world. [170] If we except the prophecy of the seventy years' captivity--which was a round number, and is in no respect parallel to the periods of Daniel--there is no other instance in the Bible of a chronological prophecy. We say no other instance, because one of the commentators who, in writing upon Daniel, objects to the remark of Nitzsch that the numbers of prophecy are mystical, yet observes on the one thousand two hundred and sixty days of Rev. xii. that the number one thousand two hundred and sixty, or three and a half years, "has no historical signification whatever, and is only to be viewed in its relation to the number seven--viz., as symbolising the apparent victory of the world over the Church." [171]

V. Alike, then, in style, in matter, and in what has been called by V. Orelli its "exoteric" manner,--alike in its definiteness and its indefiniteness--in the point from which it starts and the period at which it terminates--in its minute details and its chronological indications--in the absence of the moral and the impassioned element, and in the sense of fatalism which it must have introduced into history had it been a genuine prophecy,--the Book of Daniel differs from all the other books which compose that prophetic canon. From that canon it was rightly and deliberately excluded by the Jews. Its worth and dignity can only be rationally vindicated or rightly understood by supposing it to have been the work of an unknown moralist and patriot of the Maccabean age.

And if anything further were wanting to complete the cogency of the internal evidence which forces this conclusion upon us, it is amply found in a study of those books, confessedly apocryphal, which, although far inferior to the Book before us, are yet of value, and which we believe to have emanated from the same era.

They resemble this Book in their language, both Hebrew and Aramaic, as well as in certain recurring expressions and forms to be found in the Books of Maccabees and the Second Book of Esdras;--in their style--rhetorical rather than poetical, stately rather than ecstatic, diffuse rather than pointed, and wholly inferior to the prophets in depth and power;--in the use of an apocalyptic method, and the strange combination of dreams and symbols;--in the insertion, by way of embellishment, of speeches and formal documents which can at the best be only semi-historical;--finally, in the whole tone of thought, especially in the quite peculiar doctrine of archangels, of angels guarding kingdoms, and of opposing evil spirits. In short, the Book of Daniel may be illustrated by the Apocryphal books in every single particular. In the adoption of an illustrious name--which is the most marked characteristic of this period--it resembles the additions to the Book of Daniel, the Books of Esdras, the Letters of Baruch and

Jeremiah, and the Wisdom of Solomon. In the imaginary and quasi-legendary treatment of history it finds a parallel in Wisdom xvi.-xix., and parts of the Second Book of Maccabees and the Second Book of Esdras. As an allusive narrative bearing on contemporaneous events under the guise of describing the past, it is closely parallel to the Book of Judith, [172] while the character of Daniel bears the same relation to that of Joseph, as the representation of Judith does to that of Jael. As an ethical development of a few scattered historical data, tending to the marvellous and supernatural, but rising to the dignity of a very noble and important religious fiction, it is analogous, though incomparably superior, to Bel and the Dragon, and to the stories of Tobit and Susanna. [173]

The conclusion is obvious; and it is equally obvious that, when we suppose the name of Daniel to have been assumed, and the assumption to have been supported by an antique colouring, we do not for a moment charge the unknown author--who may very well have been Onias IV.--with any dishonesty. Indeed, it appears to us that there are many traces in the Book--phonanta sunetoisin--which exonerate the writer from any suspicion of intentional deception. They may have been meant to remove any tendency to error in understanding the artistic guise which was adopted for the better and more forcible inculcation of the lessons to be conveyed. That the stories of Daniel offered peculiar opportunities for this treatment is shown by the apocryphal additions to the Book; and that the practice was well understood even before the closing of the Canon is sufficiently shown by the Book of Ecclesiastes. The writer of that strange and fascinating book, with its alternating moods of cynicism and resignation, merely adopted the name of Solomon, and adopted it with no dishonourable purpose; for he could not have dreamed that utterances which in page after page betray to criticism their late origin would really be identified with the words of the son of David a thousand years before Christ. This may now be regarded as an indisputable, and is indeed a no longer disputed, result of all literary and philological inquiry.

It is to Porphyry, a Neoplatonist of the third century (born at Tyre, a.d. 233; died in Rome, a.d. 303), that we owe our ability to write a continuous historical commentary on the symbols of Daniel. That writer devoted the twelfth book of his Logoi kata Christianon to a proof that Daniel was not written till after the epoch which it so minutely described. [174] In order to do this he collected with great learning and industry a history of the obscure Antiochian epoch from authors most of whom have perished. Of these authors Jerome--the most valuable part of whose commentary is derived from Porphyry--gives a formidable list, mentioning among others Callinicus, Diodorus, Polybius, Posidonius, Claudius, Theo, and Andronicus. It is a strange fact that the exposition of a canonical book should have been mainly rendered possible by an avowed opponent of Christianity. It was the object of Porphyry to prove that the apocalyptic portion of the Book was not a prophecy at all. [175] It used to be a constant taunt against those who adopt his critical conclusions that their weapons are borrowed from the armoury of an infidel. The objection hardly seems worth answering. "Fas est et ab hoste doceri." If the enemies of our religion have sometimes helped us the better to understand our sacred books, or to judge more correctly respecting them, we should be grateful that their assaults have been overruled to our instruction. The reproach is wholly beside the question. We may apply to it the manly words of Grotius: "Neque me pudeat consentire Porphyrio, quando is in veram sententiam incidit." Moreover, St. Jerome himself could not have written his commentary, as he himself admits, without availing himself of the aid of the erudition of the heathen philosopher, whom no less a person than St. Augustine called "doctissimus philosophorum," though unhappily he was "acerrimus christianorum inimicus."

## Footnotes:

158. Any apparently requisite modification of these words will be considered hereafter.
159. On Revelations, vol. i., p. 408 (E. Tr.).
160. "Dient bei ihnen die Zukunft der Gegenwart, und ist selbst fortgesetzte Gegenwart" (Behrmann, Dan., p. xi).
161. See M. de Pressensé, Hist. des Trois Prem. Siècles, p. 283.
162. See some admirable remarks on this subject in Ewald, Die Proph. d. Alt. Bund., i. 23, 24; Winer, Realwörterb., s.v. "Propheten" Stähelin, Einleit., § 197.
163. Comp. Enoch i. 2.
164. Ewald, Die Proph., i. 27; Michel Nicolas, Études sur la Bible, pp. 336 ff.
165. Comp. Mic. iii. 12; Jer. xxvi. 1-19; Ezek. i. 21. Comp. xxix. 18, 19.
166. Deut. xviii. 10.
167. System der christlichen Lehre, p. 66.
168. E.g., in the case of Josiah (1 Kings xiii. 2).
169. De Coronâ, 73: idein ta pragmata archomena kai proaisthesthai kai proeipein tois allois.
170. The symbolism of numbers is carefully and learnedly worked out in Bähr's Symbolik: cf. Auberlen, p. 133. The several fulfilments of the prophesied seventy years' captivity illustrate this.
171. Hengstenberg, On Revelations, p. 609.
172. All these particulars may be found, without any allusion to the Book of Daniel, in the

admirable article on the Apocrypha by Dean Plumptre in Dr. Smith's Dict. of the Bible.

173. Ewald, Gesch. Isr., iv. 541.

174. "Et non tam Danielem ventura dixisse quam illum narrasse præterita" (Jer.).

175. "Ad intelligendas autem extremas Danielis partes multiplex Græcorum historia necessaria est" (Jer., Proæm. Explan. in Dan. Proph. ad f.). Among these Greek historians he mentions eight whom Porphyry had consulted, and adds, "Et si quando cogimur litterarum sæcularium recordari ... non nostræ est voluntatis, sed ut dicam, gravissimæ necessitatis." We know Porphyry's arguments mainly through the commentary of Jerome, who, indeed, derived from Porphyry the historic data without which the eleventh chapter, among others, would have been wholly unintelligible.

# CHAPTER VIII - EVIDENCE IN FAVOUR OF THE GENUINENESS UNCERTAIN AND INADEQUATE

We have seen that there are many circumstances which force upon us the gravest doubts as to the authenticity of the Book of Daniel. We now proceed to examine the evidence urged in its favour, and deemed adequate to refute the conclusion that in its present form it did not see the light before the time of Antiochus IV.

Taking Hengstenberg as the most learned reasoner in favour of the genuineness of Daniel, we will pass in review all the positive arguments which he has adduced. [176] They occupy no less than one hundred and ten pages (pp. 182-291) of the English translation of his work on the genuineness of Daniel. Most of them are tortuous specimens of special pleading inadequate in themselves, or refuted by increased knowledge derived from the monuments and from further inquiry. To these arguments neither Dr. Pusey nor any subsequent writer has made any material addition. Some of them have been already answered, and many of them are so unsatisfactory that they may be dismissed at once.

I. Such, for instance, are the testimony of the author himself. In one of those slovenly treatises which only serve to throw dust in the eyes of the ignorant we find it stated that, "although the name of Daniel is not prefixed to his Book, the passages in which he speaks in the first person sufficiently prove that he was the author"! Such assertions deserve no answer. If the mere assumption of a name be a sufficient proof of the authorship of a book, we are rich indeed in Jewish authors--and, not to speak of others, our list includes works by Adam, Enoch, Eldad, Medad, and Elijah. "Pseudonymity," says Behrmann, "was a very common characteristic of the literature of that day, and the conception of literary property was alien to that epoch, and especially to the circle of writings of this class."

II. The character of the language, as we have seen already, proves nothing. Hebrew and Aramaic long continued in common use side by side at least among the learned, [177] and the divergence of the Aramaic in Daniel from that of the Targums leads to no definite result, considering the late and uncertain age of those writings.

III. How any argument can be founded on the exact knowledge of history displayed by local colouring we cannot understand. Were the knowledge displayed ever so exact it would only prove that the author was a learned man, which is obvious already. But so far from any remarkable accuracy being shown by the author, it is, on the contrary, all but impossible to reconcile many of his statements with acknowledged facts. The elaborate and tortuous explanations, the frequent "subauditur," the numerous assumptions required to force the text into accordance with the certain historic data of the Babylonian and Persian empires, tell far more against the Book than for it. The methods of accounting for these inaccuracies are mostly self-confuting, for they leave the subject in hopeless confusion, and each orthodox commentator shows how untenable are the views of others.

IV. Passing over other arguments of Keil, Hengstenberg, etc., which have been either refuted already, or which are too weak to deserve repetition, we proceed to examine one or two of a more serious character. Great stress, for instance, is laid on the reception of the Book into the Canon. We acknowledge the canonicity of the Book, its high value when rightly apprehended, and its rightful acceptance as a sacred book; but this in nowise proves its authenticity. The history of the Old Testament Canon is involved in the deepest obscurity. The belief that it was finally completed by Ezra and the Great Synagogue rests on no foundation; indeed, it is irreconcilable with later historic notices and other facts connected with the Books of Ezra, Nehemiah, Esther, and the two Books of Chronicles. The Christian Fathers in this, as in some other cases, implicitly believed what came to them from the most questionable sources, and was mixed up with mere Jewish fables. One of the oldest Talmudic books, the Pirke Aboth, is entirely silent on the collection of the Old Testament, though in a vague way it connects the Great Synagogue with the preservation of the Law. The earliest mention of the legend about Ezra is in the Second Book of Esdras (xiv. 29-48). This book does not possess the slightest claim to authority, as it was not completed till a century after the Christian era; and it mingles up with this very narrative a number of particulars thoroughly fabulous and characteristic of a period when the Jewish writers were always ready to subordinate history to imaginative fables. The account of the magic cup, the forty days and forty nights' dictation, the ninety books of which seventy were secret and intended only for the learned, form part of the very passage from which we are asked to believe that Ezra established our existing Canon, though the genuine Book of Ezra is wholly silent about his having performed any such inestimable service. It adds nothing to the credit of this fable that it is echoed by Irenæus, Clemens Alexandrinus, and Tertullian.[178] Nor are there any external considerations which render it probable. The Talmudic tradition in the Baba Bathra,[179] which says (among other remarks in a passage of which "the notorious errors prove the unreliability of its testimony") that the men of the Great Synagogue wrote the Books of Ezekiel, the Twelve Minor Prophets, Daniel, and Ezra.[180] It is evident that, so far as this evidence is worth anything, it rather goes against the authenticity of Daniel than for it. The Pirke Aboth makes Simon the Just (about b.c. 290) a member of this Great Synagogue, of which the very existence is dubious.[181]

Again, the author of the forged letter at the beginning of the Second Book of Maccabees--"the work" says Hengstenberg, "of an arrant impostor"[182] --attributes the collection of certain books first to Nehemiah, and then, when they had been lost, to Judas Maccabæus (2 Macc. ii. 13, 14). The canonicity of the Old Testament books does not rest on such evidence as this,[183] and it is hardly worth while to pursue it further. That the Book of Daniel was regarded as authentic by Josephus is clear; but this by no means decides its date or authorship. It is one of the very few books of which Philo makes no mention whatever.

V. Nor can the supposed traces of the early existence of the Book be considered adequate to prove its genuineness. With the most important of these, the story of Josephus (Antt., XI. viii. 5) that the high priest Jaddua showed to Alexander the Great the prophecies of Daniel respecting himself, we shall deal later. The alleged traces of the Book in Ecclesiasticus are very uncertain, or rather wholly questionable; and the allusion to Daniel in 1 Macc. ii. 60 decides nothing, because there is nothing to prove that the speech of the dying Mattathias is authentic, and because we know nothing certain as to the date of the Greek translator of that book or of the Book of Daniel. The absence of all allusion to the prophecies of Daniel is, on the other hand, a far more cogent point against the authenticity. Whatever be the date of the Books of Maccabees, it is inconceivable that they should offer no vestige of proof that Judas and his brothers received any hope or comfort from such explicit predictions as Dan. xi., had the Book been in the hands of those pious and noble chiefs.

The First Book of Maccabees cannot be certainly dated more than a century before Christ, nor have we reason to believe that the Septuagint version of the Book is much older.[184]

VI. The badness of the Alexandrian version, and the apocryphal additions to it, seem to be rather an argument for the late age and less established authority of the Book than for its genuineness.[185] Nor can we attach much weight to the assertion (though it is endorsed by the high authority of Bishop Westcott) that "it is far more difficult to explain its composition in the Maccabean period than to meet the peculiarities which it exhibits with the exigencies of the Return." So far is this from being the case that, as we have seen already, it resembles in almost every particular the acknowledged productions of the age in which we believe it to have been written. Many of the statements made on this subject by those who defend the authenticity cannot be maintained. Thus Hengstenberg[186] remarks that (1) "at this time the Messianic hopes are dead," and (2) "that no great literary work appeared between the Restoration from the Captivity and the time of Christ." Now the facts are precisely the reverse in each instance. For (i) the little book called the Psalms of Solomon,[187] which belongs to this period, contains the strongest and clearest Messianic hopes, and the Book of Enoch most closely resembles Daniel in its Messianic predictions. Thus it speaks of the pre-existence of the Messiah (xlviii. 6, lxii. 7), of His sitting on a throne of glory (lv. 4, lxi. 8), and receiving the power of rule.

(ii) Still less can we attach any force to Hengstenberg's argument that, in the Maccabean age, the gift of prophecy was believed to have departed for ever. Indeed, that is an argument in favour of the pseudonymity of the Book. For in the age at which--for purposes of literary form--it is represented as having appeared the spirit of prophecy was far from being dead. Ezekiel was still living, or had died but recently. Zechariah, Haggai, and long afterwards Malachi, were still to continue the succession of the mighty prophets of their race. Now, if prediction be an element in the prophet's work, no prophet, nor all the prophets together, ever distantly approached any such power of minutely foretelling the events of a distant future--even the half-meaningless and all-but-trivial events of four centuries later, in kingdoms which had not yet thrown their distant shadows on the horizon--as that which Daniel must have possessed, if he were indeed the author of this Book.[188] Yet, as we have seen, he never thinks of claiming the functions of the prophets, or speaking in the prophet's commanding voice, as the foreteller of the message of God. On the contrary, he adopts the comparatively feebler and more entangled methods of the literary composers in an age when men saw not their tokens and there was no prophet more.[189]

We must postpone a closer examination of the questions as to the "four kingdoms" intended by the writer, and of his curious and enigmatic chronological calculations; but we must reject at once the monstrous assertion--excusable in the days of Sir Isaac Newton, but which has now become unwise and even portentous--that "to reject Daniel's prophecies would be to undermine the Christian religion, which is all but founded on his prophecies respecting Christ"! Happily the Christian religion is not built on such foundations of sand. Had it been so, it would long since have been swept away by the beating rain and the rushing floods. Here, again, the arguments urged by those who believe in the authenticity of Daniel recoil with tenfold force upon themselves. Sir Isaac Newton's observations on the prophecies of Daniel only show how little transcendent genius in one domain of inquiry can save a great thinker from absolute mistakes in another. In writing upon prophecy the great astronomer was writing on the assumption of baseless premisses which he had drawn from stereotyped tradition; and he was also writing at an epoch when the elements for the final solution of the problem had not as yet been discovered or elaborated. It is as certain that, had he been living now, he would have accepted the conclusion of all the ablest and most candid inquirers, as it is certain that Bacon, had he now been living, would have accepted the Copernican theory. It is absurdly false to say that "the Christian religion is all but founded on Daniel's prophecies respecting Christ." If it were not absurdly false, we might well ask, How it came that neither Christ nor His Apostles ever once alluded to the existence of any such argument, or ever pointed to the Book of Daniel and the prophecy of the seventy weeks as containing the least germ of evidence in favour of Christ's mission or the Gospel teaching? No such argument is remotely alluded to till long afterwards by some of the Fathers.

But so far from finding any agreement in the opinions of the Christian Fathers and commentators on a subject which, in Newton's view, was so momentous, we only find ourselves weltering in a chaos of uncertainties and contradictions. Thus Eusebius records the attempt of some early Christian commentators to treat the last of the seventy weeks as representing, not, like all the rest, seven years, but seventy years, in order to bring down the prophecy to the days of Trajan! Neither Jewish nor Christian exegetes have ever been able to come to the least agreement between themselves or with one another as to the beginning or end--the terminus a quo or the terminus ad quem--with reference to which the seventy weeks are to be reckoned. The Christians naturally made great efforts to make the seventy weeks end with the Crucifixion. But Julius Africanus [190] ( a.d. 232), beginning with the twentieth year of Artaxerxes (Neh. ii. 1-9, b.c. 444), gets only four hundred and seventy-five to the Crucifixion, and to escape the difficulty makes the years lunar years. [191]

Hippolytus [192] separates the last week from all the rest, and relegates it to the days of Antichrist and the end of the world. Eusebius himself refers "the anointed one" to the line of Jewish high priests, separates the last week from the others, ends it with the fourth year after the Crucifixion, and refers the ceasing of the sacrifice (Deut. ix. 27) to the rejection of Jewish sacrifices by God after the death of Christ. Apollinaris makes the seventy weeks begin with the birth of Christ, and argues that Elijah and Antichrist were to appear a.d. 490! None of these views found general acceptance. [193] Not one of them was sanctioned by Church authority. Every one, as Jerome says, argued in this direction or that pro captu ingenii sui. The climax of arbitrariness is reached by Keil--the last prominent defender of the so-called "orthodoxy" of criticism--when he makes the weeks not such commonplace things as "earthly chronological weeks," but Divine, symbolic, and therefore unknown and unascertainable periods. And are we to be told that it is on such fantastic, self-contradictory, and mutually refuting calculations that "the Christian religion is all but founded"? Thank God, the assertion is entirely wild.

## *Footnotes:*

176. Hävernick is another able and sincere supporter; but Droysen truly says (Gesch. d. Hellenismus, ii. 211), "Die Hävernickschen Auffassung kann kein vernunftiger Mensch bestimmen."

177. See Grimm, Comment., zum I. Buch der Makk., Einleit., xvii.; Mövers in Bonner Zeitschr., Heft 13, pp. 31 ff.; Stähelin, Einleit., p. 356.

178. Iren., Adv. Hæres., iv. 25; Clem., Strom. i. 21, § 146; Tert., De Cult. Fæm., i. 3; Jerome, Adv. Helv., 7; Ps. August., De Mirab., ii. 32, etc.

179. Baba Bathra, f. 13b, 14b.

180. See Oehler, s.v. "Kanon" (Herzog, Encycl.).

181. Rau, De Synag. Magna., ii. 66.

182. On Daniel, p. 195.

183. "Even after the Captivity," says Bishop Westcott, "the history of the Canon, like all Jewish history up to the date of the Maccabees, is wrapped in great obscurity. Faint traditions alone remain to interpret results which are found realised when the darkness is first cleared away" (s.v. "Canon," Smith's Dict. of Bible).

184. See König, Einleit., § 80, 2.

185. "In propheta Daniele Septuaginta interpretes multum ab Hebraica veritate discordant" (Jerome, ed. Vallarsi, v. 646). In the LXX. are first found the three apocryphal additions. For this reason the version of Theodotion was substituted for the LXX., which latter was only rediscovered in 1772 in a manuscript in the library of Cardinal Chigi.

186. On the Authenticity of Daniel, pp. 159, 290 (E. Tr.).

187. Psalms of Sol. xvii. 36, xviii. 8, etc. See Fabric., Cod. Pseudep., i. 917-972; Ewald, Gesch. d. Volkes Isr., iv. 244.

188. Even Auberlen says (Dan., p. 3, E. Tr.), "If prophecy is anywhere a history of the future, it is

here."

189. See Vitringa, De defectu Prophetiæ post Malachiæ tempora Obss. Sacr., ii. 336.
190. Demonstr. Evang., viii.
191. Of the Jews, the LXX. translators seem to make the seventy weeks end with Antiochus Epiphanes; but in Jerome's day they made the first year of "Darius the Mede" the terminus a quo, and brought down the terminus ad quem to Hadrian's destruction of the Temple. Saadia the Gaon and Rashi reckon the seventy weeks from Nebuchadrezzar to Titus, and make Cyrus the anointed one of ix. 25. Abn Ezra, on the other hand, takes Nehemiah for "the anointed one." What can be based on such varying and undemonstrable guesses? See Behrmann, Dan., p. xliii.
192. Hippolytus, Fragm. in Dan. (Migne, Patr. Græc., x.).
193. See Bevan, pp. 141-145.

# CHAPTER IX - EXTERNAL EVIDENCE AND RECEPTION INTO THE CANON

The reception of the Book of Daniel anywhere into the Canon might be regarded as an argument in favour of its authenticity, if the case of the Books of Jonah and Ecclesiastes did not sufficiently prove that canonicity, while it does constitute a proof of the value and sacred significance of a book, has no weight as to its traditional authorship. But in point of fact the position assigned by the Jews to the Book of Daniel--not among the Prophets, where, had the Book been genuine, it would have had a supreme right to stand, but only with the Book of Esther, among the latest of the Hagiographa [194] --is a strong argument for its late date. The division of the Old Testament into Law, Prophets, and Hagiographa first occurs in the Prologue to Ecclesiasticus (about b.c. 131)--"the Law, the Prophecies, and the rest of the books." [195] In spite of its peculiarities, its prophetic claims among those who accepted it as genuine were so strong that the LXX. and the later translations unhesitatingly reckon the author among the four greater prophets. If the Daniel of the Captivity had written this Book, he would have had a far greater claim to this position among the prophets than Haggai, Malachi, or the later Zechariah. Yet the Jews deliberately placed the Book among the Kethubîm, to the writers of which they indeed ascribe the Holy Spirit (Ruach Hakkodesh), but whom they did not credit with the higher degree of prophetic inspiration. Josephus expresses the Jewish conviction that, since the days of Artaxerxes onwards, the writings which had appeared had not been deemed worthy of the same reverence as those which had preceded them, because there had occurred no unquestionable succession of prophets. [196] The Jews who thus decided the true nature of the Book of Daniel must surely have been guided by strong traditional, critical, historical, or other grounds for denying (as they did) to the author the gift of prophecy. Theodoret denounces this as "shameless impudence" anaischuntian on their part; [197] but may it not rather have been fuller knowledge or simple honesty? At any rate, on any other grounds it would have been strange indeed of the Talmudists to decide that the most minutely predictive of the prophets--if indeed this were a prophecy--wrote without the gift of prophecy. [198] It can only have been the late and suspected appearance of the Book, and its marked phenomena, which led to its relegation to the lowest place in the Jewish Canon. Already in 1 Macc. iv. 46 we find that the stones of the demolished pagan altar are kept "until there should arise a prophet to show what should be done with them"; and in 1 Macc. xiv. 41 we again meet the phrase "until there should arise a faithful prophet." Before this epoch there is no trace of the existence of the Book of Daniel, and not only so, but the prophecies of the post-exilic prophets as to the future contemplate a wholly different horizon and a wholly different order of events. Had Daniel existed before the Maccabean epoch, it is impossible that the rank of the Book should have been deliberately ignored. The Jewish Rabbis of the age in which it appeared saw, quite correctly, that it had points of affinity with other pseudepigraphic apocalypses which arose in the same epoch. The Hebrew scholar Dr. Joel has pointed out how, amid its immeasurable superiority to such a poem as the enigmatic Cassandra of the Alexandrian poet Lycophron, [199] it resembles that book in its indirectness of nomenclature. Lycophron is one of the pleiad of poets in the days of Ptolemy Philadelphus; but his writings, like the Book before us, have probably received interpolations from later hands. He never calls a god or a hero by his name, but always describes him by a periphrasis, just as here we have "the King of the North" and "the King of the South," though the name "Egypt" slips in (Dan. xi. 8). Thus Hercules is "a three-nights' lion" (triesperos leon), and Alexander the Great is "a wolf." A son is always "an offshoot" (phituma), or is designated by some other metaphor. When Lycophron wants to allude to Rome, the Greek Rhome is used in its sense of "strength." The name Ptolemaios becomes by anagram apo melitos, "from honey"; and the name Arsinoë becomes ion Heras, "the violet of Hera." We may find some resemblances to these procedures when we are considering the eleventh chapter of Daniel.

It is a serious abuse of argument to pretend, as is done by Hengstenberg, by Dr. Pusey, and by many of their feebler followers, that "there are few books whose Divine authority is so fully established by the testimony of the New Testament, and in particular by our Lord Himself, as the Book of Daniel."[200] It is to the last degree dangerous, irreverent, and unwise to stake the Divine authority of our Lord on the maintenance of those ecclesiastical traditions of which so many have been scattered to the winds for ever. Our Lord, on one occasion, in the discourse on the Mount of Olives, warned His disciples that, "when they should see the abomination of desolation, spoken of by Daniel the prophet, standing in the holy place, they should flee from Jerusalem into the mountain district." [201] There is nothing to prove that He Himself uttered either the words "let him that readeth understand," or even "spoken of by Daniel the prophet." Both of those may belong to the explanatory narrative of the Evangelist, and the latter does not occur in St. Mark. Further, in St. Luke (xxi. 20) there is no specific allusion to Daniel at all; but instead of it we find, "When ye see Jerusalem being encircled by armies, then know that its desolation is near." We cannot be certain that the specific reference to Daniel may not be due to the Evangelist. But without so much as raising these questions, it is fully admitted that, whether exactly in its present form or not, the Book of Daniel formed part of the Canon in the days of Christ. If He directly refers to it as a book known to His hearers, His reference lies as wholly outside all questions of genuineness and authenticity as does St. Jude's quotation from the Book of Enoch, or St. Paul's (possible) allusions to the Assumption of Elijah, [202] or Christ's own passing reference to the Book of Jonah. Those who attempt to drag in these allusions as decisive critical dicta transfer them to a sphere wholly different from that of the moral application for which they were intended. They not only open vast and indistinct questions as to the self-imposed limitations of our Lord's human knowledge as part of His own voluntary "emptying Himself of His glory," but they also do a deadly disservice to the most essential cause of Christianity. [203] The only thing which is acceptable to the God of truth is truth; and since He has given us our reason and our conscience as lights which light every man who is born into the world, we must walk by these lights in all questions which belong to these domains. History, literature and criticism, and the interpretation of human language do belong to the domain of pure reason; and we must not be bribed by the misapplication of hypothetical exegesis to give them up for the support of traditional views which advancing knowledge no longer suffers us to maintain. It may be true or not that our Lord adopted the title "Son of Man" (Bar Enosh) from the Book of Daniel; but even if He did, which is at least disputable, that would only show, what we all already admit, that in His time the Book was an acknowledged part of the Canon. On the other hand, if our Lord and His Apostles regarded the Book of Daniel as containing the most explicit prophecies of Himself and of His kingdom, why did they never appeal or even allude to it to prove that He was the promised Messiah?

Again, Hengstenberg and his school try to prove that the Book of Daniel existed before the Maccabean age, because Josephus says that the high priest Jaddua showed to Alexander the Great, in the year b.c. 332, the prophecy of himself as the Grecian he-goat in the Book of Daniel; and that the leniency which Alexander showed towards the Jews was due to the favourable impression thus produced. [204]

The story, which is a beautiful and an interesting one, runs as follows:--

On his way from Tyre, after capturing Gaza, Alexander decided to advance to Jerusalem. The news threw Jaddua the high priest into an agony of alarm. He feared that the king was displeased with the Jews, and would inflict severe vengeance upon them. He ordered a general supplication with sacrifices, and was encouraged by God in a dream to decorate the city, throw open the gates, and go forth in procession at the head of priests and people to meet the dreaded conqueror. The procession, so unlike that of any other nation, went forth as soon as they heard that Alexander was approaching the city. They met the king on the summit of Scopas, the watch-tower--the height of Mizpah, from which the first glimpse of the city is obtained. It is the famous Blanca Guarda of the Crusaders, on the summit of which Richard I. turned away, and did not deem himself worthy to glance at the city which he was too weak to rescue from the infidel. The Phoenicians and Chaldeans in Alexander's army promised themselves that they would now be permitted to plunder the city and torment the high priest to death. But it happened far otherwise. For when the king saw the white-robed procession approaching, headed by Jaddua in his purple and golden array, and wearing on his head the golden petalon, with its inscription "Holiness to Jehovah," he advanced, saluted the priest, and adored the Divine Name. The Jews encircled and saluted him with unanimous greeting, while the King of Syria and his other followers fancied that he must be distraught. "How is it," asked Parmenio, "that you, whom all others adore, yourself adore the Jewish high priest?" "I did not adore the high priest," said Alexander, "but God, by whose priesthood He has been honoured. When I was at Dium in Macedonia, meditating on the conquest of Asia, I saw this very man in this same apparel, who invited me to march boldly and without delay, and that he would conduct me to the conquest of the Persians." Then he took Jaddua by the hand, and in the midst of the rejoicing priests entered Jerusalem, where he sacrificed to God. [205] Jaddua showed him the prediction about himself in the Book of Daniel, and in extreme satisfaction he granted to the Jews, at the high priest's request, all the petitions which they desired of him.

But this story, so grateful to Jewish vanity, is a transparent fiction. It does not find the least support from any other historic source, and is evidently one of the Jewish Haggadoth in which the intense national self-exaltation of that strange nation delighted to depict the homage which they, and their national religion, extorted from the supernaturally caused dread of the greatest heathen potentates. In this respect it resembles the earlier chapters of the Book of Daniel itself, and the numberless stories of the haughty superiority of great Rabbis to kings and emperors in which the Talmud delights. Roman Catholic historians, like Jahn and Hess, and older writers, like Prideaux, [206] accept the story, even when they reject the fable about Sanballat and the Temple on Gerizim which follows it. Stress is naturally laid upon it by apologists like Hengstenberg; but an historian like Grote does not vouchsafe to notice it by a single word, and most modern writers reject it. The Bishop of Bath and Wells thinks that these stories are "probably derived from some apocryphal book of Alexandrian growth, in which chronology and history gave way to romance and Jewish vanity." [207] All the historians except Josephus say that Alexander went straight from Gaza to Egypt, and make no mention of Jerusalem or Samaria; and Alexander was by no means "adored" by all men at that period of his career, for he never received proskunesis till after his conquest of Persia. Nor can we account for the presence of "Chaldeans" in his army at this time, for Chaldea was then under the rule of Babylon. Besides which, Daniel was expressly bidden, as Bleek observes, to "seal up his prophecy till the time of the end"; and the "time of the end" was certainly not the era of Alexander,--not to mention the circumstance that Alexander, if the prophecies were pointed out to him at all, would hardly have been content with the single verse or two about himself, and would have been anything but gratified by what immediately follows. [208]

I pass over as meaningless Hengstenberg's arguments in favour of the genuineness of the Book from the predominance of symbolism; from the moderation of tone towards Nebuchadrezzar; from the political gifts shown by the writer; and from his prediction that the Messianic Kingdom would at once appear after the death of Antiochus Epiphanes! When we are told that these circumstances "can only be explained on the assumption of a Babylonian origin"; that "they are directly opposed to the spirit of the Maccabean time"; that the artifice with which the writing is pervaded, supposing it to be a pseudepigraphic book, "far surpasses the powers of the most gifted poet"; and that "such a distinct expectation of the near advent of the Messianic Kingdom is utterly without analogy in the whole of prophetic literature,"--such arguments can only be regarded as appeals to ignorance. They are either assertions which float in the air, or are disproved at once alike by the canonical prophets and by the apocryphal literature of the Maccabean age. Symbolism is the distinguishing characteristic of apocalypses, and is found in those of the late post-exilic period. The views of the Jews about Nebuchadrezzar varied. Some writers were partially favourable to him, others were severe upon him. It does not in the least follow that a writer during the Antiochian persecution, who freely adapted traditional or imaginative elements, should necessarily represent the old potentates as irredeemably wicked, even if he meant to satirise Epiphanes in the story of their extravagances. It was necessary for his purpose to bring out the better features of their characters, in order to show the conviction wrought in them by Divine interpositions. The notion that the Book of Daniel could only have been written by a statesman or a consummate politician is mere fancy. And, lastly, in making the Messianic reign begin immediately at the close of the Seleucid persecution, the writer both expresses his own faith and hope, and follows the exact analogy of Isaiah and all the other Messianic prophets.

But though it is common with the prophets to pass at once from the warnings of destruction to the hopes of a Messianic Kingdom which is to arise immediately beyond the horizon which limits their vision, it is remarkable--and the consideration tells strongly against the authenticity of Daniel--that not one of them had the least glimpse of the four successive kingdoms or of the four hundred and ninety years;--not even those prophets who, if the Book of Daniel were genuine, must have had it in their hands. To imagine that Daniel took means to have his Book left undiscovered for some four hundred years, and then brought to light during the Maccabean struggle, is a grotesque impossibility. If the Book existed, it must have been known. Yet not only is there no real trace of its existence before b.c. 167, but the post-exilic prophets pay no sort of regard to its detailed predictions, and were evidently unaware that any such predictions had ever been uttered. What room is there for Daniel's four empires and four hundred and ninety years in such a prophecy as Zech. ii. 6-13? The pseudepigraphic Daniel possibly took the symbolism of four horns from Zech. i. 18, 19; but there is not the slightest connexion between Zechariah's symbol and that of the pseudo-Daniel. If the number four in Zechariah be not a mere number of completeness with reference to the four quarters of the world (comp. Zech. i. 18), the four horns symbolise either Assyria, Babylonia, Egypt, and Persia, or more generally the nations which had then scattered Israel (Zech. ii. 8, vi. 1-8; Ezek. xxxvii. 9); so that the following promise does not even contemplate a victorious succession of heathen powers. Again, what room is there for Daniel's four successive pagan empires in any natural interpretation of Haggai's "yet a little while and I will shake all nations" (Hag. ii. 7), and in the promise that this shaking shall take place in the lifetime of Zerubbabel (Hag. ii. 20-23)? And can we suppose that Malachi wrote that the messenger of the Lord should "suddenly" come to His Temple with such prophecies as those of Daniel before him? [209]

But if it be thought extraordinary that a pseudepigraphic prophecy should have been admitted into the Canon at all, even when placed low among the Kethubîm, and if it be argued that the Jews would never have conferred such an honour on such a composition, the answer is that even when compared with such fine books as those of Wisdom and Jesus the Son of Sirach, the Book has a right to such a place by its intrinsic superiority. Taken as a whole it is far superior in moral and spiritual instructiveness to any of the books of the Apocrypha. It was profoundly adapted to meet the needs of the age in which it originated. It was in its favour that it was written partly in Hebrew as well as in Aramaic, and it came before the Jewish Church under the sanction of a famous ancient name which was partly at least traditional and historical. There is nothing astonishing in the fact that in an age in which literature was rare and criticism unknown it soon came to be accepted as genuine. Similar phenomena are quite common in much later and more comparatively learned ages. One or two instances will suffice. Few books have exercised a more powerful influence on Christian literature than the spurious letters of Ignatius and the pseudo-Clementines. They were accepted, and their genuineness was defended for centuries; yet in these days no sane critic would imperil his reputation by an attempt to defend their genuineness. The book of the pseudo-Dionysius the Areopagite was regarded as genuine and authoritative down to the days of the Reformation, and the author professes to have seen the supernatural darkness of the Crucifixion; yet "Dionysius the Areopagite" did not write before a.d. 532! The power of the Papal usurpation was mainly built on the Forged Decretals, and for centuries no one ventured to question the genuineness and authenticity of those gross forgeries, till Laurentius Valla exposed the cheat and flung the tatters of the Decretals to the winds. In the eighteenth century Ireland could deceive even the acutest critics into the belief that his paltry Vortigern was a rediscovered play of Shakespeare; and a Cornish clergyman wrote a ballad which even Macaulay took for a genuine production of the reign of James II. Those who read the Book of Daniel in the light of Seleucid and Ptolemaic history saw that the writer was well acquainted with the events of those days, and that his words were full of hope, consolation, and instruction. After a certain lapse of time they were in no position to estimate the many indications that by no possibility could the Book have been written in the days of the Babylonian Exile; nor had it yet become manifest that all the detailed knowledge stops short with the close of the reign of Antiochus Epiphanes. The enigmatical character of the Book, and the varying elements of its calculations, led later commentators into the error that the fourth beast and the iron legs of the image stood for the Roman Empire, so that they did not expect the Messianic reign at the close of the Greek Empire, which, in the prediction, it immediately succeeds. [210]

How late was the date before the Jewish Canon was finally settled we see from the Talmudic stories that but for Hananiah ben-Hizkiah, with the help of his three hundred bottles of oil burnt in nightly studies, even the Book of Ezekiel would have been suppressed, as being contrary to the Law (Shabbath, f. 13, 2); and that but for the mystic line of interpretation adopted by Rabbi Aqiba (a.d. 120) a similar fate might have befallen the Song of Songs (Yaddayim, c. iii.; Mish., 5).

There is, then, the strongest reason to adopt the conclusion that the Book of Daniel was the production of one of the Chasidîm towards the beginning of the Maccabean struggle, and that its immediate object was to warn the Jews against the apostasies of commencing Hellenism. It was meant to encourage the faithful, who were waging a fierce battle against Greek influences and against the mighty and persecuting heathen forces by which they were supported. [211] Although the writer's knowledge of history up to the time of Alexander the Great is vague and erroneous, and his knowledge of the period which followed Antiochus entirely nebulous, on the other hand his acquaintance with the period of Antiochus Epiphanes is so extraordinarily precise as to furnish our chief information on some points of that king's reign. Guided by these indications, it is perhaps possible to fix the exact year and month in which the Book saw the light--namely, about January b.c. 164. [212]

From Dan. viii. 14 it seems that the author had lived till the cleansing of the Temple after its pollution by the Seleucid King (1 Macc. iv. 42-58). For though the Maccabean uprising is only called "a little help" (xi. 34), this is in comparison with the splendid future triumph and epiphany to which he looked forward. It is sufficiently clear from 1 Macc. v. 15, 16, that the Jews, even after the early victories of Judas, were in evil case, and that the nominal adhesion of many Hellenising Jews to the national cause was merely hypocritical (Dan. xi. 34).

Now the Temple was dedicated on December 25th, b.c. 165; and the Book appeared before the death of Antiochus, which the writer expected to happen at the end of the seventy weeks, or, as he calculated them, in June 164. The king did not actually die till the close of 164 or the beginning of 163 (1 Macc. vi. 1-16). [213]

## Footnotes:

194. Jacob Perez of Valentia accounted for this by the hatred of the Jews for Christianity! (Diestel, Gesch. d. A.T., p. 211).

195. Comp. Luke xxiv. 44; Acts xxviii. 23; Philo, De Vit. Cont., 3. See Oehler in Herzog, s.v. "Kanon."

196. Jos. c. Ap., I. 8.

197. Opp. ed. Migne, ii. 1260: Eis tosauten anaischuntian elasan hos kai tou chorou ton propheton touton aposchoinizein. He may well add, on his view of the date, ei gar tauta tes propheteias allotria, tina propheteias ta idia;

198. Megilla, 3, 1. Josephus, indeed, regards apocalyptic visions as the highest form of prophecy (Antt., X. xi. 7); but the great Rabbis Kimchi, Maimonides, Joseph Albo, etc., are strongly against him. See Behrmann, p. xxxix.

199. It has been described as "ein Versteck für Belesenheit, und ein grammatischer Monstrum."

*The Expositor's Bible: The Book of Daniel*

200. Hengstenberg, p. 209.

201. Matt. xxiv. 15; Mark xiii. 14.

202. 1 Cor. ii. 9; Eph. v. 11.

203. Hengstenberg's reference to 1 Peter i. 10-12, 1 Thess. ii. 3, 1 Cor. vi. 2, Heb. xi. 12, deserve no further notice.

204. Jos., Antt., XI. viii. 5.

205. There is nothing to surprise us in this circumstance, for Ptolemy III. (Jos. c. Ap., II. 5) and Antiochus VII. (Sidetes, Antt., XIII. viii. 2), Marcus Agrippa (id., XVI. ii. 1), and Vitellius (id., XVIII. v. 3) are said to have done the same. Comp. Suet., Aug., 93; Tert., Apolog., 6; and other passages adduced by Schürer, i., § 24.

206. Jahn, Hebr. Commonwealth, § 71; Hess, Gesch., ii. 37; Prideaux, Connection, i. 540 ff.

207. Dict. of Bible, s.v. "Jaddua." See Schürer, i. 187; Van Dale, Dissert. de LXX. Interpr., 68 ff.

208. This part of the story is a mere doublet of that about Cyrus and the prophecies of Isaiah (Antt., XI. i. 2).

209. Mal. iii. 1. LXX., exaiphnes; Vulg., statim; but it is rather "unawares" (unversehens).

210. That the fourth empire could not be the Roman has long been seen by many critics, as far back as Grotius, L'Empereur, Chamier, J. Voss, Bodinus, Becmann, etc. (Diestel, Gesch. A. T., p. 523).

211. See Hamburger, Real-Encycl., s.v. "Geheimlehre," ii. 265. The "Geheimlehre" (Heb., Sithrî Thorah) embraces a whole region of Jewish literature, of which the Book of Daniel forms the earliest beginning. See Dan. xii. 4-9. The phrases of Dan. vii. 22 are common in the Zohar.

212. "Plötzlich bei Antiochus IV. angekommen hört alle seine Wissenschaft auf, so dass wir, den Kalendar in den Hand, fast den Tag angeben können wo dies oder jenes niedergeschrieben worden ist" (Reuss, Gesch. d. Heil. Schrift., § 464).

213. For arguments in favour of this view see Cornill, Theol. Stud. aus Ostpreussen, 1889, pp. 1-32, and Einleit., p. 261. He reckons twelve generations, sixty-nine "weeks," from the destruction of Jerusalem to the murder of the high priest Onias III.

*Frederic William Farrar*

# CHAPTER X - SUMMARY AND CONCLUSION

The contents of the previous sections may be briefly summarised.

I. The objections to the authenticity and genuineness of Daniel do not arise, as is falsely asserted, from any a-priori objection to admit to the full the reality either of miracles or of genuine prediction. Hundreds of critics who have long abandoned the attempt to maintain the early date of Daniel believe both in miracles and prophecy.

II. The grounds for regarding the Book as a pseudepigraph are many and striking. The very Book which would most stand in need of overwhelming evidence in its favour is the one which furnishes the most decisive arguments against itself, and has the least external testimony in its support.

III. The historical errors in which it abounds tell overwhelmingly against it. There was no deportation in the third year of Jehoiakim; there was no King Belshazzar; the Belshazzar son of Nabunaid was not a son of Nebuchadrezzar; the names Nebuchadnezzar and Abed-nego are erroneous in form; there was no "Darius the Mede" who preceded Cyrus as king and conqueror of Babylon, though there was a later Darius, the son of Hystaspes, who conquered Babylon; the demands and decrees of Nebuchadrezzar are unlike anything which we find in history, and show every characteristic of the Jewish Haggada; and the notion that a faithful Jew could become President of the Chaldean Magi is impossible. It is not true that there were only two Babylonian kings--there were five: nor were there only four Persian kings--there were twelve. Xerxes seems to be confounded alike with Darius Hystaspis and Darius Codomannus as the last king of Persia. All correct accounts of the reign, even of Antiochus Epiphanes, seem to end about b.c. 164, and the indications in vii. 11-14, viii. 25, xi. 40-45, do not seem to accord with the historic realities of the time indicated.

IV. The philological peculiarities of the Book are no less unfavourable to its genuineness. The Hebrew is pronounced by the majority of experts to be of a later character than the time assumed for it. The Aramaic is not the Babylonian East-Aramaic, but the later Palestinian West-Aramaic. The word Kasdîm is used for "diviners," whereas at the period of the Exile it was a national name. Persian words and titles occur in the decrees attributed to Nebuchadrezzar. At least three Greek words occur, of which one is certainly of late origin, and is known to have been a favourite instrument with Antiochus Epiphanes.

V. There are no traces of the existence of the Book before the second century b.c.,[214] although there are abundant traces of the other books--Jeremiah, Ezekiel, the Second Isaiah--which belong to the period of the Exile. Even in Ecclesiasticus, while Isaiah, Jeremiah, Ezekiel, and the twelve Minor Prophets are mentioned (Ecclus. xlviii. 20-25, xlix. 6-10), not a syllable is said about Daniel, and that although the writer erroneously regards prophecy as mainly concerned with prediction. Jesus, son of Sirach, even goes out of his way to say that no man like Joseph had risen since Joseph's time, though the story of Daniel repeatedly recalls that of Joseph, and though, if Dan. i.-vi. had been authentic history, Daniel's work was far more marvellous and decisive, and his faithfulness more striking and continuous, than that of Joseph. The earliest trace of the Book is in an imaginary speech of a book written about b.c. 100 (1 Macc. ii. 59, 60).

VI. The Book was admitted by the Jews into the Canon; but so far from being placed where, if genuine, it would have had a right to stand--among the four Great Prophets---it does not even receive a place among the twelve Minor Prophets, such as is accorded to the much shorter and far inferior Book of Jonah. It is relegated to the Kethubîm, side by side with such a book as Esther. If it originated during the Babylonian Exile, Josephus might well speak of its "undeviating prophetic accuracy."[215] Yet this absolutely unparalleled and even unapproached foreteller of the minute future is not allowed by the Jews any place at all in their prophetic Canon! In the LXX. it is treated with remarkable freedom, and a number of other Haggadoth are made a part of it. It resembles Old Testament literature in very few respects, and all its peculiarities are such as abound in the later apocalypses and Apochrypha.[216] Philo, though he quotes so frequently both from the Prophets and the Hagiographa, does not even allude to the Book of Daniel.

VII. Its author seems to accept for himself the view of his age that the spirit of genuine prophecy had departed for evermore.[217] He speaks of himself as a student of the older prophecies, and alludes to the Scriptures as an authoritative Canon--Hassepharîm, "the books." His views and practices as regards three daily prayers towards Jerusalem (vi. 11); the importance attached to Levitical rules about food (i. 8-21); the expiatory and other value attached to alms and fasting (iv. 24, ix. 3, x. 3); the angelology involving even the names, distinctions, and rival offices of angels; the form taken by the Messianic hope; the twofold resurrection of good and evil,--are all in close accord with the standpoint of the second century before Christ as shown distinctly in its literature. [218]

VIII. When we have been led by decisive arguments to admit the real date of the Book of Daniel, its place among the Hagiographa confirms all our conclusions. The Law, the Prophets, and the Hagiographa represent, as Professor Sanday has pointed out, three layers or stages in the history of the collection of the Canon. If the Book of Chronicles was not accepted among the Histories (which were designated "The Former Prophets"), nor the Book of Daniel among the Greater or Lesser Prophets, the reason was that, at the date when the Prophets were formally collected into a division of the Canon, these books were not yet in existence, or at any rate had not been accepted on the same level with the other books. [219]

IX. All these circumstances, and others which have been mentioned, have come home to earnest, unprejudiced, and profoundly learned critics with so irresistible a force, and the counter-arguments which are adduced are so little valid, that the defenders of the genuineness are now an ever-dwindling body, and many of them can only support their basis at all by the hypothesis of interpolations or twofold authorship. Thus C. v. Orelli [220] can only accept a modified genuineness, for which he scarcely offers a single argument; but even he resorts to the hypothesis of a late editor in the Maccabean age who put together the traditions and general prophecies of the real Daniel. He admits that without such a supposition--by which it does not seem that we gain much--the Book of Daniel is wholly exceptional, and without a single analogy in the Old Testament. And he clearly sees that all the rays of the Book are focussed in the struggle against Antiochus as in their central point, [221] and that the best commentary on the prophetic section of the Book is the First Book of Maccabees. [222]

X. It may then be said with confidence that the critical view has finally won the day. The human mind will in the end accept that theory which covers the greatest number of facts, and harmonises best with the sum-total of knowledge. Now, in regard to the Book of Daniel, these conditions appear to be far better satisfied by the supposition that the Book was written in the second century than in the sixth. The history, imperfect as to the pseudepigraphic date, but very precise as it approaches b.c. 176-164, the late characteristics which mark the language, the notable silence respecting the Book from the sixth to the second century, and its subsequent prominence and the place which it occupies in the Kethubîm, are arguments which few candid minds can resist. The critics of Germany, even the most moderate, such as Delitzsch, Cornill, Riehm, Strack, C. v. Orelli, Meinhold, are unanimous as to the late date of, at any rate, the prophetic section of the Book; and even in the far more conservative criticism of England there is no shadow of doubt on the subject left in the minds of such scholars as Driver, Cheyne, Sanday, Bevan, and Robertson Smith. Yet, so far from detracting from the value of the Book, we add to its real value and to its accurate apprehension when we regard it, not as the work of a prophet in the Exile, but of some faithful Chasîd in the days of the Seleucid tyrant, anxious to inspire the courage and console the sufferings of his countrymen. Thus considered, the Book presents some analogy to St. Augustine's City of God. It sets forth, in strong outlines, and with magnificent originality and faith, the contrast between the kingdoms of this world and the kingdoms of our God and of His Christ, to which the eternal victory has been foreordained from the foundation of the world. In this respect we must compare it with the Apocalypse. Antiochus Epiphanes was an anticipated Nero. And just as the agonies of the Neronian persecutions wrung from the impassioned spirit of St. John the Divine those visions of glory and that denunciation of doom, in order that the hearts of Christians in Rome and Asia might be encouraged to the endurance of martyrdom, and to the certain hope that the irresistible might of their weakness would ultimately shake the world, so the folly and fury of Antiochus led the holy and gifted Jew who wrote the Book of Daniel to set forth a similar faith, partly in Haggadoth, which may, to some extent, have been drawn from tradition, and partly in prophecies, of which the central conception was that which all history teaches us--namely, that "for every false word and unrighteous deed, for cruelty and oppression, for lust and vanity, the price has to be paid at last, not always by the chief offenders, but paid by some one. Justice and truth alone endure and live. Injustice and oppression may be long-lived, but doomsday comes to them at last." [223] And when that doom has been carried to its ultimate issues, then begins the Kingdom of the Son of Man, the reign of God's Anointed, and the inheritance of the earth by the Saints of God.

## *Footnotes:*

214. It is alluded to about b.c. 140 in the Sibylline Oracles (iii. 391-416), and in 1 Macc. ii. 59, 60.
215. Jos., Antt., X. xi. 7.
216. Ewald (Hist. of Israel, v. 208) thinks that the author had read Baruch in Hebrew, because Dan. ix. 4-19 is an abbreviation of Baruch i. 15-ii. 17.
217. Psalm lxxiv. 9; 1 Macc. iv. 46, ix. 27, xiv. 41.
218. See Cornill, Einleit., pp. 257-260.
219. Sanday, Inspiration, p. 101. The name of "Earlier Prophets" was given to the two Books of

Samuel, of Kings, and of Isaiah, Jeremiah, and Ezekiel; and the twelve Minor Prophets (the latter regarded as one book) were called "The Later Prophets." Cornill places the collection of the Prophets into the Canon about b.c. 250.

220. Alttestament. Weissagung, pp. 513-530 (Vienna, 1882).

221. "Alle strahlen des Buches sich in dieser Epoche als in ihrem Brennpunkte vereinigen" (C. v. Orelli, p. 514).

222. Compare the following passages: Unclean meats, 1 Macc. i. 62-64, "Many in Israel were fully resolved not to eat any unclean thing," etc.; 2 Macc. vi. 18-31, vii. 1-42. The decrees of Nebuchadrezzar (Dan. iii. 4-6) and Darius (Dan. vi. 6-9) with the proceedings of Antiochus (1 Macc. i. 47-51). Belshazzar's profane use of the Temple vessels (Dan. v. 2) with 1 Macc. i. 23; 2 Macc. v. 16, etc.

223. Froude, Short Studies, i. 17.

# PART II – COMMENTARY ON THE HISTORIC SECTION

## CHAPTER I - THE PRELUDE

"His loyalty he kept, his faith, his love."--Milton.

The first chapter of the Book of Daniel serves as a beautiful introduction to the whole, and strikes the keynote of faithfulness to the institutions of Judaism which of all others seemed most important to the mind of a pious Hebrew in the days of Antiochus Epiphanes. At a time when many were wavering, and many had lapsed into open apostasy, the writer wished to set before his countrymen in the most winning and vivid manner the nobleness and the reward of obeying God rather than man.

He had read in 2 Kings xxiv. 1, 2, that Jehoiakim had been a vassal of Nebuchadrezzar for three years, which were not, however, the first three years of his reign, and then had rebelled, and been subdued by "bands of the Chaldeans" and their allies. In 2 Chron. xxxvi. 6 he read that Nebuchadrezzar had "bound Jehoiakim in fetters to carry him to Babylon." [224] Combining these two passages, he seems to have inferred, in the absence of more accurate historical indications, that the Chaldeans had besieged and captured Jerusalem in the third year of Jehoiakim. That the date is erroneous there can hardly be a question, for, as already stated, [225] neither Jeremiah, the contemporary of Jehoiakim, nor the Book of Kings, nor any other authority, knows anything of any siege of Jerusalem by the Babylonian King in the third year of Jehoiakim. The Chronicler, a very late writer, seems to have heard some tradition that Jehoiakim had been taken captive, but he does not date this capture; and in Jehoiakim's third year the king was a vassal, not of Babylon, but of Egypt. Nabopolassar, not Nebuchadrezzar, was then King of Babylon. It was not till the following year (b.c. 605), when Nebuchadrezzar, acting as his father's general, had defeated Egypt at the Battle of Carchemish, that any siege of Jerusalem would have been possible. Nor did Nebuchadrezzar advance against the Holy City even after the Battle of Carchemish, but dashed home across the desert to secure the crown of Babylon on hearing the news of his father's death. The only two considerable Babylonian deportations of which we know were apparently in the eighth and nineteenth years of Nebuchadrezzar's reign. In the former Jehoiachin was carried captive with ten thousand citizens (2 Kings xxiv. 14-16; Jer. xxvii. 20); in the latter Zedekiah was slain, and eight hundred and thirty-two persons carried to Babylon (Jer. lii. 29; 2 Kings xxv. 11). [226]

There seems then to be, on the very threshold, every indication of an historic inaccuracy such as could not have been committed if the historic Daniel had been the true author of this Book; and we are able, with perfect clearness, to point to the passages by which the Maccabean writer was misled into a mistaken inference. [227] To him, however, as to all Jewish writers, a mere variation in a date would have been regarded as a matter of the utmost insignificance. It in no way concerned the high purpose which he had in view, or weakened the force of his moral fiction. Nor does it in the smallest degree diminish from the instructiveness of the lessons which he has to teach to all men for all time. A fiction which is true to human experience may be as rich in spiritual meaning as a literal history. Do we degrade the majesty of the Book of Daniel if we regard it as a Haggada any more than we degrade the story of the Prodigal Son when we describe it as a Parable?

The writer proceeds to tell us that, after the siege, Nebuchadnezzar--whom the historic Daniel could never have called by the erroneous name Nebuchadnezzar--took Jehoiakim (for this seems to be implied), with some of the sacred vessels of the Temple (comp. v. 2, 3), into the land of Shinar, [228] "to the house of his god." This god, as we learn from Babylonian inscriptions, was Bel or Bel-merodach, in whose temple, built by Nebuchadrezzar, was also "the treasure-house of his kingdom." [229]

Among the captives were certain "of the king's seed, and of the princes" (Parthemîm). [230] They were chosen from among such boys as were pre-eminent for their beauty and intelligence, and the intention was to train them as pages in the royal service, and also in such a knowledge of the Chaldean language and literature as should enable them to take their places in the learned caste of priestly diviners. Their home was in the vast palace of the Babylonian King, of which the ruins are now called Kasr. Here they may have seen the hapless Jehoiachin still languishing in his long captivity.

They are called "children," and the word, together with the context, seems to imply that they were boys of the age of from twelve to fourteen. The king personally handed them over to the care of Ashpenaz, [231] the Rabsaris, or "master of the eunuchs," who held the position of lord high chamberlain. [232] It is probably implied that the boys were themselves made eunuchs, for the incident seems to be based on the rebuke given by Isaiah to the vain ostentation of Hezekiah in showing the treasures of his temple and palace to Merodach-baladan: "Behold the days come, that all that is in thine house ... shall be carried to Babylon: nothing shall be left, saith the Lord. And of thy sons that shall issue from thee, which thou shalt beget, shall they take away; and they shall be eunuchs in the palace of the King of Babylon." [233]

They were to be trained in the learning (lit. "the book") and language of Chaldea for three years; at the end of which period they were to be admitted into the king's presence, that he might see how they looked and what progress they had made. During those three years he provided them with a daily maintenance of food and wine from his table. Those who were thus maintained in Eastern courts were to be counted by hundreds, and even by thousands, and their position was often supremely wretched and degraded, as it still is in such Eastern courts. The wine was probably imported. The food consisted of meat, game, fish, joints, and wheaten bread. The word used for "provision" is interesting. It is path-bag, and seems to be a transliteration, or echo of a Persian word, patibaga (Greek potibazis), a name applied by the historian Deinon (b.c. 340) to barley bread and "mixed wine in a golden egg from which the king drinks." [234]

But among these captives were four young Jews named Daniel, Hananiah, Mishael, and Azariah.

Their very names were a witness not only to their nationality, but to their religion. Daniel means "God is my judge"; Hananiah, "Jehovah is gracious"; Mishael (perhaps), "who is equal to God?" [235] Azariah, "God is a helper."

It is hardly likely that the Chaldeans would have tolerated the use of such names among their young pupils, since every repetition of them would have sounded like a challenge to the supremacy of Bel, Merodach, and Nebo. It was a common thing to change names in heathen courts, as the name of Joseph had been changed by the Egyptians to Zaphnathpaaneah (Gen. xli. 45), and the Assyrians changed the name of Psammetichus II. into Nebo-serib-ani, "Nebo save me." They therefore made the names of the boys echo the names of the Babylonian deities. Instead of "God is my judge," Daniel was called Belteshazzar, "protect Thou his life." [236] Perhaps the prayer shows the tender regard in which he was held by Ashpenaz. Hananiah was called Shadrach, perhaps Shudur-aku, "command of Aku," the moon-deity; Mishael was called Meshach, a name which we cannot interpret; [237] and Azariah, instead of "God is a help," was called Abed-nego, a mistaken form for Abed-nebo, or "servant of Nebo." [238] Even in this slight incident there may be an allusion to Maccabean days. It appears that in that epoch the apostate Hellenising Jews were fond of changing their names into Gentile names, which had a somewhat similar sound. Thus Joshua was called "Jason," and Onias "Menelaus." [239] This was done as part of the plan of Antiochus to force upon Palestine the Greek language. So far the writer may have thought the practice a harmless one, even though imposed by heathen potentates. Such certainly was the view of the later Jews, even of the strictest sect of the Pharisees. Not only did Saul freely adopt the name of Paul, but Silas felt no scruple in being called by the name Sylvanus, though that was the name of a heathen deity.

It was far otherwise with acquiescence in the eating of heathen meats, which, in the days of the Maccabees, was forced upon many of the Jews, and which, since the institution or reinstitution of Levitism after the return from the Exile, had come to be regarded as a deadly sin. It was during the Exile that such feelings had acquired fresh intensity. At first they do not seem to have prevailed. Jehoiachin was a hero among the Jews. They remembered him with intense love and pity, and it does not seem to have been regarded as any stain upon his memory that, for years together, he had, almost in the words of Dan. i. 5, received a daily allowance from the table of the King of Babylon. [240]

In the days of Antiochus Epiphanes the ordinary feeling on this subject was very different, for the religion and nationality of the Jews were at stake. Hence we read: "Howbeit many in Israel were fully resolved and confirmed in themselves not to eat any unclean thing. Wherefore they chose rather to die, that they might not be defiled with meats, that they might not profane the holy covenant: so then they died." [241]

And in the Second Book of Maccabees we are told that on the king's birthday Jews "were constrained by bitter constraint to eat of the sacrifices," and that Eleazar, one of the principal scribes, an aged and noble-looking man, preferred rather to be tortured to death, "leaving his death for an example of noble courage, and a memorial of value, not only unto young men, but unto all his nation." [242] In the following chapter is the celebrated story of the constancy and cruel death of seven brethren and their mother, when they preferred martyrdom to tasting swine's flesh. The brave Judas Maccabæus, with some nine companions, withdrew himself into the wilderness, and "lived in the mountains after the manner of beasts with his company, who fed on herbs continually, lest they should be partakers of the pollution." The tone and object of these narratives are precisely the same as the tone and object of the stories in the Book of Daniel; and we can well imagine how the heroism of resistance would be encouraged in every Jew who read those narratives or traditions of former days of persecution and difficulty. "This Book," says Ewald, "fell like a glowing spark from a clear heaven upon a surface which was already intensely heated far and wide, and waiting to burst into flames." [243]

It may be doubtful whether such views as to ceremonial defilement were already developed at the beginning of the Babylonian Captivity. [244] The Maccabean persecution left them ingrained in the habits of the people, and Josephus tells us a contemporary story which reminds us of that of Daniel and his companions. He says that certain priests, who were friends of his own, had been imprisoned in Rome, and that he endeavoured to procure their release, "especially because I was informed that they were not unmindful of piety towards God, but supported themselves with figs and nuts," because in such eating of dry food (xerophagia, as it was called) there was no chance of heathen defilement. [245] It need hardly be added that when the time came to break down the partition-wall which separated Jewish particularism from the universal brotherhood of mankind redeemed in Christ, the Apostles--especially St. Paul--had to show the meaningless nature of many distinctions to which the Jews attached consummate importance. The Talmud abounds in stories intended to glorify the resoluteness with which the Jews maintained their stereotyped Levitism; but Christ taught, to the astonishment of the Pharisees and even of the disciples, that it is not what entereth into a man which makes him unclean, but the unclean thoughts which come from within, from the heart. [246] And this He said, katharizon panta ta bromata--i.e., abolishing thereby the Levitic Law, and "making all meats clean." Yet, even after this, it required nothing less than that Divine vision on the tanner's roof at Joppa to convince Peter that he was not to call "common" what God had cleansed, [247] and it required all the keen insight and fearless energy of St. Paul to prevent the Jews from keeping an intolerable yoke upon their own necks, and also laying it upon the necks of the Gentiles. [248]

The four princely boys--they may have been from twelve to fourteen years old [249] --determined not to share in the royal dainties, and begged the Sar-hassarîsîm to allow them to live on pulse and water, rather than on the luxuries in which--for them--lurked a heathen pollution. The eunuch not unnaturally demurred. The daily rations were provided from the royal table. He was responsible to the king for the beauty and health, as well as for the training, of his young scholars; and if Nebuchadrezzar saw them looking more meagre or haggard [250] than the rest of the captives and other pages, the chamberlain's head might pay the forfeit. [251] But Daniel, like Joseph in Egypt, had inspired affection among his captors; and since the prince of the eunuchs regarded him "with favour and tender love," he was the more willing to grant, or at least to connive at, the fulfilment of the boy's wish. So Daniel gained over the Melzar (or steward?), [252] who was in immediate charge of the boys, and begged him to try the experiment for ten days. If at the end of that time their health or beauty had suffered, the question might be reconsidered.

So for ten days the four faithful children were fed on water, and on the "seeds"--i.e., vegetables, dates, raisins, and other fruits, which are here generally called "pulse." [253] At the end of the ten days--a sort of mystic Persian week [254] --they were found to be fairer and fresher than all the other captives of the palace. [255] Thenceforth they were allowed without hindrance to keep the customs of their country.

Nor was this all. During the three probationary years they continued to flourish intellectually as well as physically. They attained to conspicuous excellence "in all kinds of books and wisdom," and Daniel also had understanding in all kinds of dreams and visions, to which the Chaldeans attached supreme importance. [256] The Jews exulted in these pictures of four youths of their own race who, though they were strangers in a strange land, excelled all their alien compeers in their own chosen fields of learning. There were already two such pictures in Jewish history,--that of the youthful Moses, learned in all the wisdom of the Egyptians, and a great man and a prince among the magicians of Pharaoh; and that of Joseph, who, though there were so many Egyptian diviners, alone could interpret dreams, whether in the dungeon or at the foot of the throne. A third picture, that of Daniel at the court of Babylon, is now added to them, and in all three cases the glory is given directly, not to them, but to the God of heaven, the God of their fathers.

At the close of the three years the prince of the eunuchs brought all his young pages into the presence of the King Nebuchadrezzar. He tested them by familiar conversation, [257] and found the four Jewish lads superior to all the rest. They were therefore chosen "to stand before the king"--in other words, to become his personal attendants. As this gave free access to his presence, it involved a position not only of high honour, but of great influence. And their superiority stood the test of time. Whenever the king consulted them on matters which required "wisdom of understanding," he found them not only better, but "ten times better," than all the "magicians" and "astrologers" that were in all his realm. [258]

The last verse of the chapter, "And Daniel continued even unto the first year of King Cyrus," is perhaps a later gloss, for it appears from x. 1 that Daniel lived, at any rate, till the third year of Cyrus. Abn Ezra adds the words "continued in Babylon," and Ewald "at the king's court." Some interpret "continued" to mean "remained alive." The reason for mentioning "the first year of Cyrus" may be to show that Daniel survived the return from the Exile, [259] and also to mark the fact that he attained a great age. For if he were about fourteen at the beginning of the narrative, he would be eighty-five in the first year of Cyrus. Dr. Pusey remarks: "Simple words, but what a volume of tried faithfulness is unrolled by them! Amid all the intrigues indigenous at all times in dynasties of Oriental despotism, amid all the envy towards a foreign captive in high office as a king's councillor, amid all the trouble incidental to the insanity of the king and the murder of two of his successors, in that whole critical period for his people, Daniel continued." [260]

The domestic anecdote of this chapter, like the other more splendid narratives which succeed it, has a value far beyond the circumstances in which it may have originated. It is a beautiful moral illustration of the blessings which attend on faithfulness and on temperance, and whether it be an Haggada or an historic tradition, it equally enshrines the same noble lesson as that which was taught to all time by the early stories of the Books of Genesis and Exodus. [261]

It teaches the crown and blessing of faithfulness. It was the highest glory of Israel "to uplift among the nations the banner of righteousness." It matters not that, in this particular instance, the Jewish boys were contending for a mere ceremonial rule which in itself was immaterial, or at any rate of no eternal significance. Suffice it that this rule presented itself to them in the guise of a principle and of a sacred duty, exactly as it did to Eleazar the Scribe, and Judas the Maccabee, and the Mother and her seven strong sons in the days of Antiochus Epiphanes. They regarded it as a duty to their laws, to their country, to their God; and therefore upon them it was sacredly incumbent. And they were faithful to it. Among the pampered minions and menials of the vast Babylonian palace--undazzled by the glitter of earthly magnificence, untempted by the allurements of pomp, pleasure, and sensuous indulgence--

*"Amid innumerable false, unmoved,*
*Unshaken, unseduced, unterrified,*
*Their loyalty they kept, their faith, their love."*

And because God loves them for their constancy, because they remain pure and true, all the Babylonian varletry around them learns the lesson of simplicity, the beauty of holiness. Amid the outpourings of the Divine favour they flourish, and are advanced to the highest honours. This is one great lesson which dominates the historic section of this Book: "Them that honour Me I will honour, and they that despise Me shall be lightly esteemed." It is the lesson of Joseph's superiority to the glamour of temptation in the house of Potiphar; of the choice of Moses, preferring to suffer affliction with the people of God rather than all the treasures of Egypt and "to be called the son of Pharaoh's daughter"; of Samuel's stainless innocence beside the corrupting example of Eli's sons; of David's strong, pure, ruddy boyhood as a shepherd-lad on Bethlehem's hills. It is the anticipated story of that yet holier childhood of Him who--subject to His parents in the sweet vale of Nazareth--blossomed "like the flower of roses in the spring of the year, and as lilies by the water-courses." The young human being who grows up in innocence and self-control grows up also in grace and beauty, in wisdom and "in favour with God and man." The Jews specially delighted in these pictures of boyish continence and piety, and they lay at the basis of all that was greatest in their national character.

But there also lay incidentally in the story a warning against corrupting luxury, the lesson of the need for, and the healthfulness of,

"The rule of not too much by temperance taught."

"The love of sumptuous food and delicious drinks is never good," says Ewald, "and with the use of the most temperate diet body and soul can flourish most admirably, as experience had at that time sufficiently taught."

To the value of this lesson the Nazarites among the Jews were a perpetual witness. Jeremiah seems to single them out for the special beauty which resulted from their youthful abstinence when he writes of Jerusalem, "Her Nazarites were purer than snow, they were whiter than milk, they were more ruddy in body than rubies, their polishing was of sapphires." [262]

It is the lesson which Milton reads in the story of Samson,--

*"O madness! to think use of strongest wines*
*And strongest drinks our chief support of health,*
*When God, with these forbidden, made choice to rear*
*His mighty champion, strong above compare,*
*Whose drink was only from the liquid brook!"*

It is the lesson which Shakespeare inculcates when he makes the old man say in As You Like It,--

*"When I was young I never did apply*

> Hot and rebellious liquors in my blood,
> Nor did not with unblushful forehead woo
> The means of weakness and debility;
> Therefore mine age is as a lusty winter,
> Frosty, yet kindly."

The writer of this Book connects intellectual advance as well as physical strength with this abstinence, and here he is supported even by ancient and pagan experience. Something of this kind may perhaps lurk in the ariston men hudor of Pindar; and certainly Horace saw that gluttony and repletion are foes to insight when he wrote,--
"Nam corpus onustum
Hesternis vitiis animum quoque prægravat una,
Atque affigit humo divinæ particulam auræ." [263]

Pythagoras was not the only ancient philosopher who recommended and practised a vegetable diet, and even Epicurus, whom so many regard as

*"The soft garden's rose-encircled child,"*

placed over his garden door the inscription that those who came would only be regaled on barley-cakes and fresh water, to satisfy, but not to allure, the appetite.

But the grand lesson of the picture is meant to be that the fair Jewish boys were kept safe in the midst of every temptation to self-indulgence, because they lived as in God's sight: and "he that holds himself in reverence and due esteem for the dignity of God's image upon him, accounts himself both a fit person to do the noblest and godliest deeds, and much better worth than to deject and defile, with such debasement and pollution as Sin is, himself so highly ransomed and ennobled to a new friendship and filial relation with God." [264]

## Footnotes:

224. Comp. Jer. xxii. 18, 19, xxxvi. 30.
225. See supra, p. 45.
226. Jeremiah (lii. 28-30) mentions three deportations, in the seventh, eighteenth, and twenty-third year of Nebuchadrezzar; but there are great difficulties about the historic verification, and the paragraph (which is of doubtful genuineness) is omitted by the LXX.
227. The manner in which the maintainers of the genuineness get over this difficulty is surely an instance of such special pleading as can convince no unbiassed inquirer. They conjecture (1) that Nebuchadrezzar had been associated with his father, and received the title of king before he really became king; (2) that by "came to Jerusalem and besieged it" is meant "set out towards Jerusalem, so that (ultimately) he besieged it"; (3) and that a vague and undated allusion in the Book of Chronicles, and a vague, unsupported, and evidently erroneous assertion in Berossus--quoted by Josephus, Antt., X. xi. 1; c. Ap., I. 19, who lived some two and a half centuries after these events, and who does not mention any siege of Jerusalem--can be so interpreted as to outweigh the fact that neither contemporary histories nor contemporary records know anything of this supposed deportation. Jeremiah (xxv. 1) says correctly that "the fourth year of Jehoiakim" was "the first year of Nebuchadrezzar"; and had Jerusalem been already captured and plundered, it is impossible that he should not have alluded to the fact in that chapter. An older subterfuge for "explaining" the error is that of Saadia the Gaon, Abn Ezra, Rashi, etc., who interpret "the third year of Jehoiakim" to mean "the third year after his rebellion from Nebuchadrezzar," which is not only impossible in itself, but also contradicts Dan. ii. 1.
228. Shinar is an archaism, supposed by Schrader to be a corruption of Sumir, or Northern Chaldea (Keilinschr., p. 34); but see Hommel, Gesch. Bab. u. Assyr., 220; F. Delitzsch, Assyr. Gram., 115. The more common name in the exilic period was Babel (Jer. li. 9, etc.) or Eretz Kasdim (Ezek. xii. 13).
229. On this god--Marduk or Maruduk (Jer. l. 2)--comp. 2 Chron. xxxvi. 7. See Schrader, K. A. T., pp. 273, 276; and Riehm, Handwörterb., ii. 982.
230. This seems to be a Persian word, fratama, "first." It is only found in Esther. Josephus says that the four boys were connected with Zedekiah (Antt., X. x. 1). Comp. Jer. xli. 1.
231. Dan. i. 3; LXX., Abiesdri. The name is of quite uncertain derivation. Lenormant connects it with Abai-Istar, "astronomer of the goddess Istar" (La Divination, p. 182). Hitzig sees in this strange rendering Abiesdri the meaning "eunuch." A eunuch could have no son to help him, so that his father is his help ('ezer). Ephræm Syrus, in his Commentary, preserves both names (Schleusner, Thesaurus, s.v. Abieser). We find the name Ashkenaz in Gen. x. 3. Theodot. has Asphanez. Among other guesses Lenormant makes Ashpenaz = Assa-ibni-zir. Dr. Joel (Notizen zum Buche Daniel, p. 17) says that since the Vulgate reads Abriesri, "ob nicht der Wort von rechts zu links gelesen müsste?"

232. Called in i. 7-11 the Sar-hassarîsîm (comp. Jer. xxxix. 3; Gen. xxxvii. 36, marg.; 2 Kings xviii. 17; Esther ii. 3). This officer now bears the title of Gyzlar Agha.

233. Isa. xxxix. 6, 7.

234. Athen., Deipnos, xi. 583. See Bevan, p. 60; Max Müller in Pusey, p. 565. How Professor Fuller can urge the presence of these Persian words in proof of the genuineness of Daniel (Speaker's Commentary, p. 250) I cannot understand. For Daniel does not seem to have survived beyond the third year of the Persian dominion, and it is extremely difficult to suppose that all these Persian words, including titles of Nebuchadrezzar's officials, were already current among the Babylonians. On the other hand, Babylonian words seem to be rare, though Daniel is represented as living nearly the whole of a long life in Babylon. There is no validity in the argument that these words could not have been known in the days of the Maccabees, "for half of them are common in Syria, though the oldest extant Syriac writers are later by three centuries than the time of the Maccabees" (Bevan, p. 41).

235. The name Daniel occurs among Ezra's contemporaries in Ezra viii. 2; Neh. x. 7, and the other names in Neh. viii. 4, x. 3, 24; 1 Esdras ix. 44.

236. Balatsu-utsur. The name in this form had nothing to do with Bel, as the writer of Daniel seems to have supposed (Dan. iv. 5), nor yet with Beltis, the wife of Bel. See supra, p. 47. Comp. the names Nabusarutsur, Sinsarutsur, Assursarutsur. Also comp. Inscr. Semit., ii. 38, etc. Pseudo-Epiphanius says that Nebuchadrezzar meant Daniel to be co-heir with his son Belshazzar.

237. F. Delitzsch calls Meshach vox hybrida. Neither "Shadrach" nor "Meshach" occurs on the monuments. "That the imposition of names is a symbol of mastership over slaves is plain" (S. Chrys., Opp., iii. 21; Pusey, p. 16). Comp. 2 Kings xxiii. 34 (Egyptians); xxiv. 17 (Babylonians); Ezra v. 14, Esther ii. 7 (Persians).

238. Comp. Obadiah, Abdiel, Abdallah, etc. Schrader says, p. 429: "The supposition that Nebo was altered to Nego, out of a contumelious desire (which Jews often displayed) to alter, avoid, and insult the names of idols, is out of place, since the other names are not altered."

239. Jos., Antt., XII. v. 1; Derenbourg, Palestine, p. 34; Ewald, Hist., v. 294 (E. Tr.); Munk, Palestine, p. 495, etc.

240. See Ewald, Gesch. Isr., vi. 654. "They shall eat unclean things in Assyria" (Hosea ix. 3). "The children of Israel shall eat their defiled bread among the Gentiles" (Ezek. iv. 13, 14).

241. 1 Macc. i. 62, 63.

242. 2 Macc. vi. 18-31. Comp. the LXX. addition to Esther iv. 14, v. 4, where she is made to plead before God that she had not tasted of the table of Haman or of the king's banquet. So Judith takes "clean" bread with her into the camp of Holofernes (Judith x. 5), and Judas and his followers live on herbs in the desert (2 Macc. v. 27). The Mishnah even forbids to take the bread, oil, or milk of the heathen.

243. Prophets of the O. T., p. 184 (E. Tr.).

244. Mr. Bevan says that the verb for "defile" (g'l), as a ritual term for the idea of ceremonial uncleanness, is post-exilic; the Pentateuch and Ezekiel used tm' (Comment., p. 61). The idea intended is that the three boys avoided meat which might have been killed with the blood and offered to idols, and therefore was not Kashar (Exod. xxxiv. 15).

245. Jos., Vit., iii. Comp. Isa. lii. 11.

246. Mark vii. 19 (according to the true reading and translation).

247. Acts x. 14.

248. 1 Cor. xi. 25. This rigorism was specially valued by the Essenes and Therapeutæ. See Derenbourg, Palestine, note, vi.

249. Plato, Alcib., i. 37; Xen., Cyrop., i. 2. Youths entered the king's service at the age of seventeen.

250. Lit. "sadder." LXX., skuthropoi.

251. LXX., kinduneuso to idio trachelo.

252. Perhaps the Assyrian matstsara, "guardian" (Delitzsch). There are various other guesses (Behrmann, p. 5).

253. Heb., zrym; LXX., spermata; Vulg., legumina. Abn Ezra took the word to mean "rice." Comp. Deut. xii. 15, 16; 1 Sam. xvii. 17, 18. Comp. Josephus (Vit., iii.), who tells us how the Jewish priests, prisoners in Rome, fed on sukois kai karuois.

254. Ewald, Antiquities, p. 131 f.

255. Pusey (p. 17) quotes from Chardin's notes in Harmer (Obs., lix.): "I have remarked that the countenance of the Kechicks (monks) are, in fact, more rosy and smooth than those of others, and that those who fast much are, notwithstanding, very beautiful, sparkling with health, with a clear and lively countenance."

256. The Chartummîm are like the Egyptian hierogrammateis. It is difficult to conceive that there was less chance of pollution in being elaborately trained in heathen magic and dream-interpretation than in eating Babylonian food. But this was, so to speak, extra fabulam. It did not enter into the writer's

scheme of moral edification. If, however, the story is meant to imply that these youths accepted the heathen training, though (as we know from tablets and inscriptions) the incantations, etc., in which it abounded were intimately connected with idolatry, and were entirely unharmed by it, this may indicate that the writer did not disapprove of the "Greek training" which Antiochus tried to introduce, so far as it merely involved an acquaintance with Greek learning and literature. This is the view of Grätz. If so, the writer belonged to the more liberal Jewish school which did not object to a study of the Chokmath Javanîth, or "Wisdom of Javan" (Derenbourg, Palestine, p. 361).

257. LXX., elalese met' auton. Considering the normal degradation of pages at Oriental courts, of which Rycaut (referred to by Pusey, p. 18) "gives a horrible account," their escape from the corruption around them was a blessed reward of their faithfulness. They may now have been seventeen, the age for entering the king's service (Xen., Cyrop., I. ii. 8). On the ordinary curse of the rule of eunuchs at Eastern courts see an interesting note in Pusey, p. 21.

258. On the names see Gesenius, Isaiah, ii. 355.
259. Alluded to in ix. 25.
260. Daniel, pp. 20, 21.
261. Comp. Gen. xxxix. 21; 1 Kings viii. 50; Neh. i. 1; Psalm cvi. 46.
262. Lam. iv. 7.
263. Hor., Sat., II. ii. 77.
264. Milton, Reason of Church Government.

## CHAPTER II - THE DREAM-IMAGE OF RUINED EMPIRES

*"With thee will I break in pieces rulers and captains."*--Jer. li. 23.

The Book of Daniel is constructed with consummate skill to teach the mighty lessons which it was designed to bring home to the minds of its readers, not only in the age of its first appearance, but for ever. It is a book which, so far from being regarded as unworthy of its place in the Canon by those who cannot accept it as either genuine or authentic, is valued by many such critics as a very noble work of inspired genius, from which all the difficulties are removed when it is considered in the light of its true date and origin. This second chapter belongs to all time. All that might be looked upon as involving harshnesses, difficulties, and glaring impossibilities, if it were meant for literal history and prediction, vanishes when we contemplate it in its real perspective as a lofty specimen of imaginative fiction, used, like the parables of our Blessed Lord, as the vehicle for the deepest truths. We shall see how the imagery of the chapter produced a deep impress on the imagination of the holiest thinkers--how magnificent a use is made of it fifteen centuries later by the great poet of mediæval Catholicism. [265] It contains the germs of the only philosophy of history which has stood the test of time. It symbolises that ultimate conviction of the Psalmist that "God is the Governor among the nations." No other conviction can suffice to give us consolation amid the perplexity which surrounds the passing phases of the destinies of empires.

The first chapter serves as a keynote of soft, simple, and delightful music by way of overture. It calms us for the contemplation of the awful and tumultuous scenes that are now in succession to be brought before us.

The model which the writer has had in view in this Haggadah is the forty-first chapter of the Book of Genesis. In both chapters we have magnificent heathen potentates--Pharaoh of Egypt, and Nebuchadrezzar of Babylon. In both chapters the kings dream dreams by which they are profoundly troubled. In both, their spirits are saddened. In both, they send for all the Chakamîm and all the Chartummîm of their kingdoms to interpret the dreams. In both, these professional magicians prove themselves entirely incompetent to furnish the interpretation. In both, the failure of the heathen oneirologists is emphasised by the immediate success of a Jewish captive. In both, the captives are described as young, gifted, and beautiful. In both, the interpretation of the king's dream is rewarded by the elevation to princely civil honours. In both, the immediate elevation to ruling position is followed by life-long faithfulness and prosperity. When we add that there are even close verbal resemblances between the chapters, it is difficult not to believe that the one has been influenced by the other.

The dream is placed "in the second year of the reign of Nebuchadnezzar." The date is surprising; for the first chapter has made Nebuchadrezzar a king of Babylon after the siege of Jerusalem "in the third year of Jehoiakim"; and setting aside the historic impossibilities involved in that date, this scene would then fall in the second year of the probation of Daniel and his companions, and at a time when Daniel could only have been a boy of fifteen. [266] The apologists get over the difficulty with the ease which suffices superficial readers who are already convinced. Thus Rashi says "the second year of Nebuchadnezzar," meaning "the second year after the destruction of the Temple," i.e., his twentieth year! Josephus, no less arbitrarily, makes it mean "the second year after the devastation of Egypt." [267] By such devices anything may stand for anything. Hengstenberg and his school, after having made Nebuchadrezzar a king, conjointly with his father--a fact of which history knows nothing, and indeed seems to exclude--say that the second year of his reign does not mean the second year after he became king, but the second year of his independent rule after the death of Nabopolassar. This style of interpretation is very familiar among harmonists, and it makes the interpretation of Scripture perpetually dependent on pure fancy. It is perhaps sufficient to say that Jewish writers, in works meant for spiritual teaching, troubled themselves extremely little with minutiæ of this kind. Like the Greek dramatists, they were unconcerned with details, to which they attached no importance, which they regarded as lying outside the immediate purpose of their narrative. But if any explanation be needful, the simplest way is, with Ewald, Herzfeld, and Lenormant, to make a slight alteration in the text, and to read "in the twelfth" instead of "in the second year of the reign of Nebuchadnezzar."

There was nothing strange in the notion that God should have vouchsafed a prophetic dream to a heathen potentate. Such instances had already been recorded in the case of Pharaoh (Gen. xli.), as well as of his chief courtiers (Gen. xl.); and in the case of Abimelech (Gen. xx. 5-7). It was also a Jewish tradition that it was in consequence of a dream that Pharaoh Necho had sent a warning to Josiah not to advance against him to the Battle of Megiddo. [268] Such dreams are recorded in the cuneiform inscriptions as having occurred to Assyrian monarchs. Ishtar, the goddess of battles, had appeared to Assur-bani-pal, and promised him safety in his war against Teumman, King of Elam; and the dream of a seer had admonished him to take severe steps against his rebel brother, the Viceroy of Babylon. Gyges, King of Lydia, had been warned in a dream to make alliance with Assur-bani-pal. In Egypt Amên-meri-hout had been warned by a dream to unite Egypt against the Assyrians. [269] Similarly in Persian history Afrasiab has an ominous dream, and summons all the astrologers to interpret it; and some of them bid him pay no attention to it. [270] Xerxes (Herod., iii. 19) and Astyages (Herod., i. 108) have dreams indicative of future prosperity or adversity. The fundamental conception of the chapter was therefore in accordance with history [271] --though to say, with the Speaker's Commentary, that these parallels "endorse the authenticity of the Biblical narratives," is either to use inaccurate terms, or to lay the unhallowed fire of false argument on the sacred altar of truth. It is impossible to think without a sigh of the vast amount which would have to be extracted from so-called "orthodox" commentaries, if such passages were rigidly reprobated as a dishonour to the cause of God.

Nebuchadrezzar then--in the second or twelfth year of his reign--dreamed a dream, by which (as in the case of Pharaoh) his spirit was troubled and his sleep interrupted. [272] His state of mind on waking is a psychological condition with which we are all familiar. We awake in a tremor. We have seen something which disquieted us, but we cannot recall what it was; we have had a frightful dream, but we can only remember the terrifying impression which it has left upon our minds.

Pharaoh, in the story of Joseph, remembered his dreams, and only asked the professors of necromancy to furnish him with its interpretation. But Nebuchadrezzar is here represented as a rasher and fiercer despot, not without a side-glance at the raging folly and tyranny of Antiochus Epiphanes. He has at his command an army of priestly prognosticators, whose main function it is to interpret the various omens of the future. Of what use were they, if they could not be relied upon in so serious an exigency? Were they to be maintained in opulence and dignity all their lives, only to fail him at a crisis? It was true that he had forgotten the dream, but it was obviously one of supreme importance; it was obviously an intimation from the gods: was it not clearly their duty to say what it meant?

So Nebuchadrezzar summoned together the whole class of Babylonian augurs in all their varieties--the Chartummîm, "magicians," or book-learned; [273] the Ashshaphîm, "enchanters"; [274] the Mekashaphîm, "sorcerers"; [275] and the Kasdîm, to which the writer gives the long later sense of "dream-interpreters," which had become prevalent in his own day. [276] In later verses he adds two further sections of the students--the Khakhamîm, "wise men," and the Gazerîm, or "soothsayers." Attempts have often been made, and most recently by Lenormant, to distinguish accurately between these classes of magi, but the attempts evaporate for the most part into shadowy etymologies. [277] It seems to have been a literary habit with the author to amass a number of names and titles together. [278] It is a part of the stateliness and leisureliness of style which he adopts, and he gives no indication of any sense of difference between the classes which he enumerates, either here or when he describes various ranks of Babylonian officials.

When they were assembled before him, the king informed them that he had dreamed an important dream, but that it produced such agitation of spirit as had caused him to forget its import. [279] He plainly expected them to supply the failure of his memory, for "a dream not interpreted," say the Rabbis, "is like a letter not read." [280]

Then spake the Chaldeans to the king, and their answer follows in Aramaic (Aramîth), a language which continues to be used till the end of chap. vii. The Western Aramaic, however, here employed could not have been the language in which they spoke, but their native Babylonian, a Semitic dialect more akin to Eastern Aramaic. The word Aramîth here, as in Ezra iv. 7, is probably a gloss or marginal note, to point out the sudden change in the language of the Book.

With the courtly phrase, "O king, live for ever," they promised to tell the king the interpretation, if he would tell them the dream.

"That I cannot do," said the king, "for it is gone from me. Nevertheless, if you do not tell me both the dream and its interpretation, you shall be hacked limb by limb, and your houses shall be made a dunghill." [281]

The language was that of brutal despotism such as had been customary for centuries among the ferocious tyrants of Assyria. The punishment of dismemberment, dichotomy, or death by mutilation was common among them, and had constantly been depicted on their monuments. It was doubtless known to the Babylonians also, being familiar to the apathetic cruelty of the East. Similarly the turning of the houses of criminals into draught-houses was a vengeance practised among other nations. [282] On the other hand, if the "Chaldeans" arose to the occasion, the king would give them rewards and great honours. It is curious to observe that the Septuagint translators, with Antiochus in their mind, render the verse in a form which would more directly remind their readers of Seleucid methods. "If you fail," they make the king say, "you shall be made an example, and your goods shall be forfeited to the crown." [283]

With "nervous servility" the magi answer to the king's extravagantly unreasonable demand, that he must tell them the dream before they can tell him the interpretation. Ewald is probably not far wrong in thinking that a subtle element of irony and humour underlies this scene. It was partly intended as a satirical reflection on the mad vagaries of Epiphanes.

For the king at once breaks out into fury, and tells them that they only want to gain (lit. "buy") time; [284] but that this should not avail them. The dream had evidently been of crucial significance and extreme urgency; something important, and perhaps even dreadful, must be in the air. The very raison d'être of these thaumaturgists and stargazers was to read the omens of the future. If the stars told of any human events, they could not fail to indicate something about the vast trouble which overshadowed the monarch's dream, even though he had forgotten its details. The king gave them to understand that he looked on them as a herd of impostors; that their plea for delay was due to mere tergiversation; [285] and that, in spite of the lying and corrupt words which they had prepared in order to gain respite "till the time be changed" [286] --that is, until they were saved by some "lucky day" or change of fortune [287] --there was but one sentence for them, which could only be averted by their vindicating their own immense pretensions, and telling him his dream.

The "Chaldeans" naturally answered that the king's request was impossible. The adoption of the Aramaic at this point may be partly due to the desire for local colouring. [288] No king or ruler in the world had ever imposed such a test on any Kartum or Ashshaph in the world. [289] No living man could possibly achieve anything so difficult. There were some gods whose dwelling is with flesh; they tenant the souls of their servants. But it is not in the power of these genii to reveal what the king demands; they are limited by the weakness of the souls which they inhabit. [290] It can only be done by those highest divinities whose dwelling is not with flesh, but who

"haunt
The lucid interspace of world and world,"

and are too far above mankind to mingle with their thoughts. [291]

Thereupon the unreasonable king was angry and very furious, and the decree went forth that the magi were to be slain en masse.

How it was that Daniel and his companions were not summoned to help the king, although they had been already declared to be "ten times wiser" than all the rest of the astrologers and magicians put together, is a feature in the story with which the writer does not trouble himself, because it in no way concerned his main purpose. Now, however, since they were prominent members of the magian guild, they are doomed to death among their fellows. Thereupon Daniel sought an interview with Arioch, "the chief of the bodyguard," [292] and asked with gentle prudence why the decree was so harshly urgent. By Arioch's intervention he gained an interview with Nebuchadrezzar, and promised to tell him the dream and its interpretation, if only the king would grant him a little time--perhaps but a single night. [293]

The delay was conceded, and Daniel went to his three companions, and urged then to join in prayer that God would make known the secret to them and spare their lives. Christ tells us that "if two shall agree on earth as touching anything that they ask, it shall be done for them." [294] The secret was revealed to Daniel in a vision of the night, and he blessed "the God of heaven." [295] Wisdom and might are His. Not dependent on "lucky" or "unlucky" days, He changeth the times and seasons; [296] He setteth down one king and putteth up another. By His revelation of deep and sacred things--for the light dwelleth with Him--He had, in answer to their common prayer, made known the secret. [297]

Accordingly Daniel bids Arioch not to execute the magians, but to go and tell the king that he will reveal to him the interpretation of his dream.

Then, by an obvious verbal inconsistency in the story, Arioch is represented as going with haste to the king, with Daniel, and saying that he had found a captive Jew who would answer the king's demands. Arioch could never have claimed any such merit, seeing that Daniel had already given his promise to Nebuchadrezzar in person, and did not need to be described. The king formally puts to Daniel the question whether he could fulfil his pledge; and Daniel answers that, though none of the Khakhamîm, Ashshaphîm, Chartummîm, or Gazerîm [298] could tell the king his dream, yet there is a God in heaven--higher, it is implied, than either the genii or those whose dwelling is not with mortals--who reveals secrets, and has made known to the king what shall be in the latter days. [299]

The king, before he fell asleep, had been deeply pondering the issues of the future; and God, "the revealer of secrets," [300] had revealed those issues to him, not because of any supreme wisdom possessed by Daniel, but simply that the interpretation might be made known. [301]

The king had seen [302] a huge gleaming, terrible colossus of many colours and of different metals, but otherwise not unlike the huge colossi which guarded the portals of his own palace. Its head was of fine gold; its torso of silver; its belly and thighs of brass; its legs of iron; its feet partly of iron and partly of clay. [303] But while he gazed upon it as it reared into the sunlight, as though in mute defiance and insolent security, its grim metallic glare, a mysterious and unforeseen fate fell upon it. [304] The fragment of a rock broke itself loose, not with hands, smote the image upon its feet of iron and clay, and broke them to pieces. It had now nothing left to stand upon, and instantly the hollow multiform monster collapsed into promiscuous ruins. [305] Its shattered fragments became like the chaff of the summer threshing-floor, and the wind swept them away; [306] but the rock, unhewn by any earthly hands, grew over the fragments into a mountain that filled the earth.

That was the haunting and portentous dream; and this was its interpretation:--

The head of gold was Nebuchadrezzar himself, the king of what Isaiah had called "the golden city" [307] --a King of kings, ruler over the beasts of the field, and the fowls of heaven, and the children of men. [308]

After him should come a second and an inferior kingdom, symbolised by the arms and heart of silver.

Then a third kingdom of brass.

Finally a fourth kingdom, strong and destructive as iron. But in this fourth kingdom was an element of weakness, symbolised by the fact that the feet are partly of iron and partly of weak clay. An attempt should be made, by intermarriages, to give greater coherency to these elements; but it should fail, because they could not intermix. In the days of these kings, indicated by the ten toes of the image, swift destruction should come upon the kingdoms from on high; for the King of heaven should set up a kingdom indestructible and eternal, which should utterly supersede all former kingdoms. "The intense nothingness and transitoriness of man's might in its highest estate, and the might of God's kingdom, are the chief subjects of this vision." [309]

Volumes have been written about the four empires indicated by the constituents of the colossus in this dream; but it is entirely needless to enter into them at length. The vast majority of the interpretations have been simply due to a-priori prepossessions, which are arbitrary and baseless. The object has been to make the interpretations fit in with preconceived theories of prophecy, and with the traditional errors about the date and object of the Book of Daniel. If we first see the irresistible evidence that the Book appeared in the days of Antiochus Epiphanes, and then observe that all its earthly "predictions" culminate in a minute description of his epoch, the general explanation of the four empires, apart from an occasional and a subordinate detail, becomes perfectly clear. In the same way the progress of criticism has elucidated in its general outlines the interpretation of the Book which has been so largely influenced by the Book of Daniel--the Revelation of St. John. The all-but-unanimous consensus of the vast majority of the sanest and most competent exegetes now agrees in the view that the Apocalypse was written in the age of Nero, and that its tone and visions were predominantly influenced by his persecution of the early Christians, as the Book of Daniel was by the ferocities of Antiochus against the faithful Jews. Ages of persecution, in which plain-speaking was impossible to the oppressed, were naturally prolific of apocalyptic cryptographs. What has been called the "futurist" interpretation of these books--which, for instance, regards the fourth empire of Daniel as some kingdom of Antichrist as yet unmanifested--is now universally abandoned. It belongs to impossible forms of exegesis, which have long been discredited by the boundless variations of absurd conjectures, and by the repeated refutation of the predictions which many have ventured to base upon these erroneous methods. Even so elaborate a work as Elliott's Horæ Apocalypticæ would now be regarded as a curious anachronism.

That the first empire, represented by the head of gold, is the Babylonian, concentrated in Nebuchadrezzar himself, is undisputed, because it is expressly stated by the writer (ii. 37, 38).

Nor can there be any serious doubt, if the Book be one coherent whole, written by one author, that by the fourth empire is meant, as in later chapters, that of Alexander and his successors--"the Diadochi," as they are often called.

For it must be regarded as certain that the four elements of the colossus, which indicate the four empires as they are presented to the imagination of the heathen despot, are closely analogous to the same four empires which in the seventh chapter present themselves as wild beasts out of the sea to the imagination of the Hebrew seer. Since the fourth empire is there, beyond all question, that of Alexander and his successors, the symmetry and purpose of the Book prove conclusively that the fourth empire here is also the Græco-Macedonian, strongly and irresistibly founded by Alexander, but gradually sinking to utter weakness by its own divisions, in the persons of the kings who split his dominion into four parts. If this needed any confirmation, we find it in the eighth chapter, which is mainly concerned with Alexander the Great and Antiochus Epiphanes; and in the eleventh chapter, which enters with startling minuteness into the wars, diplomacy, and intermarriages of the Ptolemaic and Seleucid dynasties. In viii. 21 we are expressly told that the strong he-goat is "the King of Grecia," who puts an end to the kingdoms of Media and Persia. The arguments of Hengstenberg, Pusey, etc., that the Greek Empire was a civilising and an ameliorating power, apply at least as strongly to the Roman Empire. But when Alexander thundered his way across the dreamy East, he was looked upon as a sort of shattering levin-bolt. The interconnexion of these visions is clearly marked even here, for the juxtaposition of iron and miry clay is explained by the clause "they shall mingle themselves with the seed of men: [310] but they shall not cleave one to another, even as iron is not mixed with clay." This refers to the same attempts to consolidate the rival powers of the Kings of Egypt and Syria which are referred to in xi. 6, 7, and 17. It is a definite allusion which becomes meaningless in the hands of those interpreters who attempt to explain the iron empire to be that of the Romans. "That the Greek Empire is to be the last of the Gentile empires appears from viii. 17, where the vision is said to refer to 'the time of the end.' Moreover, in the last vision of all (x.-xii.), the rise and progress of the Greek Empire are related with many details, but nothing whatever is said of any subsequent empire. Thus to introduce the Roman Empire into the Book of Daniel is to set at naught the plainest rules of exegesis." [311]

The reason of the attempt is to make the termination of the prophecy coincide with the coming of Christ, which is then--quite unhistorically--regarded as followed by the destruction of the fourth and last empire. But the interpretation can only be thus arrived at by a falsification of facts. For the victory of Christianity over Paganism, so decisive and so Divine, was in no sense a destruction of the Roman Empire. In the first place that victory was not achieved till three centuries after Christ's advent, and in the second place it was rather a continuation and defence of the Roman Empire than its destruction. The Roman Empire, in spite of Alaric and Genseric and Attila, and because of its alliance with Christianity, may be said to have practically continued down to modern times. So far from being regarded as the shatterers of the Roman Empire, the Christian popes and bishops were, and were often called, the Defensores Civitatis. That many of the Fathers, following many of the Rabbis, regarded Rome as the iron empire, and the fourth wild beast, was due to the fact that until modern days the science of criticism was unknown, and exegesis was based on the shifting sand. [312] If we are to accept their authority on this question, we must accept it on many others, respecting views and methods which have now been unanimously abandoned by the deeper insight and advancing knowledge of mankind. The influence of Jewish exegesis over the Fathers--erroneous as were its principles and fluctuating as were its conclusions--was enormous. It was not unnatural for the later Jews, living under the hatred and oppression of Rome, and still yearning for the fulfilment of Messianic promises, to identify Rome with the fourth empire. And this seems to have been the opinion of Josephus, whatever that may be worth. But it is doubtful whether it corresponds to another and earlier Jewish tradition. For among the Fathers even Ephræm Syrus identifies the Macedonian Empire with the fourth empire, and he may have borrowed this from Jewish tradition. But of how little value were early conjectures may be seen in the fact that, for reasons analogous to those which had made earlier Rabbis regard Rome as the fourth empire, two mediæval exegetes so famous as Saadia the Gaon and Abn Ezra had come to the conclusion that the fourth empire was--the Mohammedan! [313]

Every detail of the vision as regards the fourth kingdom is minutely in accord with the kingdom of Alexander. It can only be applied to Rome by deplorable shifts and sophistries, the untenability of which we are now more able to estimate than was possible in earlier centuries. So far indeed as the iron is concerned, that might by itself stand equally well for Rome or for Macedon, if Dan. vii. 7, 8, viii. 3, 4, and xi. 3 did not definitely describe the conquests of Alexander. But all which follows is meaningless as applied to Rome, nor is there anything in Roman history to explain any division of the kingdom (ii. 41), or attempt to strengthen it by intermarriage with other kingdoms (ver. 43). In the divided Græco-Macedonian Empires of the Diadochi, the dismemberment of one mighty kingdom into the four much weaker ones of Cassander, Ptolemy, Lysimachus, and Seleucus began immediately after the death of Alexander (b.c. 323). It was completed as the result of twenty-two years of war after the Battle of Ipsus (b.c. 301). The marriage of Antiochus Theos to Berenice, daughter of Ptolemy Philadelphus (b.c. 249, Dan. xi. 6), was as ineffectual as the later marriage of Ptolemy V. (Epiphanes) to Cleopatra, the daughter of Antiochus the Great (b.c. 193), to introduce strength or unity into the distracted kingdoms (xi. 17, 18).

The two legs and feet are possibly meant to indicate the two most important kingdoms--that of the Seleucidæ in Asia, and that of the Ptolemies in Egypt. If we are to press the symbolism still more closely, the ten toes may shadow forth the ten kings who are indicated by the ten horns in vii. 7.

Since, then, we are told that the first empire represents Nebuchadrezzar by the head of gold, and since we have incontestably verified the fourth empire to be the Greek Empire of Alexander and his successors, it only remains to identify the intermediate empires of silver and brass. And it becomes obvious that they can only be the Median and the Persian. That the writer of Daniel regarded these empires as distinct is clear from v. 31 and vi.

It is obvious that the silver is meant for the Median Empire, because, closely as it was allied with the Persian in the view of the writer (vi. 9, 13, 16, viii. 7), he yet spoke of the two as separate. The rule of "Darius the Mede," not of "Cyrus the Persian," is, in his point of view, the "other smaller kingdom" which arose after that of Nebuchadrezzar (v. 31). Indeed, this is also indicated in the vision of the ram (viii. 3); for it has two horns, of which the higher and stronger (the Persian Empire) rose up after the other (the Median Empire); just as in this vision the Persian Empire represented by the thighs of brass is clearly stronger than the Median Empire, which, being wealthier, is represented as being of silver, but is smaller than the other. [314] Further, the second empire is represented later on by the second beast (vii. 5), and the three ribs in its mouth may be meant for the three satrapies of vi. 2.

It may then be regarded as a certain result of exegesis that the four empires are--(1) the Babylonian; (2) the Median; (3) the Persian; (4) the Græco-Macedonian.

But what is the stone cut without hands which smote the image upon his feet? It brake them in pieces, and made the collapsing débris of the colossus like chaff scattered by the wind from the summer threshing-floor. It grew till it became a great mountain which filled the earth.

The meaning of the image being first smitten upon its feet is that the overthrow falls on the iron empire.

All alike are agreed that by the mysterious rock-fragment the writer meant the Messianic Kingdom. The "mountain" out of which (as is here first mentioned) the stone is cut is "the Mount Zion."[315] It commences "in the days of these kings." Its origin is not earthly, for it is "cut without hands." It represents "a kingdom" which "shall be set up by the God of heaven," and shall destroy and supersede all the kingdoms, and shall stand for ever.

Whether a personal Messiah was definitely prominent in the mind of the writer is a question which will come before us when we consider the seventh chapter. Here there is only a Divine Kingdom; and that this is the dominion of Israel seems to be marked by the expression, "the kingdom shall not be left to another people."

The prophecy probably indicates the glowing hopes which the writer conceived of the future of his nation, even in the days of its direst adversity, in accordance with the predictions of the mighty prophets his predecessors, whose writings he had recently studied. Very few of those predictions have as yet been literally fulfilled; not one of them was fulfilled with such immediateness as the prophets conceived, when they were "rapt into future times." To the prophetic vision was revealed the glory that should be hereafter, but not the times and seasons, which God hath kept in His own power, and which Jesus told His disciples were not even known to the Son of Man Himself in His human capacity.

Antiochus died, and his attempts to force Hellenism upon the Jews were so absolute a failure, that, in point of fact, his persecution only served to stereotype the ceremonial institutions which--not entirely proprio motu, but misled by men like the false high priests Jason and Menelaus--he had attempted to obliterate. But the magnificent expectations of a golden age to follow were indefinitely delayed. Though Antiochus died and failed, the Jews became by no means unanimous in their religious policy. Even under the Hasmonæan princes fierce elements of discord were at work in the midst of them. Foreign usurpers adroitly used these dissensions for their own objects, and in b.c. 37 Judaism acquiesced in the national acceptance of a depraved Edomite usurper in the person of Herod, and a section of the Jews attempted to represent him as the promised Messiah![316]

Not only was the Messianic prediction unfulfilled in its literal aspect "in the days of these kings,"[317] but even yet it has by no means received its complete accomplishment. The "stone cut without hands" indicated the kingdom, not--as most of the prophets seem to have imagined when they uttered words which meant more than they themselves conceived--of the literal Israel, but of that ideal Israel which is composed, not of Jews, but of Gentiles. The divinest side of Messianic prophecy is the expression of that unquenchable hope and of that indomitable faith which are the most glorious outcome of all that is most Divine in the spirit of man. That faith and hope have never found even an ideal or approximate fulfilment save in Christ and in His kingdom, which is now, and shall be without end.

But apart from the Divine predictions of the eternal sunlight visible on the horizon over vast foreshortened ages of time which to God are but as one day, let us notice how profound is the symbolism of the vision--how well it expresses the surface glare, the inward hollowness, the inherent weakness, the varying successions, the predestined transience of overgrown empires. The great poet of Catholicism makes magnificent use of Daniel's image, and sees its deep significance. He too describes the ideal of all earthly empire as a colossus of gold, silver, brass, and iron, which yet mainly rests on its right foot of baked and brittle clay. But he tells us that every part of this image, except the gold, is crannied through and through by a fissure, down which there flows a constant stream of tears.[318] These effects of misery trickle downwards, working their way through the cavern in Mount Ida in which the image stands, till, descending from rock to rock, they form those four rivers of hell,--

> "Abhorrèd Styx, the flood of deadly hate;
> Sad Acheron of sorrow, black and deep;
> Cocytus, named of lamentation loud
> Heard on the rueful stream; fierce Phlegethon
> Whose waves of torrent fire inflame with rage."[319]

There is a terrible grandeur in the emblem. Splendid and venerable looks the idol of human empire in all its pomp and pricelessness. But underneath its cracked and fissured weakness drop and trickle and stream the salt and bitter runnels of misery and anguish, till the rivers of agony are swollen into overflow by their coagulated scum.

***

It was natural that Nebuchadrezzar should have felt deeply impressed when the vanished outlines of his dream were thus recalled to him and its awful interpretation revealed. The manner in which he expresses his amazed reverence may be historically improbable, but it is psychologically true. We are told that "he fell upon his face and worshipped Daniel," and the word "worshipped" implies genuine adoration. That so magnificent a potentate should have lain on his face before a captive Jewish youth and adored him is amazing. [320] It is still more so that Daniel, without protest, should have accepted, not only his idolatrous homage, but also the offering of "an oblation and sweet incense." [321] That a Nebuchadrezzar should have been thus prostrate in the dust before their young countryman would no doubt be a delightful picture to the Jews, and if, as we believe, the story is an unconnected Haggada, it may well have been founded on such passages as Isa. xlix. 23, "Kings shall bow down to thee with their faces toward the earth, and lick up the dust of thy feet"; [322] together with Isa. lii. 15, "Kings shall shut their mouths at him: for that which had not been told them shall they see; and that which they had not heard shall they perceive."

But it is much more amazing that Daniel, who, as a boy, had been so scrupulous about the Levitic ordinance of unclean meats, in the scruple against which the gravamen lay in the possibility of their having been offered to idols, [323] should, as a man, have allowed himself to be treated exactly as the king treated his idols! To say that he accepted this worship because the king was not adoring him, but the God whose power had been manifested in him, [324] is an idle subterfuge, for that excuse is offered by all idolaters in all ages. Very different was the conduct of Paul and Barnabas when the rude population of Lystra wished to worship them as incarnations of Hermes and Zeus. The moment they heard of it they rent their clothes in horror, and leapt at once among the people, crying out, "Sirs, why do ye such things? We also are men of like passions with you, and are preaching unto you that ye should turn from these vain ones unto the Living God." [325]

That the King of Babylon should be represented as at once acknowledging the God of Daniel as "a God of gods," though he was a fanatical votary of Bel-merodach, belongs to the general plan of the Book. Daniel received in reward many great gifts, and is made "ruler of all the wise men of Babylon, and chief of the governors [signîn] over all the wise men of Babylon." About his acceptance of the civil office there is no difficulty; but there is a quite insuperable historic difficulty in his becoming a chief magian. All the wise men of Babylon, whom the king had just threatened with dismemberment as a pack of impostors, were, at any rate, a highly sacerdotal and essentially idolatrous caste. That Daniel should have objected to particular kinds of food from peril of defilement, and yet that he should have consented to be chief hierarch of a heathen cult, would indeed have been to strain at gnats and to swallow camels!

And so great was the distinction which he earned by his interpretation of the dream, that, at his further request, satrapies were conferred on his three companions; but he himself, like Mordecai, afterwards "sat in the gate of the king." [326]

## Footnotes:

265. Dante, Inferno, xiv. 94-120.

266. The Assyrian and Babylonian kings, however, only dated their reigns from the first new year after their accession.

267. Antt., X. x. 3.

268. 2 Chron. xxxv. 21. See The Second Book of Kings, p. 404 (Expositor's Bible).

269. See Professor Fuller, Speaker's Commentary, vi. 265.

270. Malcolm, Hist. of Persia, i. 39.

271. The belief that dreams come from God is not peculiar to the Jews, or to Egypt, or Assyria, or Greece (Hom., Il., i. 63; Od., iv. 841), or Rome (Cic., De Div., passim), but to every nation of mankind, even the most savage.

272. Dan. ii. 1: "His dreaming brake from him." Comp. vi. 18; Esther vi. 1: Jerome says, "Umbra quædam, et, ut ita dicam, aura somnii atque vestigium remansit in corde regis, ut, referentibus aliis posset reminisci eorum quæ viderat."

273. Gen. xli. 8; Schrader, K. A. T., p. 26; Records of the Past, i. 136.

274. The word is peculiar to Daniel, both here in the Hebrew and in the Aramaic. Pusey calls it "a common Syriac term, representing some form of divination with which Daniel had become familiar in Babylonia" (p. 40).

275. Exod. vii. 11; Deut. xviii. 10; Isa. xlvii. 9, 12. Assyrian Kashshapu.

276. As in the rule "Chaldæos ne consulito." See supra, p. 48.

277. The equivalents in the LXX., Vulgate, A.V., and other versions are mostly based on uncertain guess-work. See E. Meyer, Gesch. d. Alterth., i. 185; Hommel, Gesch. Bab. u. Assyr., v. 386;

*The Expositor's Bible: The Book of Daniel*
Behrmann, p. 2.

278. E.g., iii. 2, 3, officers of state; iii. 4, 5, etc., instruments of music; iii. 21, clothes.

279. ii. 5: "The dream is gone from me," as in ver. 8 (Theodotion, apeste). But the meaning may be the decree (or word) is "sure": for, according to Nöldeke, azda is a Persian word for "certain." Comp. Esther vii. 7; Isa. xlv. 23.

280. Berachôth, f. 10, 2. This book supplies a charm to be spoken by one who has forgotten his dream (f. 55, 2).

281. Dan. ii. 5, iii. 29. Theodot., eis apoleian esesthe. Lit. "ye shall be made into limbs." The LXX. render it by diamelizomai, membratim concidor, in frusta fio. Comp. Matt. xxiv. 51; Smith's Assurbani-pal, p. 137. The word haddam, "a limb," seems to be of Persian origin--in modern Persian andam. Hence the verb hadîm in the Targum of 1 Kings xviii. 33. Comp. 2 Macc. i. 16, mele poiein.

282. Comp. Ezra vi. 11; 2 Kings x. 27; Records of the Past, i. 27, 43.

283. In iii. 96, kai he oikia autou demeuthesetai. Comp. 2 Macc. iii. 13: "But Heliodorus, because of the king's commandment, said, That in anywise it must be brought into the king's treasury."

284. LXX. Theodot., kairon exagorazete (not in a good sense, as in Eph. v. 16; Col. iv. 5).

285. Theodot., sunethesthe. Cf. John ix. 22.

286. Theodot., eos hou ho kairos parelthe.

287. Esther iii. 7.

288. The word Aramîth may be (as Lenormant thinks) a gloss, as in Ezra iv. 7.

289. A curious parallel is adduced by Behrmann (Daniel, p. 7). Rabia-ibn-nazr, King of Yemen, has a dream which he cannot recall, and acts precisely as Nebuchadrezzar does (Wüstenfeld, p. 9).

290. See Lenormant, La Magie, pp. 181-183.

291. LXX., ii. 11: ei me tis angelos.

292. Lit. "chief of the slaughter-men" or "executioners." LXX., archimageiros. The title is perhaps taken from the story, which in this chapter is so prominently in the writer's mind, where the same title is given to Potiphar (Gen. xxxvii. 36). Comp. 2 Kings xxv. 8; Jer. xxxix. 9. The name Arioch has been derived from Erî-aku, "servant of the moon-god" (supra, p. 49), but is found in Gen. xiv. 1 as the name of "the King of Ellasar." It is also found in Judith i. 6, "Arioch, King of the Elymæans." An Erim-akû, King of Larsa, is found in cuneiform.

293. If Daniel went (as the text says) in person, he must have been already a very high official. (Comp. Esther v. 1; Herod., i. 99.) If so, it would have been strange that he should not have been consulted among the magians. All these details are regarded as insignificant, being extraneous to the general purport of the story (Ewald, Hist., iii. 194).

294. Matt. xviii. 19. The LXX. interpolate a ritual gloss: kai parengeile nesteian kai deesin kai timorian zetesai para tou Kuriou.

295. The title is found in Gen. xxiv. 7, but only became common after the Exile (Ezra i. 2, vi. 9, 10; Neh. i. 5, ii. 4).

296. Comp. Dan. vii. 12; Jer. xxvii. 7; Acts i. 7,chronoi e kairoi; 1 Thess. v. 1; Acts xvii. 26, horisas protetagmenous kairous.

297. With the phraseology of this prayer comp. Psalm xxxvi. 9, xli., cxxxix. 12; Neh. ix. 5; 1 Sam. ii. 8; Jer. xxxii. 19; Job xii. 22.

298. Here the new title Gazerîm, "prognosticators," is added to the others, and is equally vague. It may be derived from Gazar, "to cut"--that is, "to determine."

299. Comp. Gen. xx. 3, xli. 25; Numb. xxii. 35.

300. Comp. Gen. xli. 45.

301. Dan. ii. 30: "For their sakes that shall make known the interpretation to the king" (A.V.). But the phrase seems merely to be one of the vague forms for the impersonal which are common in the Mishnah. The R.V. and Ewald rightly render it as in the text.

302. Here we have (ver. 31) aloo! "behold!" as in iv. 7, 10, vii. 8; but in vii. 2, 5, 6, 7, 13, we have aroo!

303. In the four metals there is perhaps the same underlying thought as in the Hesiodic and ancient conceptions of the four ages of the world (Ewald, Hist., i. 368). Comp. the vision of Zoroaster quoted from Delitzsch by Pusey, p. 97: "Zoroaster saw a tree from whose roots sprang four trees of gold, silver, steel, and brass; and Ormuzd said to him, 'This is the world; and the four trees are the four "times" which are coming.' After the fourth comes, according to Persian doctrine, Sosiosh, the Saviour." Behrmann refers also to Bahman Yesht (Spiegel, Eran. Alterth., ii. 152); the Laws of Manu (Schröder, Ind. Litt., 448); and Roth (Mythos von den Weltaltern, 1860).

304. Much of the imagery seems to have been suggested by Jer. li.

305. Comp. Rev. xx. 11: kai topos ouch heurethe autois.

306. Psalm i. 4, ii. 9; Isa. xli. 15; Jer. li. 33, etc.

307. Isa. xiv. 4.

308. King of kings. Comp. Ezek. xxvi. 7; Ezra vii. 12; Isa. xxxvi. 4. It is the Babylonian Shar-

sharrâni, or Sharru-rabbu (Behrmann). The Rabbis tried (impossibly) to construe this title, which they thought only suitable to God, with the following clause. But Nebuchadrezzar was so addressed (Ezek. xxvi. 7), as the Assyrian kings had been before him (Isa. x. 8), and the Persian kings were after him (Ezra vii. 12). The expression seems strange, but comp. Jer. xxvii. 6, xxviii. 14. The LXX. and Theodotion mistakenly interpolate ichthues tes thalasses.

309. Pusey, p. 63.
310. Comp. Jer. xxxi. 27.
311. Bevan, p. 66.
312. The interpretation is first found, amid a chaos of false exegesis, in the Epistle of Barnabas, iv. 4, § 6.
313. See Bevan, p. 65.
314. On the distinction in the writer's mind between the Median and Persian Empires see v. 28, 31, vi. 8, 12, 15, ix. 1, xi. 1, compared with vi. 28, x. 1. In point of fact, the Persians and Medians were long spoken of as distinct, though they were closely allied; and to the Medes had been specially attributed the forthcoming overthrow of Babylon: Jer. li. 28, "Prepare against her the nations with the kings of the Medes." Comp. Jer. li. 11, and Isa. xiii. 17, xxi. 2, "Besiege, O Media."
315. See Isa. ii. 2, xxviii. 16; Matt. xxi. 42-44. "Le mot de Messie n'est pas dans Daniel. Le mot de Meshiach, ix. 26, désigne l'autorité (probablement sacerdotale) de la Judée" (Renan, Hist., iv. 358).
316. See Kuenen, The Prophets, iii.
317. No kings have been mentioned, but the ten toes symbolise ten kings. Comp. vii. 24.
318. Dante, Inferno, xiv. 94-120.
319. Milton, Paradise Lost, ii. 575.
320. It may be paralleled by the legendary prostrations of Alexander the Great before the high priest Jaddua (Jos., Antt., XI. viii. 5), and of Edwin of Deira before Paulinus of York (Bæda, Hist., ii. 14-16).
321. Isa. xlvi. 6. The same verbs, "they fall down, yea they worship," are there used of idols.
322. Comp. Isa. lx. 14: "The sons also of them that afflicted thee shall come bending unto thee; and all they that despised thee shall bow themselves down at the soles of thy feet."
323. Comp. Rom. xiv. 23; Acts xv. 29; Heb. xiii. 9; 1 Cor. viii. 1; Rev. ii. 14, 20.
324. So Jerome: "Non tam Danielem quam in Daniele adorat Deum, qui mysteria revelavit." Comp. Jos., Antt., XI. viii. 5, where Alexander answers the taunt of Parmenio about his proskunesis of the high priest: ou touton prosekunesa, ton de Theon.
325. Acts xiv. 14, 15.
326. Esther iii. 2. Comp. 1 Chron. xxvi. 30. This corresponds to what Xenophon calls hai epi tas thuras phoiteseis, and to our "right of entrée."

# CHAPTER III - THE IDOL OF GOLD, AND THE FAITHFUL THREE

*"Every goldsmith is put to shame by his molten image: for his molten image is vanity, and there is no breath in them. They are vanity, a work of delusion: in the time of their visitation they shall perish."*--Jer. li. 17, 18.

*"The angel of the Lord encampeth around them that fear Him, and shall deliver them."*--Psalm xxxiv. 7.

*"When thou walkest through the fire, thou shalt not be burnt; neither shall the flame kindle upon thee."*--Isa. xliii. 2.

Regarded as an instance of the use of historic fiction to inculcate the noblest truths, the third chapter of Daniel is not only superb in its imaginative grandeur, but still more in the manner in which it sets forth the piety of ultimate faithfulness, and of that

*"Death-defying utterance of truth"*

which is the essence of the most heroic and inspiring forms of martyrdom. So far from slighting it, because it does not come before us with adequate evidence to prove that it was even intended to be taken as literal history, I have always regarded it as one of the most precious among the narrative chapters of Scripture. It is of priceless value as illustrating the deliverance of undaunted faithfulness--as setting forth the truth that they who love God and trust in Him must love Him and trust in Him even till the end, in spite not only of the most overwhelming peril, but even when they are brought face to face with apparently hopeless defeat. Death itself, by torture or sword or flame, threatened by the priests and tyrants and multitudes of the earth set in open array against them, is impotent to shake the purpose of God's saints. When the servant of God can do nothing else against the banded forces of sin, the world, and the devil, he at least can die, and can say like the Maccabees, "Let us die in our simplicity!" He may be saved from death; but even if not, he must prefer death to apostasy, and will save his own soul. That the Jews were ever reduced to such a choice during the Babylonian exile there is no evidence; indeed, all evidence points the other way, and seems to show that they were allowed with perfect tolerance to hold and practise their own religion. [327] But in the days of Antiochus Epiphanes the question which to choose--martyrdom or apostasy--became a very burning one. Antiochus set up at Jerusalem "the abomination of desolation," and it is easy to understand what courage and conviction a tempted Jew might derive from the study of this splendid defiance. That the story is of a kind well fitted to haunt the imagination is shown by the fact that Firdausi tells a similar story from Persian tradition of "a martyr hero who came unhurt out of a fiery furnace." [328]

This immortal chapter breathes exactly the same spirit as the forty-fourth Psalm.

*"Our heart is not turned back,*
*Neither our steps gone out of Thy way:*
*No, not when Thou hast smitten us into the place of dragons,*
*And covered us with the shadow of death.*
*If we have forgotten the Name of our God,*
*And holden up our hands to any strange god,*
*Shall not God search it out?*
*For He knoweth the very secrets of the heart."*

"Nebuchadnezzar the king," we are told in one of the stately overtures in which this writer rejoices, "made an image of gold, whose height was threescore cubits, and the breadth thereof six cubits, and he set it up in the plains of Dura, in the province of Babylon."

No date is given, but the writer may well have supposed or have traditionally heard that some such event took place about the eighteenth year of Nebuchadrezzar's reign, when he had brought to conclusion a series of great victories and conquests. [329] Nor are we told whom the image represented. We may imagine that it was an idol of Bel-merodach, the patron deity of Babylon, to whom we know that he did erect an image; [330] or of Nebo, from whom the king derived his name. When it is said to be "of gold," the writer, in the grandiose character of his imaginative faculty, may have meant his words to be taken literally, or he may merely have meant that it was gilded, or overlaid with gold. [331] There were colossal images in Egypt and in Nineveh, but we never read in history of any other gilded image ninety feet high and nine feet broad. [332] The name of the plain or valley in which it was erected--Dura--has been found in several Babylonian localities. [333]

Then the king proclaimed a solemn dedicatory festival, to which he invited every sort of functionary, of which the writer, with his usual purgosis and rotundity of expression, accumulates the eight names. They were:--

1. The Princes, "satraps," or wardens of the realm. [334]
2. The Governors [335] (ii. 48).
3. The Captains. [336]
4. The Judges. [337]
5. The Treasurers or Controllers. [338]
6. The Counsellors. [339]
7. The Sheriffs. [340]
8. All the Rulers of the Provinces.

Any attempts to attach specific values to these titles are failures. They seem to be a catalogue of Assyrian, Babylonian, and Persian titles, and may perhaps (as Ewald conjectured) be meant to represent the various grades of three classes of functionaries--civil, military, and legal.

Then all these officials, who with leisurely stateliness are named again, came to the festival, and stood before the image. It is not improbable that the writer may have been a witness of some such splendid ceremony to which the Jewish magnates were invited in the reign of Antiochus Epiphanes.[341]

Then a herald (kerooza [342]) cried aloud [343] a proclamation "to all peoples, nations, and languages." Such a throng might easily have contained Greeks, Phoenicians, Jews, Arabs, and Assyrians, as well as Babylonians. At the outburst of a blast of "boisterous janizary-music" they are all to fall down and worship the golden image.

Of the six different kinds of musical instruments, which, in his usual style, the writer names and reiterates, and which it is neither possible nor very important to distinguish, three--the harp, psaltery, and bagpipe--are Greek; two, the horn and sackbut, have names derived from roots found both in Aryan and Semitic languages; and one, "the pipe," is Semitic. As to the list of officials, the writer had added "and all the rulers of the provinces"; so here he adds "and all kinds of music." [344]

Any one who refused to obey the order was to be flung, the same hour, into the burning furnace of fire. Professor Sayce, in his Hibbert Lectures, connects the whole scene with an attempt, first by Nebuchadrezzar, then by Nabunaid, to make Merodach--who, to conciliate the prejudices of the worshippers of the older deity Bel, was called Bel-merodach--the chief deity of Babylon. He sees in the king's proclamation an underlying suspicion that some would be found to oppose his attempted centralisation of worship. [345]

The music burst forth, and the vast throng all prostrated themselves, except Daniel's three companions, Shadrach, Meshach, and Abed-nego.

We naturally pause to ask where then was Daniel? If the narrative be taken for literal history, it is easy to answer with the apologist that he was ill; or was absent; or was a person of too much importance to be required to prostrate himself; or that "the Chaldeans" were afraid to accuse him. "Certainly," says Professor Fuller, "had this chapter been the composition of a pseudo-Daniel, or the record of a fictitious event, Daniel would have been introduced and his immunity explained." Apologetic literature abounds in such fanciful and valueless arguments. It would be just as true, and just as false, to say that "certainly," if the narrative were historic, his absence would have been explained; and all the more because he was expressly elected to be "in the gate of the king." But if we regard the chapter as a noble Haggada, there is not the least difficulty in accounting for Daniel's absence. The separate stories were meant to cohere to a certain extent; and though the writers of this kind of ancient imaginative literature, even in Greece, rarely trouble themselves with any questions which lie outside the immediate purpose, yet the introduction of Daniel into this story would have been to violate every vestige of verisimilitude. To represent Nebuchadrezzar worshipping Daniel as a god, and offering oblations to him on one page, and on the next to represent the king as throwing him into a furnace for refusing to worship an idol, would have involved an obvious incongruity. Daniel is represented in the other chapters as playing his part and bearing his testimony to the God of Israel; this chapter is separately devoted to the heroism and the testimony of his three friends.

Observing the defiance of the king's edict, certain Chaldeans, actuated by jealousy, came near to the king and "accused" the Jews. [346]

The word for "accused" is curious and interesting. It is literally "ate the pieces of the Jews," [347] evidently involving a metaphor of fierce devouring malice.[348] Reminding the king of his decree, they inform him that three of the Jews to whom he has given such high promotion "thought well not to regard thee; thy god will they not serve, nor worship the golden image which thou hast set up."[349]

Nebuchadrezzar, like other despots who suffer from the vertigo of autocracy, was liable to sudden outbursts of almost spasmodic fury. We read of such storms of rage in the case of Antiochus Epiphanes, of Nero, of Valentinian I., and even of Theodosius. The double insult to himself and to his god on the part of men to whom he had shown such conspicuous favour transported him out of himself. For Belmerodach, whom he had made the patron god of Babylon, was, as he says in one of his own inscriptions, "the Lord, the joy of my heart in Babylon, which is the seat of my sovereignty and empire." It seemed to him too intolerable that this god, who had crowned him with glory and victory, and that he himself, arrayed in the plenitude of his imperial power, should be defied and set at naught by three miserable and ungrateful captives.

He puts it to them whether it was their set purpose [350] that they would not serve his gods or worship his image. Then he offers them a locus poenitentiæ. The music should sound forth again. If they would then worship--but if not, they should be flung into the furnace,--"and who is that God that shall deliver you out of my hands?"

The question is a direct challenge and defiance of the God of Israel, like Pharaoh's "And who is Jehovah, that I should obey His voice?" or like Sennacherib's "Who are they among all the gods that have delivered their land out of my hand?"[351] It is answered in each instance by a decisive interposition.

The answer of Shadrach, Meshach, and Abed-nego is truly magnificent in its unflinching courage. It is: "O Nebuchadnezzar, we have no need to answer thee a word concerning this.[352] If our God whom we serve be able to deliver us, He will deliver us from the burning fiery furnace, and out of thy hand, O king. But if not, [353] be it known unto thee, O king, [354] that we will not serve thy gods, nor worship the golden image which thou hast set up."

By the phrase "if our God be able" no doubt as to God's power is expressed. The word "able" merely means "able in accordance with His own plans."[355] The three children knew well that God can deliver, and that He has repeatedly delivered His saints. Such deliverances abound on the sacred page, and are mentioned in the Dream of Gerontius:--

> "Rescue him, O Lord, in this his evil hour,
> As of old so many by Thy mighty power:--
> Enoch and Elias from the common doom;
> Noe from the waters in a saving home;
> Abraham from th' abounding guilt of Heathenesse,
> Job from all his multiform and fell distress;
> Isaac, when his father's knife was raised to slay;
> Lot from burning Sodom on its judgment-day;
> Moses from the land of bondage and despair;
> Daniel from the hungry lions in their lair;
> David from Golia, and the wrath of Saul;
> And the two Apostles from their prison-thrall."

But the willing martyrs were also well aware that in many cases it has not been God's purpose to deliver His saints out of the peril of death; and that it has been far better for them that they should be carried heavenwards on the fiery chariot of martyrdom. They were therefore perfectly prepared to find that it was the will of God that they too should perish, as thousands of God's faithful ones had perished before them, from the tyrannous and cruel hands of man; and they were cheerfully willing to confront that awful extremity. Thus regarded, the three words "And if not" are among the sublimest words uttered in all Scripture. They represent the truth that the man who trusts in God will continue to say even to the end, "Though He slay me, yet will I trust in Him." They are the triumph of faith over all adverse circumstances. It has been the glorious achievement of man to have attained, by the inspiration of the breath of the Almighty, so clear an insight into the truth that the voice of duty must be obeyed to the very end, as to lead him to defy every combination of opposing forces. The gay lyrist of heathendom expressed it in his famous ode,--

> "Justum et tenacem propositi virum
> Non civium ardor prava jubentium
> Non vultus instantis tyranni
> Mente quatit solidâ."

It is man's testimony to his indomitable belief that the things of sense are not to be valued in comparison to that high happiness which arises from obedience to the law of conscience, and that no extremities of agony are commensurate with apostasy. This it is which, more than anything else, has, in spite of appearances, shown that the spirit of man is of heavenly birth, and has enabled him to unfold

> "The wings within him wrapped, and proudly rise
> Redeemed from earth, a creature of the skies."

For wherever there is left in man any true manhood, he has never shrunk from accepting death rather than the disgrace of compliance with what he despises and abhors. This it is which sends our soldiers on the forlorn hope, and makes them march with a smile upon the batteries which vomit their cross-fires upon them; "and so die by thousands the unnamed demigods." By virtue of this it has been that all the martyrs have, "with the irresistible might of their weakness," shaken the solid world.

*\*\*\**

On hearing the defiance of the faithful Jews--absolutely firm in its decisiveness, yet perfectly respectful in its tone--the tyrant was so much beside himself, that, as he glared on Shadrach, Meshach, and Abed-nego, his very countenance was disfigured. The furnace was probably one used for the ordinary cremation of the dead. [356] He ordered that it should be heated seven times hotter than it was wont to be heated, [357] and certain men of mighty strength who were in his army were bidden to bind the three youths and fling them into the raging flames. So, bound in their hosen, their tunics, their long mantles, [358] and their other garments, they were cast into the seven-times-heated furnace. The king's commandment was so urgent, and the "tongue of flame" was darting so fiercely from the horrible kiln, that the executioners perished in planting the ladders to throw them in, but they themselves fell into the midst of the furnace.

The death of the executioners seems to have attracted no special notice, but immediately afterwards Nebuchadrezzar started in amazement and terror from his throne, and asked his chamberlains, [359] "Did we not cast three men bound into the midst of the fire?"

"True, O king," they answered.

"Behold," he said, "I see four men loose, walking in the midst of the fire, and they have no hurt, and the aspect of the fourth is like a son of the gods!" [360]

Then the king approached the door of the furnace of fire, and called, "Ye servants of the Most High God, [361] come forth." Then Shadrach, Meshach, and Abed-nego came out of the midst of the fire; and all the satraps, prefects, presidents, and court chamberlains gathered round to stare on men who were so completely untouched by the fierceness of the flames that not a hair of their heads had been singed, nor their hosen shrivelled, nor was there even the smell of burning upon them. [362] According to the version of Theodotion, the king worshipped the Lord before them, and he then published a decree in which, after blessing God for sending His angel to deliver His servants who trusted in Him, he somewhat incoherently ordained that "every people, nation, or language which spoke any blasphemy against the God of Shadrach, Meshach, and Abed-nego, should be cut in pieces, and his house made a dunghill: since there is no other god that can deliver after this sort."

Then the king--as he had done before--promoted Shadrach, Meshach, and Abed-nego in the province of Babylon. [363]

Henceforth they disappear alike from history, tradition, and legend; but the whole magnificent Haggada is the most powerful possible commentary on the words of Isa. xliii. 2: "When thou walkest through the fire thou shalt not be burned, neither shall the flame kindle upon thee." [364]

How powerfully the story struck the imagination of the Jews is shown by the not very apposite Song of the Three Children, with the other apocryphal additions. Here we are told that the furnace was heated "with rosin, pitch, tow, and small wood; so that the flame streamed forth above the furnace forty and nine cubits. And it passed through, and burned those Chaldeans it found about the furnace. But the angel of the Lord came down into the furnace together with Azarias and his fellows, and smote the flame of the fire out of the oven; and made the midst of the furnace as it had been a moist whistling wind, [365] so that the fire touched them not at all, neither hurt nor troubled them." [366]

In the Talmud the majestic limitations of the Biblical story are sometimes enriched with touches of imagination, but more often coarsened by tasteless exhibitions of triviality and rancour. Thus in the Vayyikra Rabba Nebuchadrezzar tries to persuade the youths by fantastic misquotations of Isa. x. 10, Ezek. xxiii. 14, Deut. iv. 28, Jer. xxvii. 8; and they refute him and end with clumsy plays on his name, telling him that he should bark (nabach) like a dog, swell like a water-jar (cod), and chirp like a cricket (tsirtsir), which he immediately did--i.e., he was smitten with lycanthropy. [367]

In Sanhedrin, f. 93, 1, the story is told of the adulterous false prophets Ahab and Zedekiah, and it is added that Nebuchadrezzar offered them the ordeal of fire from which the Three Children had escaped. They asked that Joshua the high priest might be with them, thinking that his sanctity would be their protection. When the king asked why Abraham, though alone, had been saved from the fire of

*The Expositor's Bible: The Book of Daniel*

Nimrod, and the Three Children from the burning furnace, and yet the high priest should have been singed (Zech. iii. 2), Joshua answered that the presence of two wicked men gave the fire power over him, and quoted the proverb, "Two dry sticks kindle one green one."

In Pesachin, f. 118, 1, there is a fine imaginative passage on the subject, attributed to Rabbi Samuel of Shiloh:--

"In the hour when Nebuchadrezzar the wicked threw Hananiah, Mishael and Azariah into the midst of the furnace of fire, Gorgemi, the prince of the hail, stood before the Holy One (blessed be He!) and said, 'Lord of the world, let me go down and cool the furnace.' 'No,' answered Gabriel; 'all men know that hail quenches fire; [368] but I, the prince of fire, will go down and make the furnace cool within and hot without, and thus work a miracle within a miracle.' The Holy One (blessed be He!) said unto him, 'Go down.' In the self-same hour Gabriel opened his mouth and said, 'And the truth of the Lord endureth for ever.'"

Mr. Ball, who quotes these passages from Wünsche's Bibliotheca Rabbinica in his Introduction to the Song of the Three Children, [369] very truly adds that many Scriptural commentators wholly lack the orientation derived from the study of Talmudic and Midrashic literature which is an indispensable preliminary to a right understanding of the treasures of Eastern thought. They do not grasp the inveterate tendency of Jewish teachers to convey doctrine by concrete stories and illustrations, and not in the form of abstract thought. "The doctrine is everything; the mode of presentation has no independent value." To make the story the first consideration, and the doctrine it was intended to convey an after-thought, as we, with our dry Western literalness are predisposed to do, is to reverse the Jewish order of thinking, and to inflict unconscious injustice on the authors of many edifying narratives of antiquity.

The part played by Daniel in the apocryphal Story of Susanna is probably suggested by the meaning of his name: "Judgment of God." Both that story and Bel and the Dragon are in their way effective fictions, though incomparably inferior to the canonical part of the Book of Daniel.

And the startling decree of Nebuchadrezzar finds its analogy in the decree published by Antiochus the Great to all his subjects in honour of the Temple at Jerusalem, in which he threatened the infliction of heavy fines on any foreigner who trespassed within the limits of the Holy Court. [370]

## *Footnotes:*

327. The false prophets Ahab and Zedekiah were "roasted in the fire" (Jer. xxix. 22), which may have suggested the idea of this punishment to the writer; but it was for committing "lewdness"--"folly," Judg. xx. 6--in Israel, and for adultery and lies, which were regarded as treasonable. In some traditions they are identified with the two elders of the Story of Susanna. Assur-bani-pal burnt Samas-sum-ucin, his brother, who was Viceroy of Babylon (about b.c. 648), and Te-Umman, who cursed his gods (Smith, Assur-bani-pal, p. 138). Comp. Ewald, Prophets, iii. 240. See supra, p. 44.

328. Malcolm, Persia, i. 29, 30.

329. Both in Theodotion and the LXX. we have etous oktokaidekatou. The siege of Jerusalem was not, however, finished till the nineteenth year of Nebuchadrezzar (2 Kings xxv. 8). Others conjecture that the scene occurred in his thirty-first year, when he was "at rest in his house, and flourishing in his palace" (Dan. iv. 4).

330. Records of the Past, v. 113. The inscriptions of Nebuchadrezzar are full of glorification of Marduk (Merodach), id., v. 115, 135, vii. 75.

331. Comp. Isa. xliv. 9-20. Mr. Hormuzd Rassan discovered a colossal statue of Nebo at Nimroud in 1853. Shalmanezer III. says on his obelisk, "I made an image of my royalty; upon it I inscribed the praise of Asshur my master, and a true account of my exploits." Herodotus (i. 183) mentions a statue of Zeus in Babylon, on which was spent eight hundred talents of gold, and of another made of "solid gold" twelve ells high.

332. By the apologists the "image" or "statue" is easily toned down into a bust on a hollow pedestal (Archdeacon Rose, Speaker's Commentary, p. 270). The colossus of Nero is said to have been a hundred and ten feet high, but was of marble. Nestle (Marginalia, 35) quotes a passage from Ammianus Marcellinus, which mentions a colossal statue of Apollo reared by Antiochus Epiphanes, to which there may be a side-allusion here.

333. Schrader, p. 430: Dur-Yagina, Dur-Sargina, etc. LXX., en pedio tou peribolou choras Babulonias.

334. LXX. and Vulg., satrapæ. Comp. Ezra viii. 36; Esther iii. 12. Supposed to be the Persian Khshatra-pawan (Bevan, p. 79).

335. Signî, Babylonian word (Schrader, p. 411).

336. LXX., toparchai. Comp. Pechah, Ezra v. 14. An Assyrian word (Schrader, p. 577).

337. LXX., hegoumenoi. Perhaps the Persian endarzgar, or "counseller."

338. LXX., dioiketai. Comp. Ezra vii. 21; but Grätz thinks there is a mere scribe's mistake for the gadbarî of vv. 24 and 27.

339. This word is perhaps the old Persian dàtabard.

340. The word is found here alone. Perhaps "advisers." On these words see Bevan, p. 79; Speaker's Commentary, pp. 278, 279; Sayce, Assyr. Gr., p. 110.

341. Ewald, Prophets, v. 209; Hist., v. 294.

342. The word has often been compared with the Greek kerux, but the root is freely found in Assyrian inscriptions (Karaz, "an edict").

343. Comp. Rev. xviii. 2, ekraxen en ischui.

344. See supra, p. 22. The qar'na (horn, keras) and sab'ka (sambuke) are in root both Greek and Aramean. The "pipe" (mash'rôkîtha) is Semitic. Brandig tries to prove that even in Nebuchadrezzar's time these three Greek names (even the symphonia) had been borrowed by the Babylonians from the Greeks; but the combined weight of philological authority is against him.

345. See Hibbert Lectures, chap. lxxxix., etc.

346. Comp. vi. 13, 14.

347. Akaloo Qar'tsîhîn.

348. It is "found in the Targum rendering of Lev. xix. 16 for a talebearer, and is frequent as a Syriac and Arabic idiom" (Fuller).

349. Jerome emphasises the element of jealousy, "Quos prætulisti nobis et captivos ac servos principes fecisti, ii elati in superbiam tua præcepta contemnunt."

350. The phrase is unique and of uncertain meaning.

351. Exod. v. 2; Isa. xxxvi. 20; 2 Chron. xxxii. 13-17.

352. Dan. iii. 16. LXX., ou chreian echomen; Vulg., non oportet nos. To soften the brusqueness of the address, in which the Rabbis (e.g., Rashi) rejoice, the LXX. add another Basileu.

353. Jerome explains "But if not" by Quodsi noluerit; and Theodoret by eite oun rhuetai eite kai me.

354. iii. 18. LXX., kai tote phaneron soi estai. Tert., from the Vet. Itala, "tunc manifestum erit tibi" (Scorp., 8).

355. Comp. Gen. xix. 22: "I cannot do anything until thou be come thither."

356. Cremation prevailed among the Accadians, and was adopted by the Babylonians (G. Bertin, Bab. and Orient. Records, i. 17-21). Fire was regarded as the great purifier. In the Catacombs the scene of the Three Children in the fire is common. They are painted walking in a sort of open cistern full of flames, with doors beneath. The Greek word is kaminos (Matt. xiii. 42), "a calcining furnace."

357. It seems very needless to introduce here, as Mr. Deane does in Bishop Ellicott's commentary, the notion of the seven Maskîm or demons of Babylonian mythology. In the Song of the Three Children the flames stream out forty-nine ($7 \times 7$) cubits. Comp. Isa. xxx. 26.

358. The meaning of these articles of dress is only conjectural: they are--(1) Sarbalîn, perhaps "trousers," LXX. sarabaroi, Vulg. braccæ; (2) Patîsh, LXX. tiarai, Vulg. tiaræ; (3) Kar'bla, LXX. periknemides, Vulg. calceamenta. It is useless to repeat all the guesses. Sarbala is a "tunic" in the Talmud, Arab. sirbal; and some connect Patîsh with the Greek petasos. Judging from Assyrian and Babylonian dress as represented on the monuments, the youths were probably clad in turbans (the Median kaunake), an inner tunic (the Median kandus), an outer mantle, and some sort of leggings (anaxurides). It is interesting to compare with the passage the chapter of Herodotus (i. 190) about the Babylonian dress. He says they wore a linen tunic reaching to the feet, a woollen over-tunic, a white shawl, and slippers. It was said to be borrowed from the dress of Semiramis.

359. Chald., haddab'rîn; LXX., hoi philoi tou basileos.

360. The A.V., "like the Son of God," is quite untenable. The expression may mean a heavenly or an angelic being (Gen. vi. 2; Job i. 6). So ordinary an expression does not need to be superfluously illustrated by references to the Assyrian and Babylonian inscriptions, but they may be found in Sayce, Hibbert Lectures, 128 and passim.

361. LXX., ho Theos ton theon, ho hupsistos. Comp. 2 Macc. iii. 31; Mark v. 7; Luke viii. 28; Acts xvi. 17, from which it will be seen that it was not a Jewish expression, though it often occurs in the Book of Enoch (Dillmann, p. 98).

362. So in Persian history the Prince Siawash clears himself from a false accusation in the reign of his father Kai Kaoos by passing through the fire (Malcolm, Hist. of Persia, i. 38).

363. Comp. Psalm xvi. 12: "We went through fire and water, and Thou broughtest us out into a safe place."

364. Comp. Gen. xxiv. 7; Exod. xxiii. 20; Deut. xxxvi. 1. The phrase applied to Joshua the high priest (Zech. iii. 2), "Is not this a brand plucked out of the burning?" originated the legend that, when the false prophets Ahab and Zedekiah had been burnt by Nebuchadrezzar (Jer. xxix. 22), Joshua had been saved, though singed. This and other apocryphal stories illustrate the evolution of Haggadoth out of metaphoric allusions.

365. pneuma notion diasurizon, "a dewy wind, whistling continually."

366. Song of the Three Children, 23-27.

367. Vay. Rab., xxv. 1 (Wünsche, Bibliotheca Rabbinica).

368. Ecclus. xviii. 16: "Shall not the dew assuage the heat?"
369. Speaker's Commentary, on the Apocrypha, ii. 305-307.
370. Jos., Antt., XII. iii. 3; Jahn, Hebr. Commonwealth, § xc.

# CHAPTER IV - THE BABYLONIAN CEDAR, AND THE STRICKEN DESPOT

*"Pride goeth before destruction, and a haughty spirit before a fall."*--Prov. xvi. 18.

Thrice already, in these magnificent stories, had Nebuchadrezzar been taught to recognise the existence and to reverence the power of God. In this chapter he is represented as having been brought to a still more overwhelming conviction, and to an open acknowledgment of God's supremacy, by the lightning-stroke of terrible calamity.

The chapter is dramatically thrown into the form of a decree which, after his recovery and shortly before his death, the king is represented as having promulgated to "all people, nations, and languages that dwell in all the earth." [371] But the literary form is so absolutely subordinated to the general purpose--which is to show that where God's "judgments are in the earth the inhabitants of the earth will learn righteousness," [372] --that the writer passes without any difficulty from the first to the third person (iv. 20-30). He does not hesitate to represent Nebuchadrezzar as addressing all the subject nations in favour of the God of Israel, even placing in his imperial decree a cento of Scriptural phraseology.

Readers unbiassed by a-priori assumptions, which are broken to pieces at every step, will ask, "Is it even historically conceivable that Nebuchadrezzar (to whom the later Jews commonly gave the title of Ha-Rashang, 'the wicked') could ever have issued such a decree?" [373] They will further ask, "Is there any shadow of evidence to show that the king's degrading madness and recovery rest upon any real tradition?"

As to the monuments and inscriptions, they are entirely silent upon the subject; nor is there any trace of these events in any historic record. Those who, with the school of Hengstenberg and Pusey, think that the narrative receives support from the phrase of Berossus that Nebuchadrezzar "fell sick and departed this life when he had reigned forty-three years," must be easily satisfied, since he says very nearly the same of Nabopolassar. [374] Such writers too much assume that immemorial prejudices on the subject have so completely weakened the independent intelligence of their readers, that they may safely make assertions which, in matters of secular criticism, would be set aside as almost childishly nugatory.

It is different with the testimony of Abydenus, quoted by Eusebius. [375] Abydenus, in his book on the Assyrians, quoted from Megasthenes the story that, after great conquests, "Nebuchadrezzar" (as the Chaldean story goes), "when he had ascended the roof of his palace, was inspired by some god or other, and cried aloud, 'I, Nebuchadrezzar, announce to you the future calamity which neither Bel my ancestor, nor our queen Beltis, can persuade the Fates to avert. There shall come a Persian, a mule, who shall have your own gods as his allies, and he shall make you slaves. Moreover, he who shall help to bring this about shall be the son of a Median woman, the boast of the Assyrian. Would that before his countrymen perish some whirlpool or flood might seize him and destroy him utterly; [376] or else would that he might betake himself to some other place, and might be driven to the desert, where is no city nor track of men, where wild beasts seek their food and birds fly hither and thither! Would that among rocks and mountain clefts he might wander alone! And as for me, may I, before he imagines this, meet with some happier end!' When he had thus prophesied, he suddenly vanished."

I have italicised the passages which, amid immense differences, bear a remote analogy to the story of this chapter. To quote the passage as any proof that the writer of Daniel is narrating literal history is an extraordinary misuse of it.

Megasthenes flourished b.c. 323, and wrote a book which contained many fabulous stories, three centuries after the events to which he alludes. Abydenus, author of Assyriaca, was a Greek historian of still later, and uncertain, date. The writer of Daniel may have met with their works, or, quite independently of them, he may have learned from the Babylonian Jews that there was some strange legend or other about the death of Nebuchadrezzar. The Jews in Babylonia were more numerous and more distinguished than those in Palestine, and kept up constant communication with them. So far from any historical accuracy about Babylon in a Palestinian Jew of the age of the Maccabees being strange, or furnishing any proof that he was a contemporary of Nebuchadrezzar, the only subject of astonishment would be that he should have fallen into so many mistakes and inaccuracies, were it not that the ancients in general, and the Jews particularly, paid little attention to such matters.

Aware, then, of some dim traditions that Nebuchadrezzar at the close of his life ascended his palace roof and there received some sort of inspiration, after which he mysteriously disappeared, the writer, giving free play to his imagination for didactic purposes, after the common fashion of his age and nation, worked up these slight elements into the stately and striking Midrash of this chapter. He too makes the king mount his palace roof and receive an inspiration; but in his pages the inspiration does not refer to "the mule" or half-breed, Cyrus, nor to Nabunaid, the son of a Median woman, nor to any imprecation pronounced upon them, but is an admonition to himself; and the imprecation which he denounced upon the future subverters of Babylon is dimly analogous to the fate which fell on his own head. Instead of making him "vanish" immediately afterwards, the writer makes him fall into a beast-madness for "seven times," after which he suddenly recovers and publishes a decree that all mankind should honour the true God.

Ewald thinks that a verse has been lost at the beginning of the chapter, indicating the nature of the document which follows; but it seems more probable that the author began this, as he begins other chapters, with the sort of imposing overture of the first verse.

Like Assur-bani-pal and the ancient despots, Nebuchadrezzar addresses himself to "all people in the earth," and after the salutation of peace [377] says that he thought it right to tell them "the signs and wonders that the High God hath wrought towards me. How great are His signs, and how mighty are His wonders! His kingdom is an everlasting kingdom, and His dominion is from generation to generation."[378]

He goes on to relate that, while he was at ease and secure in his palace, [379] he saw a dream which affrighted him, and left a train of gloomy forebodings. As usual he summoned the whole train of Khakhamîm, Ashshaphîm, Mekashshaphîm, Kasdîm, Chartummîm, and Gazerîm, to interpret his dream, and as usual they failed to do so. Then lastly, Daniel, surnamed Belteshazzar, after Bel, Nebuchradrezzar's god, [380] and "chief of the magicians," [381] in whom was "the spirit of the holy gods," is summoned. To him the king tells his dream.

The writer probably derives the images of the dream from the magnificent description of the King of Assyria as a spreading cedar in Ezek. xxxi. 3-18:--

"Behold, the Assyrian was a cedar in Lebanon with fair branches, and with a shadowing shroud, and of an high stature; and his top was among the thick boughs. The waters nourished him, the deep made him to grow.... Therefore his stature was exalted above all the trees of the field; and his boughs were multiplied, and his branches became long by reason of many waters. All the fowls of the air made their nests in his boughs, and under his branches did all the beasts of the field bring forth their young, and under his shadow dwelt all great nations.... The cedars in the garden of God could not hide him ... nor was any tree in the garden of God like him in his beauty.... Therefore thus saith the Lord God: Because thou art exalted in stature ... I will deliver him into the hand of the mighty one of the nations.... And strangers, the terrible of the nations, have cut him off, and have left him. Upon the mountains and in all the valleys his branches are broken ... and all the people of the earth are gone down from his shadow, and have left him.... I made the nations to shake at the sound of his fall."

We may also compare this dream with that of Cambyses narrated by Herodotus [382] : "He fancied that a vine grew from the womb of his daughter and overshadowed the whole of Asia.... The magian interpreter expounded the vision to foreshow that the offspring of his daughter would reign over Asia in his stead."

So too Nebuchadrezzar in his dream had seen a tree in the midst of the earth, of stately height, which reached to heaven and overshadowed the world, with fair leaves and abundant fruit, giving large nourishment to all mankind, and shade to the beasts of the field and fowls of the heaven. The LXX. adds with glowing exaggeration, "The sun and moon dwelled in it, and gave light to the whole earth. And, behold, a watcher ['îr] [383] and a holy one [qaddîsh] [384] came down from heaven, and bade, Hew down, and lop, and strip the tree, and scatter his fruit, and scare away the beasts and birds from it, but leave the stump in the greening turf bound by a band of brass and iron, and let it be wet with heaven's dews,"-- and then, passing from the image to the thing signified, "and let his portion be with the beasts in the grass of the earth. Let his heart be changed from man's, and let a beast's heart be given unto him, and let seven times pass over him." We are not told to whom the mandate is given--that is left magnificently vague. The object of this "sentence of the watchers, and utterance of the holy ones," is that the living may know that the Most High is the Supreme King, and can, if He will, give rule even to the lowliest. Nebuchadrezzar, who tells us in his inscription that "he never forgave impiety," has to learn that he is nothing, and that God is all,--that "He pulleth down the mighty from their seat, and exalteth the humble and meek." [385]

This dream Nebuchadrezzar bids Daniel to interpret, "because thou hast the spirit of a Holy God in thee."

Before we proceed let us pause for a moment to notice the agents of the doom. It is one of the never-sleeping ones--an 'îr and a holy one--who flashes down from heaven with the mandate; and he is only the mouthpiece of the whole body of the watchers and holy ones.

Generally, no doubt, the phrase means an angelic denizen of heaven. The LXX. translates watcher by "angel." Theodotion, feeling that there is something technical in the word, which only occurs in this chapter, renders it by eir. This is the first appearance of the term in Jewish literature, but it becomes extremely common in later Jewish writings--as, for instance, in the Book of Enoch. The term "a holy one" [386] connotes the dedicated separation of the angels; for in the Old Testament holiness is used to express consecration and setting apart, rather than moral stainlessness. [387] The "seven watchers" are alluded to in the post-exilic Zechariah (iv. 10): "They see with joy the plummet in the hand of Zerubbabel, even those seven, the eyes of the Lord; they run to and fro through the whole earth." In this verse Kohut [388] and Kuenen read "watchers" ('îrîm) for "eyes" ('înîm), and we find these seven watchers in the Book of Enoch (chap. xx.). We see as an historic fact that the familiarity of the Jews with Persian angelology and demonology seems to have developed their views on the subject. It is only after the Exile that we find angels and demons playing a more prominent part than before, divided into classes, and even marked out by special names. The Apocrypha becomes more precise than the canonical books, and the later pseudepigraphic books, which advance still further, are left behind by the Talmud. Some have supposed a connexion between the seven watchers and the Persian amschashpands.[389] The shedîm, or evil spirits, are also seven in number,--

*"Seven are they, seven are they!*
*In the channel of the deep seven are they,*
*In the radiance of heaven seven are they!"* [390]

It is true that in Enoch (xc. 91) the prophet sees "the first six white ones," and we find six also in Ezek. ix. 2. On the other hand, we find seven in Tobit: "I am Raphael, one of the seven holy angels which present the prayers of the saints, and which go in and out before the glory of the Holy One." [391] The names are variously given; but perhaps the commonest are Michael, Gabriel, Uriel, Raphael, and Raguel. [392] In the Babylonian mythology seven deities stood at the head of all Divine beings, and the seven planetary spirits watched the gates of Hades. [393]

To Daniel, when he had heard the dream, it seemed so full of portentous omen that "he was astonished for one hour." [394] Seeing his agitation, the king bids him take courage and fearlessly interpret the dream. But it is an augury of fearful visitation; so he begins with a formula intended as it were to avert the threatened consequences. "My Lord," he exclaimed, on recovering voice, "the dream be to them that hate thee, and the interpretation to thine enemies." [395] The king would regard it as a sort of appeal to the averting deities (the Roman Dî Averrunci), and as analogous to the current formula of his hymns, "From the noxious spirit may the King of heaven and the king of earth preserve thee!" [396] He then proceeds to tell the king that the fair, stately, sheltering tree--"it is thou, O king"; and the interpretation of the doom pronounced upon it is that he should be driven from men, and should dwell with the beasts of the field, and be reduced to eat grass like the oxen, and be wet with the dew of heaven, "and seven times shall pass over thee, till thou shalt know that the Most High ruleth in the kingdom of men, and giveth it to whomsoever He will." But as the stump of the tree was to be left in the fresh green grass, so the kingdom should be restored to him when he had learnt that the Heavens do rule.

The only feature of the dream which is left uninterpreted is the binding of the stump with bands of iron and brass. Most commentators follow Jerome in making it refer to the fetters with which maniacs are bound, [397] but there is no evidence that Nebuchadrezzar was so restrained, and the bands round the stump are for its protection from injury. This seems preferable to the view which explains them as "the stern and crushing sentence under which the king is to lie." [398] Josephus and the Jewish exegetes take the "seven times" to be "seven years"; but the phrase is vague, and the event is evidently represented as taking place at the close of the king's reign. Instead of using the awful name of Jehovah, the prophet uses the distant periphrasis of "the Heavens." It was a phrase which became common in later Jewish literature, and a Babylonian king would be familiar with it; for in the inscriptions we find Maruduk addressed as the "great Heavens," the father of the gods. [399]

Having faithfully interpreted the fearful warning of the dream, Daniel points out that the menaces of doom are sometimes conditional, and may be averted or delayed. "Wherefore," he says, "O king, let my counsel be acceptable unto thee, and break off thy sins by righteousness, and thine iniquities by showing mercy to the poor; if so be there may be a healing of thy error." [400]

This pious exhortation of Daniel has been severely criticised from opposite directions.

The Jewish Rabbis, in the very spirit of bigotry and false religion, said that Daniel was subsequently thrown into the den of lions to punish him for the crime of tendering good advice to Nebuchadrezzar; [401] and, moreover, the advice could not be of any real use; "for even if the nations of the world do righteousness and mercy to prolong their dominion, it is only sin to them." [402]

On the other hand, the Roman Catholics have made it their chief support for the doctrine of good works, which is so severely condemned in the twelfth of our Articles.

Probably no such theological questions remotely entered into the mind of the writer. Perhaps the words should be rendered "break off thy sins by righteousness," rather than (as Theodotion renders them) "redeem thy sins by almsgiving." [403] It is, however, certain that among the Pharisees and the later Rabbis there was a grievous limitation of the sense of the word tzedakah, "righteousness," to mean merely almsgiving. In Matt. vi. 1 it is well known that the reading "alms" (eleemosunen) has in the received text displaced the reading "righteousness" (dikaiosunen); and in the Talmud "righteousness"--like our shrunken misuse of the word "charity"--means almsgiving. The value of "alms" has often been extravagantly exalted. Thus we read: "Whoever shears his substance for the poor escapes the condemnation of hell" (Nedarîm, f. 22, 1).

In Baba Bathra, f. 10, 1, and Rosh Hashanah, f. 16, 2, we have "alms delivereth from death," as a gloss on the meaning of Prov. xi. 4. [404]

We cannot tell that the writer shared these views. He probably meant no more than that cruelty and injustice were the chief vices of despots, and that the only way to avert a threatened calamity was by repenting of them. The necessity for compassion in the abstract was recognised even by the most brutal Assyrian kings.

\*\*\*

We are next told the fulfilment of the dark dream. The interpretation had been meant to warn the king; but the warning was soon forgotten by one arrayed in such absolutism of imperial power. The intoxication of pride had become habitual in his heart, and twelve months sufficed to obliterate all solemn thoughts. The Septuagint adds that "he kept the words in his heart"; but the absence of any mention of rewards or honours paid to Daniel is perhaps a sign that he was rather offended than impressed.

A year later he was walking on the flat roof of the great palace of the kingdom of Babylon. The sight of that golden city in the zenith of its splendour may well have dazzled the soul of its founder. He tells us in an inscription that he regarded that city as the apple of his eye, and that the palace was its most glorious ornament. [405] It was in the centre of the whole country; it covered a vast space, and was visible far and wide. It was built of brick and bitumen, enriched with cedar and iron, decorated with inscriptions and paintings. The tower "contained the treasures of my imperishable royalty; and silver, gold, metals, gems, nameless and priceless, and immense treasures of rare value," had been lavished upon it. Begun "in a happy month, and on an auspicious day," it had been finished in fifteen days by armies of slaves. This palace and its celebrated hanging gardens were one of the wonders of the world.

Beyond this superb edifice, where now the hyæna prowls amid miles of débris and mounds of ruin, and where the bittern builds amid pools of water, lay the unequalled city. Its walls were three hundred and eighty feet high and eighty-five feet thick, and each side of the quadrilateral they enclosed was fifteen miles in length. The mighty Euphrates flowed through the midst of the city, which is said to have covered a space of two hundred square miles; and on its farther bank, terrace above terrace, up to its central altar, rose the huge Temple of Bel, with all its dependent temples and palaces. [406] The vast circuit of the walls enclosed no mere wilderness of houses, but there were interspaces of gardens, and palm-groves, and orchards, and cornland, sufficient to maintain the whole population. Here and there rose the temples reared to Nebo, and Sin the moon-god, and Mylitta, and Nana, and Samas, and other deities; and there were aqueducts or conduits for water, and forts and palaces; and the walls were pierced with a hundred brazen gates. When Milton wanted to find some parallel to the city of Pandemonium in Paradise Lost, he could only say,--

> "Not Babylon,
> Nor great Alcairo such magnificence
> Equall'd in all their glories, to enshrine
> Belus or Serapis their gods, or seat
> Their kings, when Egypt with Assyria strove
> In wealth and luxury."

Babylon, to use the phrase of Aristotle, included, not a city, but a nation. [407]

Enchanted by the glorious spectacle of this house of his royalty and abode of his majesty, the despot exclaimed almost in the words of some of his own inscriptions, "Is not this great Babylon that I have built for the house of the kingdom by the might of my treasures and for the honour of my majesty?"

The Bible always represents to us that pride and arrogant self-confidence are an offence against God. The doom fell on Nebuchadrezzar "while the haughty boast was still in the king's mouth." The suddenness of the Nemesis of pride is closely paralleled by the scene in the Acts of the Apostles in which Herod Agrippa I. is represented as entering the theatre at Cæsarea to receive the deputies of Tyre and Sidon. He was clad, says Josephus, in a robe of intertissued silver, and when the sun shone upon it he was surrounded with a blaze of splendour. Struck by the scene, the people, when he had ended his harangue to them, shouted, "It is the voice of a god, and not of a man!" Herod, too, in the story of Josephus, had received, just before, an ominous warning; but it came to him in vain. He accepted the blasphemous adulation, and immediately, smitten by the angel of God, he was eaten of worms, and in three days was dead. [408]

And something like this we see again and again in what the late Bishop Thirlwall called the "irony of history"--the very cases in which men seem to have been elevated to the very summit of power only to heighten the dreadful precipice over which they immediately fall. He mentions the cases of Persia, which was on the verge of ruin, when with lordly arrogance she dictated the Peace of Antalcidas; of Boniface VIII., in the Jubilee of 1300, immediately preceding his deadly overthrow; of Spain, under Philip II., struck down by the ruin of the Armada at the zenith of her wealth and pride. He might have added the instances of Ahab, Sennacherib, Nebuchadrezzar, and Herod Antipas; of Alexander the Great, dying as the fool dieth, drunken and miserable, in the supreme hour of his conquests; of Napoleon, hurled into the dust, first by the retreat from Moscow, then by the overthrow at Waterloo.

"While the word was yet in the king's mouth, there fell a voice from heaven." It was what the Talmudists alluded to so frequently as the Bath Qôl, or "daughter of a voice," which came sometimes for the consolation of suffering, sometimes for the admonition of overweening arrogance. It announced to him the fulfilment of the dream and its interpretation. As with one lightning-flash the glorious cedar was blasted, its leaves scattered, its fruits destroyed, its shelter reduced to burning and barrenness. Then somehow the man's heart was taken from him. He was driven forth to dwell among the beasts of the field, to eat grass like oxen. Taking himself for an animal in his degrading humiliation he lived in the open field. The dews of heaven fell upon him. His unkempt locks grew rough like eagles' feathers, his uncut nails like claws. In this condition he remained till "seven times"--some vague and sacred cycle of days--passed over him.

His penalty was nothing absolutely abnormal. His illness is well known to science and national tradition as that form of hypochondriasis in which a man takes himself for a wolf (lycanthropy), or a dog (kynanthropy), or some other animal. [409] Probably the fifth-century monks, who were known as Boskoi, from feeding on grass, may have been, in many cases, half maniacs who in time took themselves for oxen. Cornill, so far as I know, is the first to point out the curious circumstance that a notion as to the points of analogy between Nebuchadnezzar (thus spelt) and Antiochus Epiphanes may have been strengthened by the Jewish method of mystic commentary known in the Talmud as Gematria, and in Greek as Isopsephism. That such methods, in other forms, were known and practised in early times we find from the substitution of Sheshach for Babel in Jer. xxv. 26, li. 41, and of Tabeal (by some cryptogram) for Remaliah in Isa. vii. 6; and of lebh kamai ("them that dwell in the midst of them") for Kasdîm (Chaldeans) in Jer. li. 1. These forms are only explicable by the interchange of letters known as Athbash, Albam, etc. Now Nebuchadnezzar = 423:--

$n = 50; v = 2; v = 6; k = 20; d = 4; n = 50; ' = 1; ts = 90; r = 200 = 423.$

And Antiochus Epiphanes = 423:--

$' = 1; n = 50; t = 9; y = 10; v = 6; k = 20; v = 6; s = 60 =?\,?\,.\,?\,.\,?\,.\,?\,.\,?\,.\,?\,.\,?\,.\,??\,162\} ' = 1; ph = 70; y = 10; ph = 70; n = 50; s = 60 = 261\} = 423.$

The madness of Antiochus was recognised in the popular change of his name from Epiphanes to Epimanes. But there were obvious points of resemblance between these potentates. Both of them conquered Jerusalem. Both of them robbed the Temple of its holy vessels. Both of them were liable to madness. Both of them tried to dictate the religion of their subjects.

What happened to the kingdom of Babylon during the interim is a point with which the writer does not trouble himself. It formed no part of his story or of his moral. There is, however, no difficulty in supposing that the chief mages and courtiers may have continued to rule in the king's name--a course rendered all the more easy by the extreme seclusion in which most Eastern monarchs pass their lives, often unseen by their subjects from one year's end to the other. Alike in ancient days as in modern--witness the cases of Charles VI. of France, Christian VII. of Denmark, George III. of England, and Otho of Bavaria--a king's madness is not allowed to interfere with the normal administration of the kingdom.

When the seven "times"--whether years or brief periods--were concluded, Nebuchadrezzar "lifted up his eyes to heaven," and his understanding returned to him. No further light is thrown on his recovery, which (as is not infrequently the case in madness) was as sudden as his aberration. Perhaps the calm of the infinite azure over his head flowed into his troubled soul, and reminded him that (as the inscriptions say) "the Heavens" are "the father of the gods." [410] At any rate, with that upward glance came the restoration of his reason.

He instantly blessed the Most High, "and praised and honoured Him who liveth for ever, whose dominion is an everlasting dominion, and His kingdom is from generation to generation. [411] And all the inhabitants of the earth are reputed as nothing; and He doeth according to His will [412] in the army of heaven, and among the inhabitants of the earth; [413] and none can stay His hand, or say unto Him, What doest Thou?" [414]

Then his lords and counsellors reinstated him in his former majesty; his honour and brightness returned to him; he was once more "that head of gold" in his kingdom. [415]

He concludes the story with the words: "Now I Nebuchadnezzar praise and extol and honour the King of heaven, all whose works are truth and His ways judgment; [416] and those that walk in pride He is able to abase." [417]

He died b.c. 561, and was deified, leaving behind him an invincible name.

## Footnotes:

371. Comp. 1 Macc. i. 41, 42: "And the king [Antiochus Epiphanes] wrote to his whole kingdom, that all should be one people, and every one should leave his laws."

372. Isa. xxvi. 9.

373. Professor Fuller follows them in supposing that the decree is really a letter written by Daniel, as is shown by the analogy of similar documents, and the attestation (!) of the LXX. (arche tes epistoles). He adds, "The undertone of genuineness which makes itself so inobtrusively felt to the Assyrian scholar when reading it, is quite sufficient to decide the question of authenticity"! Such remarks are meant only for a certain circle of readers already convinced. If they were true, it would be singular that scarcely one living Assyriologist accepts the authenticity of Daniel; and Mr. Bevan calls this "a narrative which contains scarcely anything specifically Babylonian."

374. See Jos. c. Ap., I. 20, empeson eis arrhostian, metellaxato ton bion (of Nebuchadrezzar); and I. 19 of Nabopolassar.

375. Præp. Ev., lx. 41.

376. I follow the better readings which Mr. Bevan adopts from Von Gutschmid and Toup.

377. Comp. Ezra iv. 7, vii. 12.

378. If Nebuchadrezzar wrote this edict, he must have been very familiar with the language of Scripture. See Deut. vi. 22; Isa. viii. 18; Psalm lxxviii. 12-16, cvi. 2; Mic. iv. 7, etc.

379. Heykal, "palace"; Bab., ikallu. Comp. Amos viii. 3. See the palace described in Layard, Nineveh and Babylon.

380. A mistake of the writer. See supra, p. 129.

381. Rab-chartummaya.

382. Herod., i. 108.

383. yr. Comp. Mal. ii. 12 (perhaps "the watchman and him that answereth"). LXX., angelos; Theodot., egregoros.

384. Comp. Deut. xxxiii. 2; Zech. xiv. 5; Psalm lxxxix. 6; Job v. 1, etc.

385. The LXX., in its free manipulation of the original, adds that the king saw the dream fulfilled. In one day the tree was cut down, and its destruction completed in one hour.

386. Comp. Zech. xiv. 5; Psalm lxxxix. 6.

387. See Job xv. 15.

388. Dr. A. Kohut, Die jüdische Angelologie, p. 6, n. 17.

389. For a full examination of the subject see Oehler, Theol. of the O. T., § 59, pp. 195 ff.; Schultz, Alttest. Theol., p. 555; Hamburger, Real-Encycl., i., s.v. "Engel"; Professor Fuller, Speaker's Commentary, on the Apocrypha, Tobit, i., 171-183.

390. Sayce, Records of the Past, ix. 140.

391. The number seven is not, however, found in all texts.

392. The Jewish tradition admits that the names of the angels came from Persia (Rosh Hashanah, f. 56, 1; Bereshîth Rabba, c. 48; Riehm, R. W. B., i. 381).

393. Descent of Ishtar, Records of the Past, i. 141. Botta found seven rude figures buried under the thresholds of doors.

394. The Targum understands it "for a moment."

395. The wish was quite natural. It is needless to follow Rashi, etc., in making this an address to God, as though it were a prayer to Him that ruin might fall on His enemy Nebuchadrezzar. Comp. Ov., Fast., iii. 494: "Eveniat nostris hostibus ille color."

396. Records of the Past, i. 133.

397. Mark v. 3.

398. Bevan, p. 92.

399. In the Mishnah often Shamayîm; N. T., he basileia ton ouranon.

400. Or, as in A.V. and Hitzig, "if it may be a lengthening of thy tranquillity"; but Ewald reads arukah, "healing" (Isa. lviii. 8), for ar'kah.

401. Baba Bathra, f. 4, 1.

402. Berachôth, f. 10, 2; f. 57, 2.
403. Theodot., tas hamartias sou en eleemosunais lutrosai; Vulg., peccata tua eleemosynis redime. Comp. Psalm cxii. 9. This exaltation of almsgiving is a characteristic of later Judaism (Ecclus. iv. 5-10; Tobit iv. 11).
404. Comp. Prov. x. 2, xvi. 6; Sukka, f. 49, 2. The theological and ethical question involved is discussed by Calvin, Instt., iii. 4; Bellarmine, De Poenitent., ii. 6 (Behrmann).
405. It is now called Kasr, but the Arabs call it Mujelibé, "The Ruined."
406. Birs-Nimrod (Grote, Hist. of Greece, III., chap. xix.; Layard, Nin. and Bab., chap. ii.).
407. Arist., Polit., III. i. 12. He says that three days after its capture some of its inhabitants were still unaware of the fact.
408. Acts xii. 20-23; Jos., Antt., XIV. viii. 2.
409. For further information on this subject I may refer to my paper on "Rabbinic Exegesis," Expositor, v. 362-378. The fact that there are slight variations in spelling Nebuchadnezzar and Antiochus Epiphanes is of no importance.
410. Psalm cxxiii. 1. See Eurypides, Bacchæ, 699.
411. Exod. xvii. 16.
412. Psalm cxlv. 13.
413. Isa. xxiv. 21, xl. 15, 17. For the "host of heaven" (stratia ouranios, Luke ii. 13) see Isa. xl. 26; Job. xxxviii. 7; 1 Kings xxii. 19; Enoch xviii. 14-16; Matt. xi. 25.
414. Isa. xliii. 13, xlv. 9; Psalm cxxxv. 6; Job ix. 12; Eccles. viii. 4. The phrase for "to reprove" is literally "to strike on the hand," and is common in later Jewish writers.
415. Dan. ii. 38.
416. Psalm xxxiii. 4.
417. Exod. xviii. 11.

## CHAPTER V - THE FIERY INSCRIPTION

*"That night they slew him on his father's throne*
*He died unnoticed, and the hand unknown:*
*Crownless and sceptreless Belshazzar lay,*
*A robe of purple round a form of clay."*
Sir E. Arnold.

In this chapter again we have another magnificent fresco-picture, intended, as was the last--but under circumstances of aggravated guilt and more terrible menace--to teach the lesson that "verily there is a God that judgeth the earth."

The truest way to enjoy the chapter, and to grasp the lessons which it is meant to inculcate in their proper force and vividness, is to consider it wholly apart from the difficulties as to its literal truth. To read it aright, and duly to estimate its grandeur, we must relegate to the conclusion of the story all worrying questions, impossible of final solution, as to whom the writer intended by Belshazzar, or whom by Darius the Mede. [418] All such discussions are extraneous to edification, and in no way affect either the consummate skill of the picture or the eternal truths of which it is the symbolic expression. To those who, with the present writer, are convinced, by evidence from every quarter--from philology, history, the testimony of the inscriptions, and the manifold results obtained by the Higher Criticism-- that the Book of Daniel is the work of some holy and highly gifted Chasîd in the days of Antiochus Epiphanes, it becomes clear that the story of Belshazzar, whatever dim fragments of Babylonian tradition it may enshrine, is really suggested by the profanity of Antiochus Epiphanes in carrying off, and doubtless subjecting to profane usage, many of the sacred vessels of the Temple of Jerusalem. [419] The retribution which awaited the wayward Seleucid tyrant is prophetically intimated by the menace of doom which received such immediate fulfilment in the case of the Babylonian King. The humiliation of the guilty conqueror, "Nebuchadrezzar the Wicked," who founded the Empire of Babylon, is followed by the overthrow of his dynasty in the person of his "son," and the capture of his vast capital.

"It is natural," says Ewald, "that thus the picture drawn in this narrative should become, under the hands of our author, a true night-piece, with all the colours of the dissolute, extravagant riot of luxurious passion and growing madness, of ruinous bewilderment, and of the mysterious horror and terror of such a night of revelry and death."

The description of the scene begins with one of those crashing overtures of which the writer duly estimated the effect upon the imagination.

"Belshazzar the king made a great feast to a thousand of his lords, and drank wine before the thousand." [420] The banquet may have been intended as some propitiatory feast in honour of Bel-merodach. It was celebrated in that palace which was a wonder of the world, with its winged statues and splendid spacious halls. The walls were rich with images of the Chaldeans, painted in vermilion and exceeding in dyed attire--those images of goodly youths riding on goodly horses, as in the Panathenaic procession on the frieze of the Acropolis--the frescoed pictures, on which, in the prophet's vision, Aholah and Aholibah, gloated in the chambers of secret imagery. [421] Belshazzar's princes were there, and his wives, and his concubines, whose presence the Babylonian custom admitted, though the Persian regarded it as unseemly. [422] The Babylonian banquets, like those of the Greeks, usually ended by a KOmos or revelry, in which intoxication was regarded as no disgrace. Wine flowed freely. Doubtless, as in the grandiose picture of Martin, there were brasiers of precious metal, which breathed forth the fumes of incense; [423] and doubtless, too, there were women and boys and girls with flutes and cymbals, to which the dancers danced in all the orgiastic abandonment of Eastern passion. All this was regarded as an element in the religious solemnity; and while the revellers drank their wine, hymns were being chanted, in which they praised "the gods of gold and of silver, of brass, of iron, of wood, and of stone." That the king drank wine before the thousand is the more remarkable because usually the kings of the East banquet in solitary state in their own apartments. [424]

Then the wild king, with just such a burst of folly and irreverence as characterised the banquets of Antiochus Epiphanes, bethought him of yet another element of splendour with which he might make his banquet memorable, and prove the superiority of his own victorious gods over those of other nations. The Temple of Jerusalem was famous over all the world, and there were few monarchs who had not heard of the marvels and the majesty of the God of Israel. Belshazzar, as the "son" of Nebuchadrezzar, must--if there was any historic reality in the events narrated in the previous chapter--have heard of the "signs and wonders" displayed by the King of heaven, whose unparalleled awfulness his "father" had publicly attested in edicts addressed to all the world. He must have known of the Rab-mag Daniel, whose wisdom, even as a boy, had been found superior to that of all the Chartummîm and Ashshaphîm; and how his three companions had been elevated to supreme satrapies; and how they had been delivered unsinged from the seven-times-heated furnace, whose flames had killed his father's executioners. Under no conceivable circumstances could such marvels have been forgotten; under no circumstances could they have possibly failed to create an intense and a profound impression. And Belshazzar could hardly fail to have heard of the dreams of the golden image and of the shattered cedar, and of Nebuchadrezzar's unspeakably degrading lycanthropy. His "father" had publicly acknowledged--in a decree published "to all peoples, nations, and languages that dwell in all the earth"--that humiliation had come upon him as a punishment for his overweening pride. In that same decree the mighty Nebuchadrezzar--only a year or two before, if Belshazzar succeeded him--had proclaimed his allegiance to the King of heaven; and in all previous decrees he had threatened "all people, nations, and languages" that, if they spake anything amiss against the God of Shadrach, Meshach, and Abed-nego, they should be cut in pieces, and their houses made a dunghill. [425] Yet now Belshazzar, in the flush of pride and drunkenness, [426] gives his order to insult this God with deadly impiety by publicly defiling the vessels of His awful Temple,[427] at a feast in honour of his own idol deities!

Similarly Antiochus Epiphanes, if he had not been half mad, might have taken warning, before he insulted the Temple and the sacred vessels of Jerusalem, from the fact that his father, Antiochus the Great, had met his death in attempting to plunder the Temple at Elymais (b.c. 187). He might also have recalled the celebrated discomfiture--however caused--of Heliodorus in the Temple of Jerusalem. [428]

Such insulting and reckless blasphemy could not go unpunished. It is fitting that the Divine retribution should overtake the king on the same night, and that the same lips which thus profaned with this wine the holiest things should sip the wine of the Divine poison-cup, whose fierce heat must in the same night prove fatal to himself. But even such sinners, drinking as it were over the pit of hell, "according to a metaphor used elsewhere, [429] must still at the last moment be warned by a suitable Divine sign, that it may be known whether they will honour the truth." [430] Nebuchadrezzar had received his warning, and in the end it had not been wholly in vain. Even for Belshazzar it might perhaps not prove to be too late.

For at this very moment [431] when the revelry was at its zenith, when the whirl of excited self-exaltation was most intense, when Judah's gold was "treading heavy on the lips"--the profane lips--of satraps and concubines, there appeared a portent, which seems at first to have been visible to the king alone.

Seated on his lofty and jewelled throne, which

*"Outshone the wealth of Ormuz or of Ind,*
*Or where the gorgeous East with richest hand*
*Showers on its kings barbaric pearl and gold,"*

his eye caught something visible on the white stucco of the wall above the line of frescoes. [432] He saw it over the lights which crowned the huge golden Nebrashta, or chandelier. [433] The fingers of a man's hand were writing letters on the wall, and the king saw the hollow of that gigantic supernatural palm. [434]

The portent astounded and horrified him. The flush of youth and of wine faded from his cheek;-- "his brightnesses were changed"; his thoughts troubled him; the bands of his loins were loosed; [435] his knees smote one against another in his trembling attitude, [436] as he stood arrested by the awful sight.

With a terrible cry he ordered that the whole familiar tribe of astrologers and soothsayers should be summoned. For though the hand had vanished, its trace was left on the wall of the banqueting-chamber in letters of fire. And the stricken king, anxious to know above all things the purport of that strange writing, proclaims that he who could interpret it should be clothed in scarlet, and have a chain of gold about his neck, and should be one of the triumvirs of the kingdom. [437]

It was the usual resource; and it failed as it had done in every previous instance. The Babylonian magi in the Book of Daniel prove themselves to be more futile even than Pharaoh's magicians with their enchantments.

The dream-interpreters in all their divisions entered the banquet-hall. The king was perturbed, the omen urgent, the reward magnificent. But it was all in vain. As usual they failed, as in every instance in which they are introduced in the Old Testament. And their failure added to the visible confusion of the king, whose livid countenance retained its pallor. The banquet, in all its royal magnificence, seemed likely to end in tumult and confusion; for the princes, and satraps, and wives, and concubines all shared in the agitation and bewilderment of their sovereign.

Meanwhile the tidings of the startling prodigy had reached the ears of the Gebîrah--the queen-mother--who, as always in the East, held a higher rank than even the reigning sultana. [438] She had not been present at--perhaps had not approved of--the luxurious revel, held when the Persians were at the very gates. But now, in her young son's extremity, she comes forward to help and advise him. Entering the hall with her attendant maidens, she bids the king to be no longer troubled, for there is a man of the highest rank--invariably, as would appear, overlooked and forgotten till the critical moment, in spite of his long series of triumphs and achievements--who was quite able to read the fearful augury, as he had often done before, when all others had been foiled by Him who "frustrateth the tokens of the liars and maketh diviners mad." [439] Strange that he should not have been thought of, though "the king thy father, the king, I say, thy father, made him master of the whole college of mages and astrologers. Let Belshazzar send for Belteshazzar, and he would untie the knot and read the awful enigma." [440]

Then, Daniel was summoned; and since the king "has heard of him, that the spirit of the gods is in him, and that light and understanding and excellent wisdom is found in him," and that he is one who can interpret dreams, and unriddle hard sentences and untie knots, he shall have the scarlet robe, and the golden chain, and the seat among the triumvirs, if he will read and interpret the writing.

"Let thy gifts be thine, and thy rewards to another," [441] answered the seer, with fearless forthrightness: "yet, O king, I will read and interpret the writing." Then, after reminding him of the consummate power and majesty of his father Nebuchadrezzar; and how his mind had become indurated with pride; and how he had been stricken with lycanthropy, "till he knew that the Most High God ruled in the kingdom of men"; and that, in spite of all this, he, Belshazzar, in his infatuation, had insulted the Most High God by profaning the holy vessels of His Temple in a licentious revelry in honour of idols of gold, silver, brass, iron, and stone, which neither see, nor know, nor hear,--for this reason (said the seer) had the hollow hand been sent and the writing stamped upon the wall.

And now what was the writing? Daniel at the first glance had read that fiery quadrilateral of letters, looking like the twelve gems of the high priest's ephod with the mystic light gleaming upon them.

M. N. A. M. N. A. T. Q. L. P. R. S.

Four names of weight. [442]
A Mina. A Mina. A Shekel. A Half-mina. [443].

What possible meaning could there be in that? Did it need an archangel's colossal hand, flashing forth upon a palace-wall to write the menace of doom, to have inscribed no more than the names of four coins or weights? No wonder that the Chaldeans could not interpret such writing!

It may be asked why they could not even read it, since the words are evidently Aramaic, and Aramaic was the common language of trade. The Rabbis say that the words, instead of being written from right to left, were written kionedon, "pillar-wise," as the Greeks called it, from above downwards: thus--

p h t m m r
q n n s
l ' '

Read from left to right, they would look like gibberish; read from above downwards, they became clear as far as the reading was concerned, though their interpretation might still be surpassingly enigmatic.

But words may stand for all sorts of mysterious meanings; and in the views of analogists--as those are called who not only believe in the mysterious force and fascination of words, but even in the physiological quality of sounds--they may hide awful indications under harmless vocables. Herein lay the secret.

A mina! a mina! Yes; but the names of the weights recall the word m'nah, "hath numbered": and "God hath numbered thy kingdom and finished it."

A shekel! Yes; t'qilta: "Thou hast been weighed in a balance and found wanting."

Peres--a half-mina! Yes; but p'rîsath: "Thy kingdom has been divided, and given to the Medes and Persians." [444]

At this point the story is very swiftly brought to a conclusion, for its essence has been already given. Daniel is clothed in scarlet, and ornamented with the chain of gold, and proclaimed triumvir.[445]

But the king's doom is sealed! "That night was Belshazzar, king of the Chaldeans, slain." His name meant, "Bel! preserve thou the king!" But Bel bowed down, and Nebo stooped, and gave no help to their votary.

"Evil things in robes of sorrow
Assailed the monarch's high estate;

*Ah, woe is me! for never morrow*
*Shall dawn upon him desolate!*
*And all about his throne the glory*
*That blushed and bloomed*
*Is but an ill-remembered story*
*Of the old time entombed."*

"And Darius the Mede took the kingdom, being about sixty-two years old."

As there is no such person known as "Darius the Mede," the age assigned to him must be due either to some tradition about some other Darius, or to chronological calculations to which we no longer possess the key. [446]

He is called the son of Achashverosh, Ahasuerus (ix. 1), or Xerxes. The apologists have argued that--

1. Darius was Cyaxares II., father of Cyrus, on the authority of Xenophon's romance, [447] and Josephus's echo of it. [448] But the Cyropædia is no authority, being, as Cicero said, a non-historic fiction written to describe an ideal kingdom. [449] History knows nothing of a Cyaxares II.

2. Darius was Astyages. [450] Not to mention other impossibilities which attach to this view, Astyages would have been far older than sixty-two at the capture of Babylon by Cyrus. Cyrus had suppressed the Median dynasty altogether some years before he took Babylon.

3. Darius was the satrap Gobryas, who, so far as we know, only acted as governor for a few months. But he is represented on the contrary as an extremely absolute king, setting one hundred and twenty princes "over the whole kingdom," and issuing mandates to "all people, nations, and languages that dwell in all the earth." Even if such an identification were admissible, it would not in the least save the historic accuracy of the writer. This "Darius the Mede" is ignored by history, and Cyrus is represented by the ancient records as having been the sole and undisputed king of Babylon from the time of his conquest. [451] "Darius the Mede" probably owes his existence to a literal understanding of the prophecies of Isaiah (xiii. 17) and Jeremiah (li. 11, 28).

We can now proceed to the examination of the next chapter unimpeded by impossible and half-hearted hypotheses. We understand it, and it was meant to be understood, as a moral and spiritual parable, in which unverified historic names and traditions are utilised for the purpose of inculcating lessons of courage and faithfulness. The picture, however, falls far below those of the other chapters in power, finish, and even an approach to natural verisimilitude.

## *Footnotes:*

418. The question has already been fully discussed (supra, pp. 54-57). The apologists say that-- 1. Belshazzar was Evil-merodach (Niebuhr, Wolff, Bishop Westcott, Zöckler, Keil, etc.), as the son of Nebuchadrezzar (Dan. v. 2, 11, 18, 22), and his successor (Baruch i. 11, 12, where he is called Balthasar, as in the LXX.). The identification is impossible (see Dan. v. 28, 31); for Evil-merodach (b.c. 561) was murdered by his brother-in-law Neriglissar (b.c. 559). Besides, the Jews were well acquainted with Evil-merodach (2 Kings xxv. 27; Jer. lii. 31.) 2. Belshazzar was Nabunaid (St. Jerome, Ewald, Winer, Herzfeld, Auberlen, etc.). But the usurper Nabunaid, son of a Rab-mag, was wholly unlike Belshazzar; and so far from being slain, he was pardoned, and sent by Cyrus to be Governor of Karmania, in which position he died. 3. Belshazzar was the son of Nabunaid. But though Nabunaid had a son of the name he was never king. We know nothing of any relationship between him and Nebuchadrezzar, nor does Cyrus in his records make the most distant allusion to him. The attempt to identify Nebuchadrezzar with an unknown Marduk-sar-utsur, mentioned in Babylonian tablets, breaks down; for Mr. Boscawen (Soc. Bibl., in § vi., p. 108) finds that he reigned before Nabunaid. Further, the son of Nabunaid perished, not in Babylon, but in Accad.

419. See 1 Macc. i. 21-24. He "entered proudly into the sanctuary, and took away the golden altar, and the candlestick of light, and all the vessels thereof, and the table of the shewbread, and the pouring vessels, and the vials, and the censers of gold.... He took also the silver and the gold, and the precious vessels: also he took the hidden treasures which he found," etc. Comp. 2 Macc. v. 11-14; Diod. Sic., XXXI. i. 48. The value of precious metals which he carried off was estimated at one thousand eight hundred silver talents--about £350,000 (2 Macc. v. 21).

420. The LXX. says "two thousand." Comp. Esther i. 3, 4. Jerome adds, "Unusquisque secundum suam bibit ætatem."

421. Ezek. xxiii. 15.

422. Herod., i. 191, v. 18; Xen., Cyrop., V. ii. 28; Q. Curt., V. i. 38. Theodotion, perhaps scandalised by the fact, omits the wives, and the LXX. omits both wives and concubines.

423. Layard, Nin. and Bab., ii. 262-269.

424. Athen., Deipnos, iv. 145. See the bas-relief in the British Museum of King Assur-bani-pal

drinking wine with his queen, while the head of his vanquished enemy, Te-Umman, King of Elam, dangles from a palm-branch full in his view, so that he can feast his eyes upon it. None others are present except the attendant eunuchs.

425. Dan. iii. 29.

426. The Babylonians were notorious for drunken revels. Q. Curt., V. i., "Babylonii maxime in vinum et quæ ebrietatem sequuntur, effusi sunt."

427. Dan. i. 2. Comp. 1 Macc. i. 21 ff.

428. 2 Macc. iii.

429. Psalm lv. 15.

430. Ewald.

431. Comp. Dan. iii. 7.

432. See Layard, Nin. and Bab., ii. 269.

433. A word of uncertain origin. The Talmud uses it for the word lmphds (the Greek lampas).

434. "Hollow." Heb., pas; Theodot., astragalous; Vulg., articulos. The word may mean "palm" of the hand, or sole of the foot (Bevan).

435. Psalm lxix. 23. "Bands"--lit. "fastenings"; Theodot., sundesmoi; Vulg., compages.

436. Comp. Ezek. vii. 17, and the Homeric luto gounata, Od., iv. 703; Ov., Met., ii. 180, "genua intremuere timore."

437. Doubtless suggested by Gen. xli. 42 (comp. Herod., iii. 20; Xen., Anab., I. ii. 27; Cyrop., VIII. v. 18), as other parts of Daniel's story recall that of Joseph. Comp. Esther vi. 8, 9. The word for "scarlet" or red-purple is argona. The word for "chain" (Q'rî. ham'nîka) is in Theodotion rendered maniakes, and occurs in later Aramaic. The phrase rendered "third ruler" is very uncertain. The inference drawn from it in the Speaker's Commentary--that Nabunaid was king, and Belshazzar second ruler--is purely nugatory. For the Hebrew word taltî cannot mean "third," which would be tlyty. Ewald and most Hebraists take it to mean "rule, as one of the board of three." For "triumvir" comp. vi. 2.

438. 1 Kings xv. 13. She is precariously identified by the apologists with the Nitocris of Herodotus; and it is imagined that she may have been a daughter of Nebuchadrezzar, married to Nabunaid before the murder of Neriglissar.

439. Isa. xliv. 25.

440. The word Qistrîn, "knots," may mean "hard questions"; but Mr. Bevan (p. 104) thinks there may be an allusion to knots used as magic spells. (Comp. Sen., OEdip., 101, "Nodosa sortis verba et implexos dolos.") He quotes Al-Baidawi on the Koran, lxiii. 4, who says that "a Jew casts a spell on Mohammed by tying knots in a cord, and hiding it in a well." But Gabriel told the prophet to send for the cord, and at each verse of the Koran recited over it a knot untied itself. See Records of the Past, iii. 141; and Duke, Rabb. Blumenlehre, 231.

441. So Elisha, 2 Kings v. 16.

442. The Menê is repeated for emphasis. In the Upharsîn (ver. 25) the u is merely the "and," and the word is slightly altered, perhaps to make the paronomasia with "Persians" more obvious. According to Buxtorf and Gesenius, peras, in the sense of "divide," is very rare in the Targums.

443. Journal Asiatique, 1886. (Comp. Nöldeke, Ztschr. für Assyriologie, i. 414-418; Kamphausen, p. 46.) It is M. Clermont-Ganneau who has the credit of discovering what seems to be the true interpretation of these mysterious words. M'nê (Heb. Maneh) is the Greek mna, Lat. mina, which the Greeks borrowed from the Assyrians. Tekel (in the Targum of Onkelos tîkla) is the Hebrew shekel. In the Mishnah a half-mina is called peras, and an Assyrian weight in the British Museum bears the inscription perash in the Aramaic character. (See Bevan, p. 106; Schrader, s.v. "Mene" in Riehm, R.W.B.) Peres is used for a half-mina in Yoma, f. 4, 4; often in the Talmud; and in Corp. Inscr. Sem., ii. 10 (Behrmann).

444. The word occurs in Perez Uzza. There still, however, remain some obviously unexplored mysteries about these words. Paronomasia, as I showed long ago in other works, plays a noble and profound part in the language of emotion; and that the interpretation should here be made to turn upon it is not surprising by any means. We find it in the older prophets. Thus in Jer. i. 11, 12: "What seest thou? And I said, I see a rod of an almond tree. Then said the Lord unto me, Thou hast well seen: for I will hasten My word to perform it." The meaning here depends on the resemblance in Hebrew between shaqeed, "an almond tree" ("a wakeful, or early tree"), and shoqeed, "I will hasten," or "am wakeful over." And that the same use of plays on words was still common in the Maccabean epoch we see in the Story of Susanna. There Daniel plays on the resemblance between schinos, "a mastick tree," and schisei, "shall cut thee in two"; and prinos, "a holm oak," and prisai, "to cut asunder." We may also point to the fine paronomasia in the Hebrew of Isa. v. 7, Mic. i. 10-15, and other passages. "Such a conceit," says Mr. Ball, "may seem to us far-fetched and inappropriate; but the Oriental mind delights in such lusus verborum, and the peculiar force of all such passages in the Hebrew prophets is lost in our version because they have not been preserved in translation." As regards the Medes, they are placed after the Persians in Isa. xxi. 2, Esther i. 3, but generally before them.

445. LXX., edoken exousian auto tou tritou merous; Theodot., archonta triton. See supra, p. 210.

446. The LXX. evidently felt some difficulty or followed some other text, for they render it, "And Artaxerxes of the Medes took the kingdom, and Darius full of days and glorious in old age." So, too, Josephus (Antt., X. xi. 4), who says that "he was called by another name among the Greeks."

447. Cyrop., I. v. 2.

448. Antt., X. xi. 4. This was the view of Vitringa, Bertholdt, Gesenius, Winer, Keil, Hengstenberg, Hävernick, etc.

449. Ad. Q. Fratr., i. 8.

450. The view of Niebuhr and Westcott.

451. See Herod., i. 109. The Median Empire fell b.c. 559; Babylon was taken about b.c. 539. It is regarded as "important" that a late Greek lexicographer, long after the Christian era, makes the vague and wholly unsupported assertion that the "Daric" was named after some Darius other than the father of Xerxes! See supra, pp. 57-60.

# CHAPTER VI - STOPPING THE MOUTHS OF LIONS

*"Thou shalt tread upon the lion ... the young lion shalt thou trample under thy feet."*--Psalm xci. 13.

On the view which regards these pictures as powerful parables, rich in spiritual instructiveness, but not primarily concerned with historic accuracy, nor even necessarily with ancient tradition, we have seen how easily "the great strong fresco-strokes" which the narrator loves to use "may have been suggested to him by his diligent study of the Scriptures."

The first chapter is a beautiful picture which serves to set forth the glory of moderation and to furnish a vivid concrete illustration of such passages as those of Jeremiah: "Her Nazarites were purer than snow; they were whiter than milk; they were more ruddy in body than rubies; their polishing was of sapphire." [452]

The second chapter, closely reflecting in many of its details the story of Joseph, illustrated how God "frustrateth the tokens of the liars, and maketh diviners mad; turneth wise men backward, and maketh their knowledge foolish; confirmeth the word of His servant, and performeth the counsel of His messengers." [453]

The third chapter gives vividness to the promise, "When thou walkest through the fire, thou shalt not be burned, neither shall the flame kindle upon thee." [454]

The fourth chapter repeats the apologue of Ezekiel, in which he compares the King of Assyria to a cedar in Lebanon with fine branches, and with a shadowy shroud, and fair by the multitude of his branches, so that all the trees of Eden that were in the garden of God envied him, but whose boughs were "broken by all the watercourses until the peoples of the earth left his shadow." [455] It was also meant to show that "pride goeth before destruction, and a haughty spirit before a fall." [456] It illustrates the words of Isaiah: "Behold, the Lord, the Lord of hosts, shall lop the bough with terror; and the high ones of stature shall be hewn down, and the haughty shall be humbled." [457]

The fifth chapter gives a vivid answer to Isaiah's challenge: "Let now the astrologers, the stargazers, the monthly prognosticators, stand up and save thee from these things which shall come upon thee." [458] It describes a fulfilment of his vision: "A grievous vision is declared unto thee; the treacherous dealer dealeth treacherously, and the spoiler spoileth. Go up, O Elam: besiege, O Media." [459] The more detailed prophecy of Jeremiah had said: "Prepare against Babylon the nations with the kings of the Medes.... The mighty men of Babylon have forborne to fight.... One post shall run to meet another, and one messenger to meet another, to show the King of Babylon that his city is taken at one end.... In their heat I will make their feasts, and I will make them drunken, that they shall rejoice, and sleep a perpetual sleep, and not wake, saith the Lord.... How is Sheshach taken! [460] and how is the praise of the whole earth surprised!... And I will make drunk her princes, and her wise men, her captains, and her rulers, and her mighty men; and they shall sleep a perpetual sleep, and not wake, saith the King, whose name is the Lord of hosts." [461]

The sixth chapter puts into concrete form such passages of the Psalmist as: "My soul is among lions: and I lie even among them that are set on fire, even the sons of men, whose teeth are spears and arrows, and their tongue a sharp sword"; [462] and--"Break the jaw-bones of the lions, O Lord"; [463] and-- "They have cut off my life in the dungeon, and cast a stone upon me" [464] :--and more generally such promises as those in Isaiah: "No weapon that is formed against thee shall prosper; and every tongue that shall rise against thee in judgment thou shalt condemn. This is the heritage of the servants of the Lord, and their righteousness is of Me, saith the Lord." [465]

This genesis of Haggadoth is remarkably illustrated by the apocryphal additions to Daniel. Thus the History of Susanna was very probably suggested by Jeremiah's allusion (xxix. 22) to the two false prophets Ahab and Zedekiah, whom Nebuchadrezzar burnt. [466] Similarly the story of Bel and the Dragon is a fiction which expounds Jer. li. 44: "And I will punish Bel in Babylon, and I will bring forth out of his mouth that which he hath swallowed up." [467]

Hitherto the career of Daniel had been personally prosperous. We have seen him in perpetual honour and exaltation, and he had not even incurred--though he may now have been ninety years old-- such early trials and privations in a heathen land as had fallen to the lot of Joseph, his youthful prototype. His three companions had been potential martyrs; he had not even been a confessor. Terrible as was the doom which he had twice been called upon to pronounce upon Nebuchadrezzar and upon his kingdom, the stern messages of prophecy, so far from involving him in ruin, had only helped to uplift him to the supremest honours. Not even the sternness of his bearing, and the terrible severity of his interpretations of the flaming message to Belshazzar, had prevented him from being proclaimed triumvir, and clothed in scarlet, and decorated with a chain of gold, on the last night of the Babylonian Empire. And now a new king of a new dynasty is represented as seated on the throne; and it might well have seemed that Daniel was destined to close his days, not only in peace, but in consummate outward felicity.

Darius the Mede began his reign by appointing one hundred and twenty princes over the whole kingdom; [468] and over these he placed three presidents. Daniel is one of these "eyes" of the king.[469] "Because an excellent spirit was in him," he acquired preponderant influence among the presidents; and the king, considering that Daniel's integrity would secure him from damage in the royal accounts, designed to set him over the whole realm.

But assuming that the writer is dealing, not with the real, but with the ideal, something would be lacking to Daniel's eminent saintliness, if he were not set forth as no less capable of martyrdom on behalf of his convictions than his three companions had been. From the fiery trial in which their faithfulness had been proved like gold in the furnace he had been exempt. His life thus far had been a course of unbroken prosperity. But the career of a pre-eminent prophet and saint hardly seems to have won its final crown, unless he also be called upon to mount his Calvary, and to share with all prophets and all saints the persecutions which are the invariable concomitants of the hundredfold reward. [470] Shadrach, Meshach, and Abed-nego had been tested in early youth: the trial of Daniel is reserved for his extreme old age. It is not, it could not be, a severer trial than that which his friends braved, nor could his deliverance be represented as more supernatural or more complete, unless it were that they endured only for a few moments the semblable violence of the fire, while he was shut up for all the long hours of night alone in the savage lions' den. There are, nevertheless, two respects in which this chapter serves as a climax to those which preceded it. On the one hand, the virtue of Daniel is of a marked character in that it is positive, and not negative--in that it consists, not in rejecting an overt sin of idolatry, but in continuing the private duty of prayer; on the other, the decree of Darius surpasses even those of Nebuchadrezzar in the intensity of its acknowledgment of the supremacy of Israel's God.

Daniel's age--for by this time he must have passed the allotted limit of man's threescore years and ten--might have exempted him from envy, even if, as the LXX. adds, "he was clad in purple." But jealous that a captive Jew should be exalted above all the native satraps and potentates by the king's favour, his colleagues the presidents (whom the LXX. calls "two young men") and the princes "rushed" before the king with a request which they thought would enable them to overthrow Daniel by subtlety. Faithfulness is required in stewards; [471] and they knew that his faithfulness and wisdom were such that they would be unable to undermine him in any ordinary way. There was but one point at which they considered him to be vulnerable, and that was in any matter which affected his allegiance to an alien worship. But it was difficult to invent an incident which would give them the sought-for opportunity. All polytheisms are as tolerant as their priests will let them be. The worship of the Jews in the Exile was of a necessarily private nature. They had no Temple, and such religious gatherings as they held were in no sense unlawful. The problem of the writer was to manage his Haggada in such a way as to make private prayer an act of treason; and the difficulty is met--not, indeed, without violent improbability, for which, however, Jewish haggadists cared little, but with as much skill as the circumstances permitted.

The phrase that they "made a tumult" or "rushed" [472] before the king, which recurs in vi. 11 and 18, is singular, and looks as if it were intentionally grotesque by way of satire. The etiquette of Oriental courts is always most elaborately stately, and requires solemn obeisance. This is why Æschylus makes Agamemnon say, in answer to the too-obsequious fulsomeness of his false wife,--

"*kai talla, me gunaikos en tropois eme
habrune, mede barbarou photos diken
chamaipetes boama proschanes emoi.*"

"*Besides, prithee, use not too fond a care
To me, as to some virgin whom thou strivest
To deck with ornaments, whose softness looks
Softer, hung round the softness of her youth;
Ope not the mouth to me, nor cry amain
As at the footstool of a man of the East
Prone on the ground: so stoop not thou to me!*"

That these "presidents and satraps," instead of trying to win the king by such flatteries and "gaping upon him an earth-grovelling howl," should on each occasion have "rushed" into his presence, must be regarded either as a touch of intentional sarcasm, or, at any rate, as being more in accord with the rude familiarities of licence permitted to the courtiers of the half-mad Antiochus, than with the prostrations and solemn approaches which since the days of Deïoces would alone have been permitted by any conceivable "Darius the Mede."

However, after this tumultuous intrusion into the king's presence, "all the presidents, governors, chief chamberlains," present to him the monstrous but unanimous request that he would, by an irrevocable interdict, forbid that any man should, for thirty days, ask any petition of any god or man, on peril of being cast into the den of lions. [473]

Professor Fuller, in the Speaker's Commentary, considers that "this chapter gives a valuable as well as an interesting insight into Median customs," because the king is represented as living a secluded life, and keeps lions, and is practically deified! The importance of the remark is far from obvious. The chapter presents no particular picture of a secluded life. On the contrary, the king moves about freely, and his courtiers seem to have free access to him whenever they choose. As for the semi-deification of kings, it was universal throughout the East, and even Antiochus II. had openly taken the surname of Theos, the "god." Again, every Jew throughout the world must have been very well aware, since the days of the Exile, that Assyrian and other monarchs kept dens of lions, and occasionally flung their enemies to them. [474] But so far as the decree of Darius is concerned, it may well be said that throughout all history no single parallel to it can be quoted. Kings have very often been deified in absolutism; but not even a mad Antiochus, a mad Caligula, a mad Elagabalus, or a mad Commodus ever dreamt of passing an interdict that no one was to prefer any petition either to God or man for thirty days, except to himself! A decree so preposterous, which might be violated by millions many times a day without the king being cognisant of it, would be a proof of positive imbecility in any king who should dream of making it. Strange, too--though a matter of indifference to the writer, because it did not affect his moral lesson--that Darius should not have noticed the absence of his chief official, and the one man in whom he placed the fullest and deepest confidence.

The king, without giving another thought to the matter, at once signs the irrevocable decree.

It naturally does not make the least difference to the practices or the purpose of Daniel. His duty towards God transcends his duty to man. He has been accustomed, thrice a day, to kneel and pray to God, with the window of his upper chamber open, looking towards the Kibleh of Jerusalem; [475] and the king's decree makes no change in his manner of daily worship.

Then the princes "rushed" thither again, and found Daniel praying and asking petitions before his God.

Instantly they go before the king, and denounce Daniel for his triple daily defiance of the sacrosanct decree, showing that "he regardeth not thee, O king, nor the decree that thou hast signed."

Their denunciations produced an effect very different from what they had intended. They had hoped to raise the king's wrath and jealousy against Daniel, as one who lightly esteemed his divine autocracy. But so far from having any such ignoble feeling, the king only sees that he has been an utter fool, the dupe of the worthlessness of his designing courtiers. [476] All his anger was against himself for his own folly; his sole desire was to save the man whom for his integrity and ability he valued more than the whole crew of base plotters who had entrapped him against his will into a stupid act of injustice. All day, till sunset, he laboured hard to deliver Daniel. [477] The whole band of satraps and chamberlains feel that this will not do at all; so they again "rush" to the king to remind him of the Median and Persian law that no decree which the king has passed can be altered. [478] To alter it would be a confession of fallibility, and therefore an abnegation of godhead! Yet the strenuous action which he afterwards adopted shows that he might, even then, have acted on the principle which the mages laid down to Cambyses, son of Cyrus, that "the king can do no wrong." There seems to be no reason why he should not have told these "tumultuous" princes that if they interfered with Daniel they should be flung into the lions' den. This would probably have altered their opinion as to pressing the royal infallibility of irreversible decrees.

But as this resource did not suggest itself to Darius, nothing could be done except to cast Daniel into the den or "pit" of lions; but in sentencing him the king offers the prayer, "May the God whom thou servest continually deliver thee!" [479] Then a stone is laid over the mouth of the pit, and, for the sake of double security, that even the king may not have the power of tampering with it, it is sealed, not only with his own seal, but also with that of his lords. [480]

From the lion-pit the king went back to his palace, but only to spend a miserable night. He could take no food. [481] No dancing-women were summoned to his harem; [482] no sleep visited his eyelids. At the first glimpse of morning he rose, [483] and went with haste to the den--taking the satraps with him, adds the LXX.--and cried with a sorrowful voice, "O Daniel, servant of the living God, hath thy God whom thou servest continually been able to deliver thee from the lions?"

And the voice of the prophet answered, "O king, live for ever! My God sent His angel, [484] and shut the mouths of the lions, that they should not destroy me: forasmuch as before Him innocency was found in me; and also before thee, O king, have I committed no offence."

Thereupon the happy king ordered that Daniel should be taken up out of the lion-pit; and he was found to be unhurt, because he believed in his God.

We would have gladly spared the touch of savagery with which the story ends. The deliverance of Daniel made no difference in the guilt of his accusers. What they had charged him with was a fact, and was a transgression of the ridiculous decree which they had caused the king to pass. But his deliverance was regarded as a Divine judgment upon them--as proof that vengeance should fall on them. Accordingly, not they only, but, with the brutal solidarity of revenge and punishment which, in savage and semi-civilised races, confounds the innocent with the guilty, their wives and even their children were also cast into the den of lions, and they did not reach the bottom of the pit before "the lions got hold of them and crushed all their bones." [485] They are devoured, or caught, by the hungry lions in mid-air.

"Then King Darius wrote to all the nations, communities, and tongues who dwell in the whole world, May your peace be multiplied! I make a decree, That in every dominion of my kingdom men tremble and fear before the God of Daniel: for He is the living God, and steadfast for ever, and His kingdom that which shall not be destroyed, and His dominion even unto the end. He delivereth and He rescueth, and He worketh signs and wonders in heaven and in earth, who delivered Daniel from the power of the lions."

The language, as in Nebuchadrezzar's decrees, is purely Scriptural. [486] What the Median mages and the Persian fire-worshippers would think of such a decree, and whether it produced the slightest effect before it vanished without leaving a trace behind, are questions with which the author of the story is not concerned.

He merely adds that Daniel prospered in the reign of Darius and of Cyrus the Persian.

## *Footnotes:*

452. Lam. iv. 7.
453. Isa. xliv. 25, 26.
454. Isa. xliii. 2.
455. Ezek. xxxi. 2-15.
456. Prov. xvi. 18.
457. Isa. x. 33.
458. Isa. xlvii. 13.
459. Isa. xxi. 2.
460. The word is a cabalistic cryptogram--an instance of Gematria--for Babel.
461. Jer. li. 28-57.
462. Psalm lvii. 4.
463. Psalm lviii. 6.
464. Lam. iii. 53.
465. Isa. liv. 17.
466. Sanhedrin, f. 93, 1. See another story in Vayyikra Rabba, c. xix.
467. Bereshîth Rabba, § 68.
468. The LXX. says 127, and Josephus (Antt., X. xi. 4) says 360 (comp. Esther i. 1, viii. 9, ix. 3). Under Darius, son of Hystaspes, there were only twenty divisions of the empire (Herod., iii. 89).
469. Dan. vi. 2: "Of whom Daniel was"--not "first," as in A.V., but "one," R.V.
470. Matt. xix. 29.
471. 1 Cor. iv. 2.
472. Dan. vi. 6, char'ggishoo; Vulg., surripuerunt regi; A.V. marg., "came tumultuously." The word is found in the Targum in Ruth i. 19 (Bevan).
473. The den (goob or gubba) seems to mean a vault. The Hebrew word for "pit" is boor.
474. See Layard, Nin. and Bab., i. 335, 447, 475; Smith, Hist. of Assur-bani-pal, xxiv.
475. The chamber was perhaps supposed to be a huperoon on the roof. The "kneeling" in prayer (as in 1 Kings viii. 54; 2 Chron. vi. 13; Ezra ix. 5) is in the East a less common attitude than standing. See 1 Sam. i. 26; Mark xi. 25; Luke xviii. 11: but see Neh. viii. 6; Gen. xxiv. 26. The Temple, and Jerusalem, was the Kibleh, or sacred direction of devotion (1 Kings viii. 44; Ezek. viii. 16; Psalm v. 7, xxviii. 2, lv. 17, etc.).
476. Comp. Mark vi. 26.
477. Theodot., agonizomenos.
478. Esther i. 19, viii. 8.
479. "Courage, till to-morrow" (heos proi tharrhei), adds the LXX.
480. Comp. Lam. iii. 53. Seal-rings are very ancient (Herod., i. 195). It is useless to speculate on the construction of the lion-pit. The only opening mentioned seems to have been at the top; but there

*The Expositor's Bible: The Book of Daniel*
must necessarily have been side-openings also.

481. Theodot., ekoimethe adeipnos. Daniel, on the other hand, in the apocryphal Haggada, gets his dinner miraculously from the Prophet Habakkuk.

482. Heb., dachavan; R.V., "instruments of music"; R.V. marg., "dancing-girls"; Gesenius, Zöckler, etc., "concubines."

483. Theodot., to proi en to photi.

484. Comp. Dan. iii. 8; Psalm xxxiv. 7-10; Acts xii. 11.

485. Comp. Esther ix. 13, 14; Josh. vii. 24; 2 Sam. xxi. 1-6. The LXX. modifies the savagery of the story by making the vengeance fall only on the two young men who were Daniel's fellow-presidents. But comp. Herod., iii. 119; Am. Marcell., xxiii. 6; and "Ob noxam unius omnis propinquitas perit," etc.

486. Psalm xxix. 1, x. 16, etc. Professor Fuller calls it "a Mazdean colouring in the language"!

# PART III - THE PROPHETIC SECTION OF THE BOOK

## CHAPTER I - VISION OF THE FOUR WILD BEASTS

We now enter upon the second division of the Book of Daniel--the apocalyptic. It is unquestionably inferior to the first part in grandeur and importance as a whole, but it contains not a few great conceptions, and it was well adapted to inspire the hopes and arouse the heroic courage of the persecuted Jews in the terrible days of Antiochus Epiphanes. Daniel now speaks in the first person, [487] whereas throughout the historic section of the Book the third person has been used.

In the form of apocalypse which he adopts he had already had partial precursors in Ezekiel and Zechariah; but their symbolic visions were far less detailed and developed--it may be added far more poetic and classical--than his. And in later apocalypses, for which this served as a model, little regard is paid to the grotesqueness or incongruity of the symbols, if only the intended conception is conveyed. In no previous writer of the grander days of Hebrew literature would such symbols have been permitted as horns which have eyes and speak, or lions from which the wings are plucked, and which thereafter stand on their feet as a man, and have a man's heart given to them.

The vision is dated, "In the first year of Belshazzar, King of Babylon." It therefore comes chronologically between the fourth and fifth chapters. On the pseudepigraphic view of the Book we may suppose that this date is merely a touch of literary verisimilitude, designed to assimilate the prophecies to the form of those uttered by the ancient prophets; or perhaps it may be intended to indicate that with three of the four empires--the Babylonian, the Median, and the Persian--Daniel had a personal acquaintance. Beyond this we can see no significance in the date; for the predictions which are here recorded have none of that immediate relation to the year in which they originated which we see in the writings of Isaiah and Jeremiah. Perhaps the verse itself is a later guess or gloss, since there are slight variations in Theodotion and the LXX. Daniel, we are told, both saw and wrote and narrated the dream. [488]

In the vision of the night he had seen the four winds of heaven travailing, or bursting forth, on the great sea; [489] and from those tumultuous waves came four immense wild beasts, each unlike the other.

The first was a lion, with four eagles' wings. The wings were plucked off, and it then raised itself from the earth, stood on its feet like a man, and a man's heart was given to it.

The second was like a bear, raising itself on one side, and having three ribs between its teeth; and it is bidden to "arise and devour much flesh."

The third is a leopard, or panther, with four wings and four heads, to which dominion is given.

The fourth--a yet more terrible monster, which is left undescribed, as though indescribable--has great devouring teeth of iron, and feet that stamp and crush. [490] It has ten horns, and among them came up a little horn, before which three of the others are plucked up by the roots; and this horn has eyes, and a mouth speaking great things.

Then the thrones were set for the Divine judges, [491] and the Ancient of Days seats Himself--His raiment as white snow, His hair as bright wool, His throne of flames, His wheels of burning fire. A stream of dazzling fire goes out before Him. Thousand thousands stand before Him; ten thousand times ten thousand minister to Him. The judgment is set; the books are opened. The fourth monster is then slain and burned because of the blaspheming horn; the other beasts are suffered to live for a season and a time, but their dominion is taken away. [492]

\*\*\*

But then, in the night vision, there came "one even as a son of man" with the clouds of heaven, and is brought before the Ancient of Days, and receives from Him power and glory and a kingdom--an everlasting dominion, a kingdom that shall not be destroyed--over all people, nations, and languages.

Such is the vision, and its interpretation follows. The heart of Daniel "is pierced in the midst of its sheath" by what he has seen, and the visions of his head troubled him. Coming near to one of them that stood by--the angelic ministrants of the Ancient of Days--he begs for an interpretation of the vision.

It is given him with extreme brevity.

The four wild beasts represent four kings, the founders of four successive kingdoms. But the ultimate and eternal dominion is not to be with them. It is to be given, till the eternities of the eternities, to "the holy ones of the Lofty One." [493]

What follows is surely an indication of the date of the Book. Daniel is quite satisfied with this meagre interpretation, in which no single detail is given as regards the first three world-empires, which one would have supposed would chiefly interest the real Daniel. His whole curiosity is absorbed in a detail of the vision of the fourth monster. It is all but inconceivable that a contemporary prophet should have felt no further interest in the destinies which affected the great golden Empire of Babylon under which he lived, nor in those of Media and Persia, which were already beginning to loom large on the horizon, and should have cared only for an incident in the story of a fourth empire as yet unheard of, which was only to be fulfilled four centuries later. The interests of every other Hebrew prophet are always mainly absorbed, so far as earthly things are concerned, in the immediate or not-far-distant future. That is true also of the author of Daniel, if, as we have had reason to see, he wrote under the rule of the persecuting and blaspheming horn.

In his appeal for the interpretation of this symbol there are fresh particulars about this horn which had eyes and spake very great things. We are told that "his look was more stout than his fellows"; and that "he made war against the saints and prevailed against them, until the Ancient of Days came. Then judgment was given to the saints, and the time came that the saints possessed the kingdom."

The interpretation is that the fourth beast is an earth-devouring, trampling, shattering kingdom, diverse from all kingdoms; its ten horns are ten kings that shall arise from it. [494] Then another king shall arise, diverse from the first, who shall subdue three kings, shall speak blasphemies, shall wear out the saints, and will strive to change times and laws. But after "a time, two times, and a half," [495] the judgment shall sit, and he will be annihilated, and his dominion shall be given for ever to the people of the saints of the Most High.

Such was the vision; such its interpretation; and there can be no difficulty as to its general significance.

I. That the four empires, and their founders, are not identical with the four empires of the metal colossus in Nebuchadrezzar's dream, is an inference which, apart from dogmatic bias, would scarcely have occurred to any unsophisticated reader. To the imagination of Nebuchadrezzar, the heathen potentate, they would naturally present themselves in their strength and towering grandeur, splendid and impassive and secure, till the mysterious destruction smites them. To the Jewish seer they present themselves in their cruel ferocity and headstrong ambition as destroying wild beasts. The symbolism would naturally occur to all who were familiar with the winged bulls and lions and other gigantic representations of monsters which decorated the palace-walls of Nineveh and Babylon. Indeed, similar imagery had already found a place on the prophetic page. [496]

II. The turbulent sea, from which the immense beasts emerge after the struggling of the four winds of heaven upon its surface, is the sea of nations. [497]

III. The first great beast is Nebuchadrezzar and the Babylonian Empire. [498] There is nothing strange in the fact that there should be a certain transfusion or overlapping of the symbols, the object not being literary congruity, but the creation of a general impression. He is represented as a lion, because lions were prevalent in Babylonia, and were specially prominent in Babylonian decorations. His eagle-wings symbolise rapacity and swiftness. [499] But, according to the narrative already given, a change had come over the spirit of Nebuchadrezzar in his latter days. That subduing and softening by the influence of a Divine power is represented by the plucking off of the lion's eagle-wings, and its fall to earth. But it was not left to lie there in impotent degradation. It is lifted up from the earth, and humanised, and made to stand on its feet as a man, and a man's heart is given to it. [500]

IV. The bear, which places itself upon one side, is the Median Empire, smaller than the Chaldean, as the bear is smaller and less formidable than the lion. The crouching on one side is obscure. It is explained by some as implying that it was lower in exaltation than the Babylonian Empire; by others that "it gravitated, as regards its power, only towards the countries west of the Tigris and Euphrates." [501] The meaning of the "three ribs in its mouth" is also uncertain. Some regard the number three as a vague round number; others refer it to the three countries over which the Median dominion extended--Babylonia, Assyria, and Syria; others, less probably, to the three chief cities. The command, "Arise, devour much flesh," refers to the prophecies of Median conquest, [502] and perhaps to uncertain historical reminiscences which confused "Darius the Mede" with Darius the son of Hystaspes. Those who explain this monster as an emblem, not of the Median but of the Medo-Persian Empire, neglect the plain indications of the Book itself, for the author regards the Median and Persian Empires as distinct. [503]

V. The leopard or panther represents the Persian kingdom. [504] It has four wings on its back, to indicate how freely and swiftly it soared to the four quarters of the world. Its four heads indicate four kings. There were indeed twelve or thirteen kings of Persia between b.c. 536 and b.c. 333; but the author of the Book of Daniel, who of course had no books of history before him, only thinks of the four who were most prominent in popular tradition--namely (as it would seem), Cyrus, Darius, Artaxerxes, and Xerxes. [505] These are the only four names which the writer knew, because they are the only ones which occur in Scripture. It is true that the Darius of Neh. xii. 22 is not the Great Darius, son of Hystaspes, but Darius Codomannus (b.c. 424-404). But this fact may most easily have been overlooked in uncritical and unhistoric times. And "power was given to it," for it was far stronger than the preceding kingdom of the Medes.

VI. The fourth monster won its chief aspect of terribleness from the conquests of Alexander, which blazed over the East with such irresistible force and suddenness. [506] The great Macedonian, after his massacres at Tyre, struck into the Eastern world the intense feeling of terror which we still can recognise in the narrative of Josephus. His rule is therefore symbolised by a monster diverse from all the beasts before it in its sudden leap out of obscurity, in the lightning-like rapidity of its flash from West to East, and in its instantaneous disintegration into four separate kingdoms. It is with one only of those four kingdoms of the Diadochi, the one which so terribly affected the fortunes of the Holy Land, that the writer is predominantly concerned--namely, the empire of the Seleucid kings. It is in that portion of the kingdom--namely, from the Euxine to the confines of Arabia--that the ten horns arise which, we are told, symbolise ten kings. It seems almost certain that these ten kings are intended for:--

b.c. 1. Seleucus I. (Nicator) [507] 312-280 2. Antiochus I. (Soter) 280-261 3. Antiochus II. (Theos) 261-246 4. Seleucus II. (Kallinikos)246-226 5. Seleucus III. (Keraunos) 226-223 6. Antiochus III. (Megas)223-187 7. Seleucus IV. (Philopator)223-187

Then followed the three kings (actual or potential) who were plucked up before the little horn: namely--

8. Demetrius.175 9. Heliodorus. 176 10. Ptolemy Philometor. 181-146

Of these three who succumbed to the machinations of Antiochus Epiphanes, or the little horn, [508] the first, Demetrius, was the only son of Seleucus Philopator, and true heir to the crown. His father sent him to Rome as a hostage, and released his brother Antiochus. So far from showing gratitude for this generosity, Antiochus, on the murder of Seleucus IV. (b.c. 175), usurped the rights of his nephew (Dan. xi. 21).

The second, Heliodorus, seeing that Demetrius the heir was out of the way, poisoned Seleucus Philopator, and himself usurped the kingdom. [509]

Ptolemy Philometor was the son of Cleopatra, the sister of Seleucus Philopator. A large party was in favour of uniting Egypt and Persia under his rule. But Antiochus Epiphanes ignored the compact which had made Coele-Syria and Phoenicia the dower of Cleopatra, and not only kept Philometor from his rights, but would have deprived him of Egypt also but for the strenuous interposition of the Romans and their ambassador M. Popilius Lænas. [510]

When the three horns had thus fallen before him, the little horn--Antiochus Epiphanes--sprang into prominence. The mention of his "eyes" seems to be a reference to his shrewdness, cunning, and vigilance. [511] The "mouth that spoke very great things" [512] alludes to the boastful arrogance which led him to assume the title of Epiphanes, or "the illustrious"--which his scornful subjects changed into Epimanes, "the mad"--and to his assumption even of the title Theos, "the god," on some of his coins. [513] His look "was bigger than his fellows," for he inspired the kings of Egypt and other countries with terror. "He made war against the saints," with the aid of "Jason and Menelaus, those ungodly wretches," and "prevailed against them." He "wore out the saints of the Most High," for he took Jerusalem by storm, plundered it, slew eighty thousand men, women, and children, took forty thousand prisoners, and sold as many into slavery (b.c. 170). [514] "As he entered the sanctuary to plunder it, under the guidance of the apostate high priest Menelaus, he uttered words of blasphemy, and he carried off all the gold and silver he could find, including the golden table, altar of incense, candlesticks, and vessels, and even rifled the subterranean vaults, so that he seized no less than eighteen hundred talents of gold." [515] He then sacrificed swine upon the altar, and sprinkled the whole Temple with the broth.

Further than all this, "he thought to change times and laws"; and they were "given into his hand until a time, and two times, and a half." For he made a determined attempt to put down the Jewish feasts, the Sabbath, circumcision, and all the most distinctive Jewish ordinances. [516] In b.c. 167, two years after his cruel devastation of the city, he sent Apollonius, his chief collector of tribute, against Jerusalem, with an army of twenty-two thousand men. On the first Sabbath after his arrival, Apollonius sent his soldiers to massacre all the men whom they met in the streets, and to seize the women and children as slaves. He occupied the castle on Mount Zion, and prevented the Jews from attending the public ordinances of their sanctuary. Hence in June b.c. 167 the daily sacrifice ceased, and the Jews fled for their lives from the Holy City. Antiochus then published an edict forbidding all his subjects in Syria and elsewhere--even the Zoroastrians in Armenia and Persia--to worship any gods, or acknowledge any religion but his. [517] The Jewish sacred books were burnt, and not only the Samaritans but many Jews apostatised, while others hid themselves in mountains and deserts. [518] He sent an old philosopher named Athenæus to instruct the Jews in the Greek religion, and to enforce its observance. He dedicated the Temple to Zeus Olympios, and built on the altar of Jehovah a smaller altar for sacrifice to Zeus, to whom he must also have erected a statue. This heathen altar was set up on Kisleu (December) 15, and the heathen sacrifice began on Kisleu 25. All observance of the Jewish Law was now treated as a capital crime. The Jews were forced to sacrifice in heathen groves at heathen altars, and to walk, crowned with ivy, in Bacchic processions. Two women who had braved the despot's wrath by circumcising their children were flung from the Temple battlements into the vale below. [519]

The triumph of this blasphemous and despotic savagery was arrested, first by the irresistible force of determined martyrdom which preferred death to unfaithfulness, and next by the armed resistance evoked by the heroism of Mattathias, the priest at Modin. When Apelles visited the town, and ordered the Jews to sacrifice, Mattathias struck down with his own hand a Jew who was preparing to obey. Then, aided by his strong heroic sons, he attacked Apelles, slew him and his soldiers, tore down the idolatrous altar, and with his sons and adherents fled into the wilderness, where they were joined by many of the Jews.

The news of this revolt brought Antiochus to Palestine in b.c. 166, and among his other atrocities he ordered the execution by torture of the venerable scribe Eleazar, and of the pious mother with her seven sons. In spite of all his efforts the party of the Chasidîm grew in numbers and in strength. When Mattathias died, Judas the Maccabee became their leader, and his brother Simon their counsellor. [520] While Antiochus was celebrating his mad and licentious festival at Daphne, Judas inflicted a severe defeat on Apollonius, and won other battles, which made Antiochus vow in an access of fury that he would exterminate the nation (Dan. xi. 44). But he found himself bankrupt, and the Persians and Armenians were revolting from him in disgust. He therefore sent Lysias as his general to Judæa, and Lysias assembled an immense army of forty thousand foot and seven thousand horse, to whom Judas could only oppose six thousand men. [521] Lysias pitched his camp at Beth-shur, south of Jerusalem. There Judas attacked him with irresistible valour and confidence, slew five thousand of his soldiers, and drove the rest to flight.

Lysias retired to Antioch, intending to renew the invasion next year. Thereupon Judas and his army recaptured Jerusalem, and restored and cleansed and reconsecrated the dilapidated and desecrated sanctuary. He made a new shewbread-table, incense-altar, and candlestick of gold in place of those which Antiochus had carried off, and new vessels of gold, and a new veil before the Holiest Place. All this was completed on Kisleu 25, b.c. 165, about the time of the winter solstice, "on the same day of the year on which, three years before, it had been profaned by Antiochus, and just three years and a half--'a time, two times, and half a time'--after the city and Temple had been desolated by Apollonius." [522] They began the day by renewing the sacrifices, kindling the altar and the candlestick by pure fire struck by flints. The whole law of the Temple service continued thenceforward without interruption till the destruction of the Temple by the Romans. It was a feast in commemoration of this dedication--called the Encænia and "the Lights"--which Christ honoured by His presence at Jerusalem. [523]

The neighbouring nations, when they heard of this revolt of the Jews, and its splendid success, proposed to join with Antiochus for their extermination. But meanwhile the king, having been shamefully repulsed in his sacrilegious attack on the Temple of Artemis at Elymais, retired in deep chagrin to Ecbatana, in Media. It was there that he heard of the Jewish successes and set out to chastise the rebels. On his way he heard of the recovery of Jerusalem, the destruction of his heathen altars, and the purification of the Temple. The news flung him into one of those paroxysms of fury to which he was liable, and, breathing out threatenings and slaughter, he declared that he would turn Jerusalem into one vast cemetery for the whole Jewish race. Suddenly smitten with a violent internal malady, he would not stay his course, but still urged his charioteer to the utmost speed. [524] In consequence of this the chariot was overturned, and he was flung violently to the ground, receiving severe injuries. He was placed in a litter, but, unable to bear the agonies caused by its motion, he stopped at Tabæ, in the mountains of Parætacene, on the borders of Persia and Babylonia, where he died, b.c. 164, in very evil case, half mad with the furies of a remorseful conscience. [525] The Jewish historians say that, before his death, he repented, acknowledged the crimes he had committed against the Jews, and vowed that he would repair them if he survived. The stories of his death resemble those of the deaths of Herod, of Galerius, of Philip II., and of other bitter persecutors of the saints of God. Judas the Maccabee, who had overthrown his power in Palestine, died at Eleasa in b.c. 161, after a series of brilliant victories.

Such were the fortunes of the king whom the writer shadows forth under the emblem of the little horn with human eyes and a mouth which spake blasphemies, whose power was to be made transitory, and to be annihilated and destroyed unto the end. [526] And when this wild beast was slain, and its body given to the burning fire, the rest of the beasts were indeed to be deprived of their splendid dominions, but a respite of life is given them, and they are suffered to endure for a time and a period. [527]

But the eternal life, and the imperishable dominion, which were denied to them, are given to another in the epiphany of the Ancient of Days. The vision of the seer is one of a great scene of judgment. Thrones are set for the heavenly assessors, and the Almighty appears in snow-white raiment, and on His chariot-throne of burning flame which flashes round Him like a vast photosphere. [528] The books of everlasting record are opened before the glittering faces of the myriads of saints who accompany Him, and the fiery doom is passed on the monstrous world-powers who would fain usurp His authority. [529]

But who is the "one even as a son of man," who "comes with the clouds of heaven," and who "is brought before the Ancient of Days," [530] to whom is given the imperishable dominion? That he is not an angel appears from the fact that he seems to be separate from all the ten thousand times ten thousand who stand around the cherubic chariot. He is not a man, but something more. In this respect he resembles the angels described in Dan. viii. 15, x. 16-18. He has "the appearance of a man," and is "like the similitude of the sons of men." [531]

We should naturally answer, in accordance with the multitude of ancient and modern commentators both Jewish and Christian, that the Messiah is intended; [532] and, indeed, our Lord alludes to the prophecy in Matt. xxvi. 64. That the vision is meant to indicate the establishment of the Messianic theocracy cannot be doubted. But if we follow the interpretation given by the angel himself in answer to Daniel's entreaty, the personality of the Messiah seems to be at least somewhat subordinate or indistinct. For the interpretation, without mentioning any person, seems to point only to the saints of Israel who are to inherit and maintain that Divine kingdom which has been already thrice asserted and prophesied. It is the "holy ones" (Qaddîshîn), "the holy ones of the Most High" (Qaddîshî Elîonîn), upon whom the never-ending sovereignty is conferred; [533] and who these are cannot be misunderstood, for they are the very same as those against whom the little horn has been engaged in war. [534] The Messianic kingdom is here predominantly represented as the spiritual supremacy of the chosen people. Neither here, nor in ii. 44, nor in xii. 3, does the writer separately indicate any Davidic king, or priest upon his throne, as had been already done by so many previous prophets. [535] This vision does not seem to have brought into prominence the rule of any Divinely Incarnate Christ over the kingdom of the Highest. In this respect the interpretation of the "one even as a son of man" comes upon us as a surprise, and seems to indicate that the true interpretation of that element of the vision is that the kingdom of the saints is there personified; so that as wild beasts were appropriate emblems of the world-powers, the reasonableness and sanctity of the saintly theocracy are indicated by a human form, which has its origin in the clouds of heaven, not in the miry and troubled sea. This is the view of the Christian father Ephræm Syrus, as well as of the Jewish exegete Abn Ezra; and it is supported by the fact that in other apocryphal books of the later epoch, as in the Assumption of Moses and the Book of Jubilees, the Messianic hope is concentrated in the conception that the holy nation is to have the dominance over the Gentiles. At any rate, it seems that, if truth is to guide us rather than theological prepossession, we must take the significance of the writer, not from the emblems of the vision, but from the divinely imparted interpretation of it; and there the figure of "one as a son of man" is persistently (vv. 18, 22, 27) explained to stand, not for the Christ Himself, but for "the holy ones of the Most High," [536] whose dominion Christ's coming should inaugurate and secure.

The chapter closes with the words: "Here is the end of the matter. As for me, Daniel, my thoughts much troubled me, and my brightness was changed in me: but I kept the matter in my heart."

## *Footnotes:*

487. Except in the heading of chap. x.

488. In the opinion of Lagarde and others this chapter--which is not noticed by Josephus, and which Meinhold thinks cannot have been written by the author of chap. ii., since it says nothing of the sufferings or deliverance of Israel--did not belong to the original form of the Book. Lagarde thinks that it was written a.d. 69, after the persecution of the Christians by Nero.

489. St. Ephræm Syrus says, "The sea is the world." Isa. xvii. 12, xxvii. 1, xxxii. 2. But compare Dan. vii. 17; Ezek. xxix. 3; Rev. xiii. 1, xvii. 1-8, xxi. 1.

490. In the vision of the colossus in ii. 41-43 stress is laid on the division of the fourth empire into stronger and weaker elements (iron and clay). That point is here passed over.

491. A.V., "the thrones were cast down."

492. In ii. 35, 44, the four empires are represented as finally destroyed.

493. A.V. marg., "high ones"--i.e., things or places.

494. Not kingdoms, as in viii. 8.

495. Comp. Rev. xii. 14; Luke iv. 25; James v. 17.

496. Isa. xxvii. 1, li. 9; Ezek. xxix. 3, xxxii. 2.

497. Comp. Job xxxviii. 16, 17; Isa. viii. 7, xvii. 12.

498. Comp. Dan. ii. 38. Jeremiah had likened Nebuchadrezzar both to the lion (iv. 7, xlix. 19, etc.) and to the eagle (xlviii. 40, xlix. 22). Ezekiel had compared the king (xvii. 3), and Habakkuk his armies

(i. 8), as also Jeremiah (iv. 13; Lam. iv. 19), to the eagle (Pusey, p. 690). See too Layard, Nin. and Bab., ii. 460. For other beast-symbols see Isa. xxvii. 1, li. 9; Ezek. xxix. 3; Psalm lxxiv. 13.

499. Comp. Jer. iv. 7, 13, xlix. 16; Ezek. xvii. 3, 12; Hab. i. 8; Lam. iv. 19.

500. The use of enôsh--not eesh--indicates chastening and weakness.

501. Ewald.

502. Isa. xiii. 17; Jer. li. 11, 28. Aristotle, H. N., viii. 5, calls the bear pamphagos, "all-devouring." A bear appears as a dream-symbol in an Assyrian book of auguries (Lenormant, Magie, 492).

503. Dan. v. 28, 31, vi. 8, 12, 15, 28, viii. 20, ix. 1, xi. 1.

504. The composite beast of Rev. xiii. 2 combines leopard, bear, and lion.

505. Comp. viii. 4-8.

506. Battle of the Granicus, b.c. 334; Battle of Issus, 333; Siege of Tyre, 332; Battle of Arbela, 331; Death of Darius, 330. Alexander died b.c. 323.

507. This was the interpretation given by the great father Ephræm Syrus in the first century. Hitzig, Kuenen, and others count from Alexander the Great, and omit Ptolemy Philometor.

508. Dan. xi. 21.

509. Appian, Syr., 45; Liv., xli. 24. The story of his attempt to rob the Temple at Jerusalem, rendered so famous by the great picture of Raphael in the Vatican stanze, is not mentioned by Josephus, but only in 2 Macc. iii. 24-40. In 4 Macc. it is told, without the miracle, of Apollonius. There can be little doubt that something of the kind happened, but it was perhaps due to an imposture of the Jewish high priest.

510. Porphyry interpreted the three kings who succumbed to the little horn to be Ptolemy Philometor, Ptolemy Euergetes II., and Artaxias, King of Armenia. The critics who begin the ten kings with Alexander the Great count Seleucus IV. (Philopator) as one of the three who were supplanted by Antiochus. Von Gutschmid counts as one of the three a younger brother of Demetrius, said to have been murdered by Antiochus (Müller, Fr. Hist. Græc., iv. 558).

511. Comp. viii. 23.

512. Comp. lalein megala (Rev. xiii. 5); Hom., Od., xvi. 243.

513. Comp. xi. 36.

514. Jos., B. J., I. i. 2, VI. x. 1. In Antt., XII. v. 3, Josephus says he took Jerusalem by stratagem.

515. Jahn, Hebr. Commonwealth, § xciv.; Ewald, Hist. of Isr., v. 293-300.

516. 2 Macc. iv. 9-15: "The priests had no courage to serve any more at the altar, but despising the Temple, and neglecting the sacrifices, hastened to be partakers of the unlawful allowance in the place of exercise, after the game of Discus ... not setting by the honours of their fathers, but liking the glory of the Grecians best of all."

517. 1 Macc. i. 29-40; 2 Macc. v. 24-26; Jos., Antt., XII. v. 4. Comp. Dan. xi. 30, 31. See Schürer, i. 155 ff.

518. Jerome, Comm. in Dan., viii., ix.; Tac., Hist., v. 8; 1 Macc. i. 41-53; 2 Macc. v. 27, vi. 2; Jos., Antt., XII. v. 4.

519. 1 Macc. ii. 41-64, iv. 54; 2 Macc. vi. 1-9, x. 5; Jos., Antt., XII. v. 4; Dan. xi. 31.

520. Maccabee perhaps means "the Hammerer" (comp. the names Charles Martel and Malleus hæreticorum). Simeon was called Tadshî, "he increases" (? Gk., Thassis).

521. The numbers vary in the records.

522. Prideaux, Connection, ii. 212. Comp. Rev. xii. 14, xi. 2, 3.

523. John x. 22.

524. On the death of Antiochus see 1 Macc. vi. 8; 2 Macc. ix.; Polybius, xxxi. 11; Jos., Antt., XII. ix. 1, 2.

525. Polybius, De Virt. et Vit., Exc. Vales, p. 144; Q. Curtius, v. 13; Strabo, xi. 522; Appian, Syriaca, xlvi. 80; 1 Macc. vi.; 2 Macc. ix.; Jos., Antt., XII. ix. 1; Prideaux, ii. 217; Jahn, Hebr. Commonwealth § xcvi.

526. Dan. vii. 26.

527. Dan. vii. 12. This is only explicable at all--and then not clearly--on the supposition that the fourth beast represents Alexander and the Diadochi. See even Pusey, p. 78.

528. Ezek. i. 26; Psalm l. 3. Comp. the adaptation of this vision in Enoch xlvi. 1-3.

529. Isa. l. 11, lx. 10-12, lxvi. 24, Joel iii. 1, 2. See Rev. i. 13. In the Gospels it is not "a son of man," but generally ho huios tou anthropou. Comp. Matt. xvi. 13, xxiv. 30; John xii. 34; Acts vii. 56; Justin, Dial. c. Tryph., 31.

530. Comp. Mark xiv. 62; Rev. i. 7; Hom., Il., v. 867, homou nepheessin.

531. Comp. Ezek. i. 26.

532. It is so understood by the Book of Enoch; the Talmud (Sanhedrin, f. 98, 1); the early father Justin Martyr, Dial. c. Tryph., 31, etc. Some of the Jewish commentators (e.g., Abn Ezra) understood it of the people of God, and so Hofmann, Hitzig, Meinhold, etc. See Behrmann, Dan., p. 48.

533. Dan. iv. 3, 34, vi. 26. See Schürer, ii. 247; Wellhausen, Die Pharis. u. Sadd., 24 ff.

534. Dan. vii. 16, 22, 23, 27.
535. Zech. ix. 9.
536. See Schürer, ii. 138-187, "The Messianic Hope": he refers to Ecclus. xxxii. 18, 19, xxxiii. 1-11, xl. 13, l. 24; Judith xvi. 12; 2 Macc. ii. 18; Baruch ii. 27-35; Tobit xiii, 11-18; Wisdom iii. 8, v. 1, etc. The Messianic King appears more distinctly in Orac. Sibyll., iii.; in parts of the Book of Enoch (of which, however, xlv.-lvii. are of unknown date); and the Psalms of Solomon. In Philo we seem to have traces of the King as well as of the kingdom. See Drummond, The Jewish Messiah, pp. 196 ff.; Stanton, The Jewish and Christian Messiah, pp. 109-118.

# CHAPTER II - THE RAM AND THE HE-GOAT

This vision is dated as having occurred in the third year of Belshazzar; but it is not easy to see the significance of the date, since it is almost exclusively occupied with the establishment of the Greek Empire, its dissolution into the kingdoms of the Diadochi, and the godless despotism of King Antiochus Epiphanes.

The seer imagines himself to be in the palace of Shushan: "As I beheld I was in the castle of Shushan." [537] It has been supposed by some that Daniel was really there upon some business connected with the kingdom of Babylon. But this view creates a needless difficulty. Shushan, which the Greeks called Susa, and the Persians Shush (now Shushter), "the city of the lily," was "the palace" or fortress (bîrah [538]) of the Achæmenid kings of Persia, and it is most unlikely that a chief officer of the kingdom of Babylon should have been there in the third year of the imaginary King Belshazzar, just when Cyrus was on the eve of capturing Babylon without a blow. If Belshazzar is some dim reflection of the son of Nabunaid (though he never reigned), Shushan was not then subject to the King of Babylonia. But the ideal presence of the prophet there, in vision, is analogous to the presence of the exile Ezekiel in Jerusalem (Ezek. xl. 1); and these transferences of the prophets to the scenes of their operation were sometimes even regarded as bodily, as in the legend of Habakkuk taken to the lions' den to support Daniel.

Shushan is described as being in the province of Elam or Elymais, which may be here used as a general designation of the district in which Susiana was included. The prophet imagines himself as standing by the river-basin (oobâl [539]) of the Ulai, which shows that we must take the words "in the castle of Shushan" in an ideal sense; for, as Ewald says, "it is only in a dream that images and places are changed so rapidly." The Ulai is the river called by the Greeks the Eulæus, now the Karûn. [540]

Shushan is said by Pliny and Arrian to have been on the river Eulæus, and by Herodotus to have been on the banks of

*"Choaspes, amber stream,*
*The drink of none but kings."*

It seems now to have been proved that the Ulai was merely a branch of the Choaspes or Kerkhah.[541]

Lifting up his eyes, Daniel sees a ram standing eastward of the river-basin. It has two lofty horns, the loftier of the two being the later in origin. It butts westward, northward, and southward, and does great things. [542] But in the midst of its successes a he-goat, with a conspicuous horn between its eyes, [543] comes from the West so swiftly over the face of all the earth that it scarcely seems even to touch the ground, [544] and runs upon the ram in the fury of his strength, [545] conquering and trampling upon him, and smashing in pieces his two horns. But his impetuosity was short-lived, for the great horn was speedily broken, and four others [546] rose in its place towards the four winds of heaven. Out of these four horns shot up a puny horn, [547] which grew exceedingly great towards the South, and towards the East, and towards "the Glory"--i.e., towards the Holy Land. [548] It became great even to the host of heaven, and cast down some of the host and of the stars to the ground, and trampled on them. [549] He even behaved proudly against the prince of the host, took away from him [550] "the daily" (sacrifice), polluted the dismantled sanctuary with sacrilegious arms, [551] and cast the truth to the ground and prospered. Then "one holy one called to another and asked, For how long is the vision of the daily [sacrifice], and the horrible sacrilege, that thus both the sanctuary and host are surrendered to be trampled underfoot?" [552] And the answer is, "Until two thousand three hundred 'erebh-bôqer, 'evening-morning'; then will the sanctuary be justified."

Daniel sought to understand the vision, and immediately there stood before him one in the semblance of a man, and he hears the distant voice of some one [553] standing between the Ulai--i.e., between its two banks, [554] or perhaps between its two branches, the Eulæus and the Choaspes--who called aloud to "Gabriel." The archangel Gabriel is here first mentioned in Scripture. [555] "Gabriel," cried the voice, "explain to him what he has seen." So Gabriel came and stood beside him; but he was terrified, and fell on his face. "Observe, thou son of man," [556] said the angel to him; "for unto the time of the end is the vision." But since Daniel still lay prostrate on his face, and sank into a swoon, the angel touched him, and raised him up, and said that the great wrath was only for a fixed time, and he would tell him what would happen at the end of it.

The two-horned ram, he said, the Baal-keranaîm, or "lord of two horns," represents the King of Media and Persia; the shaggy goat is the Empire of Greece; and the great horn is its first king--Alexander the Great. [557]

The four horns rising out of the broken great horn are four inferior kingdoms. In one of these, sacrilege would culminate in the person of a king of bold face, [558] and skilled in cunning, who would become powerful, though not by his own strength. [559] He would prosper and destroy mighty men and the people of the holy ones, [560] and deceit would succeed by his double-dealing. He would contend against the Prince of princes, [561] and yet without a hand would he be broken in pieces.

Such is the vision and its interpretation; and though there is here and there a difficulty in the details and translation, and though there is a necessary crudeness in the emblematic imagery, the general significance of the whole is perfectly clear.

The scene of the vision is ideally placed in Shushan, because the Jews regarded it as the royal capital of the Persian dominion, and the dream begins with the overthrow of the Medo-Persian Empire. [562] The ram is a natural symbol of power and strength, as in Isa. lx. 7. The two horns represent the two divisions of the empire, of which the later--the Persian--is the loftier and the stronger. It is regarded as being already the lord of the East, but it extends its conquests by butting westward over the Tigris into Europe, and southwards to Egypt and Africa, and northwards towards Scythia, with magnificent success.

The he-goat is Greece. [563] Its one great horn represents "the great Emathian conqueror." [564] So swift was the career of Alexander's conquests, that the goat seems to speed along without so much as touching the ground. [565] With irresistible fury, in the great battles of the Granicus (b.c. 334), Issus (b.c. 333), and Arbela (b.c. 331), he stamps to pieces the power of Persia and of its king, Darius Codomannus. [566] In this short space of time Alexander conquers Syria, Phoenicia, Cyprus, Tyre, Gaza, Egypt, Babylonia, Persia, Media, Hyrcania, Aria, and Arachosia. In b.c. 330 Darius was murdered by Bessus, and Alexander became lord of his kingdom. In b.c. 329 the Greek King conquered Bactria, crossed the Oxus and Jaxartes, and defeated the Scythians. In b.c. 328 he conquered Sogdiana. In b.c. 327 and 326 he crossed the Indus, Hydaspes, and Akesines, subdued Northern and Western India, and--compelled by the discontent of his troops to pause in his career of victory--sailed down the Hydaspes and Indus to the Ocean. He then returned by land through Gedrosia, Karmania, Persia, and Susiana to Babylon.

There the great horn is suddenly broken without hand. [567] Alexander in b.c. 323, after a reign of twelve years and eight months, died as a fool dieth, of a fever brought on by fatigue, exposure, drunkenness, and debauchery. He was only thirty-two years old.

The dismemberment of his empire immediately followed. In b.c. 322 its vast extent was divided among his principal generals. Twenty-two years of war ensued; and in b.c. 301, after the defeat of Antigonus and his son Demetrius at the Battle of Ipsus, four horns are visible in the place of one. The battle was won by the confederacy of Cassander, Lysimachus, Ptolemy, and Seleucus, and they founded four kingdoms. Cassander ruled in Greece and Macedonia; Lysimachus in Asia Minor; Ptolemy in Egypt, Coele-Syria, and Palestine; Seleucus in Upper Asia.

With one only of the four kingdoms, and with one only of its kings, is the vision further concerned--with the kingdom of the Seleucidæ, and with the eighth king of the dynasty, Antiochus Epiphanes. In this chapter, however, a brief sketch only of him is furnished. Many details of the minutest kind are subsequently added.

He is called "a puny horn," because, in his youth, no one could have anticipated his future greatness. He was only a younger son of Antiochus III. (the Great). When Antiochus III. was defeated in the Battle of Magnesia under Mount Sipylus (b.c. 190), his loss was terrible. Fifty thousand foot and four thousand horse were slain on the battlefield, and fourteen hundred were taken prisoners. He was forced to make peace with the Romans, and to give them hostages, one of whom was Antiochus the Younger, brother of Seleucus, who was heir to the throne. Antiochus for thirteen years languished miserably as a hostage at Rome. His father, Antiochus the Great, was either slain in b.c. 187 by the people of Elymais, after his sacrilegious plundering of the Temple of Jupiter-Belus; [568] or murdered by some of his own attendants whom he had beaten during a fit of drunkenness. [569] Seleucus Philopator succeeded him, and after having reigned for thirteen years, wished to see his brother Antiochus again. He therefore sent his son Demetrius in exchange for him, perhaps desiring that the boy, who was then twelve years old, should enjoy the advantage of a Roman education, or thinking that Antiochus would be of more use to him in his designs against Ptolemy Philometor, the child-king of Egypt. When Demetrius was on his way to Rome, and Antiochus had not yet reached Antioch, Heliodorus the treasurer seized the opportunity to poison Seleucus and usurp the crown.

The chances, therefore, of Antiochus seemed very forlorn. But he was a man of ability, though with a taint of folly and madness in his veins. By allying himself with Eumenes, King of Pergamum, as we shall see hereafter, he suppressed Heliodorus, secured the kingdom, and "becoming very great," though only by fraud, cruelty, and stratagem, assumed the title of Epiphanes "the Illustrious." He extended his power "towards the South" by intriguing and warring against Egypt and his young nephew, Ptolemy Philometor; [570] and "towards the Sunrising" by his successes in the direction of Media and Persia; [571] and towards "the Glory" or "Ornament" (hatstsebî)--i.e., the Holy Land. [572] Inflated with insolence, he now set himself against the stars, the host of heaven--i.e., against the chosen people of God and their leaders. He cast down and trampled on them, [573] and defied the Prince of the host; for he

> "Not e'en against the Holy One of heaven
> Refrained his tongue blasphémous."

His chief enormity was the abolition of "the daily" (tamîd)--i.e., the sacrifice daily offered in the Temple; and the desecration of the sanctuary itself by violence and sacrilege, which will be more fully set forth in the next chapters. He also seized and destroyed the sacred books of the Jews. As he forbade the reading of the Law--of which the daily lesson was called the Parashah--there began from this time the custom of selecting a lesson from the Prophets, which was called the Haphtarah. [574]

It was natural to make one of the holy ones, who are supposed to witness this horrible iniquity, [575] inquire how long it was to be permitted. The enigmatic answer is, "Until an evening-morning two thousand three hundred."

In the further explanation given to Daniel by Gabriel a few more touches are added.

Antiochus Epiphanes is described as a king "bold of visage, and skilled in enigmas." His boldness is sufficiently illustrated by his many campaigns and battles, and his braggart insolence has been already alluded to in vii. 8. His skill in enigmas is illustrated by his dark and tortuous diplomacy, which was exhibited in all his proceedings, [576] and especially in the whole of his dealings with Egypt, in which country he desired to usurp the throne from his young nephew Ptolemy Philometor. The statement that "he will have mighty strength, but not by his own strength," may either mean that his transient prosperity was due only to the permission of God, or that his successes were won rather by cunning than by prowess. After an allusion to his cruel persecution of the holy people, Gabriel adds that "without a hand shall he be broken in pieces"; in other words, his retribution and destruction shall be due to no human intervention, but will come from God Himself. [577]

Daniel is bidden to hide the vision for many days--a sentence which is due to the literary plan of the Book; and he is assured that the vision concerning the "evening-morning" was true. He adds that the vision exhausted and almost annihilated him; but, afterwards, he arose and did the king's business. He was silent about the vision, for neither he nor any one else understood it. [578] Of course, had the real date of the chapter been in the reign of Belshazzar, it was wholly impossible that either the seer or any one else should have been able to attach any significance to it. [579]

Emphasis is evidently attached to the "two thousand three hundred evening-morning" during which the desolation of the sanctuary is to continue.

What does the phrase "evening-morning" ('erebh-bôqer) mean?

In ver. 26 it is called "the vision concerning the evening and the morning."

Does "evening-morning" mean a whole day, like the Greek nuchthemeron, or half a day? The expression is doubly perplexing. If the writer meant "days," why does he not say "days," as in xii. 11, 12? [580] And why, in any case, does he here use the solecism 'erebh-bôqer (Abendmorgen), and not, as in ver. 26, "evening and morning"? Does the expression mean two thousand three hundred days? or eleven hundred and fifty days?

It is a natural supposition that the time is meant to correspond with the three years and a half ("a time, two times, and half a time") of vii. 25. But here again all certainty of detail is precluded by our ignorance as to the exact length of years by which the writer reckoned; and how he treated the month Ve-adar, a month of thirty days, which was intercalated once in every six years.

Supposing that he allowed an intercalary fifteen days for three and a half years, and took the Babylonian reckoning of twelve months of thirty days, then three and a half years gives us twelve hundred and seventy-five days, or, omitting any allowance for intercalation, twelve hundred and sixty days.

If, then, "two thousand three hundred evening-morning" means two thousand three hundred half days, we have one hundred and ten days too many for the three and a half years.

And if the phrase means two thousand three hundred full days, that gives us (counting thirty intercalary days for Ve-adar) too little for seven years by two hundred and fifty days. Some see in this a mystic intimation that the period of chastisement shall for the elect's sake be shortened. [581] Some commentators reckon seven years roughly, from the elevation of Menelaus to the high-priesthood (Kisleu, b.c. 168; 2 Macc. v. 11) to the victory of Judas Maccabæus over Nicanor at Adasa, March, b.c. 161 (1 Macc. vii. 25-50; 2 Macc. xv. 20-35).

In neither case do the calculations agree with the twelve hundred and ninety or the thirteen hundred and thirty-five days of xii. 12, 13.

*Frederic William Farrar*

Entire volumes of tedious and wholly inconclusive comment have been written on these combinations, but by no reasonable supposition can we arrive at close accuracy. Strict chronological accuracy was difficult of attainment in those days, and was never a matter about which the Jews, in particular, greatly troubled themselves. We do not know either the terminus a quo from which or the terminus ad quem to which the writer reckoned. All that can be said is that it is perfectly impossible for us to identify or exactly equiparate the three and a half years (vii. 25), the "two thousand three hundred evening-morning" (viii. 14), the seventy-two weeks (ix. 26), and the twelve hundred and ninety days (xii. 11). Yet all those dates have this point of resemblance about them, that they very roughly indicate a space of about three and a half years (more or less) as the time during which the daily sacrifice should cease, and the Temple be polluted and desolate. [582]

Turning now to the dates, we know that Judas the Maccabee cleansed [583] ("justified" or "vindicated," viii. 14) the Temple on Kisleu 25 (December 25th, b.c. 165). If we reckon back two thousand three hundred full days from this date, it brings us to b.c. 171, in which Menelaus, who bribed Antiochus to appoint him high priest, robbed the Temple of some of its treasures, and procured the murder of the high priest Onias III. In this year Antiochus sacrificed a great sow on the altar of burnt offerings, and sprinkled its broth over the sacred building. These crimes provoked the revolt of the Jews, in which they killed Lysimachus, governor of Syria, and brought on themselves a heavy retribution. [584]

If we reckon back two thousand three hundred half-days, eleven hundred and fifty whole days, we must go back three years and seventy days, but we cannot tell what exact event the writer had in mind as the starting-point of his calculations. The actual time which elapsed from the final defilement of the Temple by Apollonius, the general of Antiochus, in b.c. 168, till its repurification was roughly three years. Perhaps, however--for all is uncertain--the writer reckoned from the earliest steps taken, or contemplated, by Antiochus for the suppression of Judaism. The purification of the Temple did not end the time of persecution, which was to continue, first, for one hundred and forty days longer, and then forty-five days more (xii. 11, 12). It is clear from this that the writer reckoned the beginning and the end of troubles from different epochs which we have no longer sufficient data to discover.

It must, however, be borne in mind that no minute certainty about the exact dates is attainable. Many authorities, from Prideaux [585] down to Schürer, [586] place the desecration of the Temple towards the close of b.c. 168. Kuenen sees reason to place it a year later. Our authorities for this period of history are numerous, but they are fragmentary, abbreviated, and often inexact. Fortunately, so far as we are able to see, no very important lesson is lost by our inability to furnish an undoubted or a rigidly scientific explanation of the minuter details.

Approximate Dates, as inferred by Cornill and Others [587]

b.c. Jeremiah's prophecy in Jer. xxv. 12 605 Jeremiah's prophecy in Jer. xxix. 10 594 Destruction of the Temple 586 or 588 Return of the Jewish exiles 537 Decree of Artaxerxes Longimanus (Ezra vii. 1) 458 Second decree (Neh. ii. 1) 445 Accession of Antiochus Epiphanes (August, Clinton) 175 Usurpation of the high-priesthood by Jason 175 Jason displaced by Menelaus 172(?) Murder of Onias III. (June) 171 Apollonius defiles the Temple 168 War of independence 166 Purification of the Temple by Judas the Maccabee (December) 165 Death of Antiochus 163

## Footnotes:

537. Ezra vi. 2; Neh. i. 1; Herod., v. 49; Polyb., v. 48. A supposed tomb of Daniel has long been revered at Shushan.

538. Pers., baru; Skr., bura; Assyr., birtu; Gk., baris. Comp. Æsch., Pers., 554; Herod., ii. 96.

539. Theodot., oubal; Ewald, Stromgebiet--a place where several rivers meet. The Jews prayed on river-banks (Acts xvi. 13), and Ezekiel had seen his vision on the Chebar (Ezek. i. 1, iii. 15, etc.); but this Ulai is here mentioned because the palace stood on its bank. Both the LXX. and Theodotion omit the word Ulai.

540. "Susianam ab Elymaide disterminat amnis Eulæus" (Plin., H. N., vi. 27).

541. See Loftus, Chaldæa, p. 346, who visited Shush in 1854; Herzog, R. E., s.v. "Susa." A tile was found by Layard at Kuyunjik representing a large city between two rivers. It probably represents Susa. Loftus says that the city stood between the Choaspes and the Kopratas (now the Dizful).

542. The Latin word for "to butt" is arietare, from aries, "a ram." It butts in three directions (comp. Dan. vii. 5). Its conquests in the East were apart from the writer's purpose. Croesus called the Persians hubristai, and Æschylus huperkompoi agan, Pers., 795 (Stuart). For horns as the symbol of strength see Amos vi. 13; Psalm lxxv. 5.

543. Unicorns are often represented on Assyrio-Babylonian sculptures.

544. 1 Macc. i. 1-3; Isa. xli. 2; Hosea xiii. 7, 8; Hab. i. 6.

545. Fury (chemah), "heat," "violence"--also of deadly venom (Deut. xxxii. 24).

546. A.V., "four notable horns"; but the word chazoth means literally "a sight of four"--i.e., "four other horns" (comp. ver. 8). Grätz reads acheroth; LXX., hetera tessara (comp. xi. 4).

547. Lit. "out of littleness."

548. Hatstsebî. Comp. xi. 45; Ezek. xx. 6; Jer. iii. 19; Zech. vii. 14; Psalm cvi. 24. The Rabbis make the word mean "the gazelle" for fanciful reasons (Taanîth, 69, a).

549. The physical image implies the war against the spiritual host of heaven, the holy people with their leaders. See 1 Macc. i. 24-30; 2 Macc. ix. 10. The Tsebaoth mean primarily the stars and angels, but next the Israelites (Exod. vii. 4).

550. So in the Hebrew margin (Q'rî), followed by Theodoret and Ewald; but in the text (Kethîbh) it is, "by him the daily was abolished"; and with this reading the Peshito and Vulgate agree. Hattamîd, "the daily" sacrifice; LXX., endelechismos; Numb. xxviii. 3; 1 Macc. i. 39, 45, iii. 45.

551. The Hebrew is here corrupt. The R.V. renders it, "And the host was given over to it, together with the continual burnt offering through transgression; and it cast down truth to the ground, and it did its pleasure and prospered."

552. Dan. viii. 13. I follow Ewald in this difficult verse, and with him Von Lengerke and Hitzig substantially agree; but the text is again corrupt, as appears also in the LXX. It would be useless here to enter into minute philological criticism. "How long?" (comp. Isa. vi. 11).

553. LXX., phelmoni; nescio quis (Vulg., viri).

554. Comp. for the expression xii. 6.

555. We find no names in Gen. xxxii. 30; Judg. xiii. 18. For the presence of angels at the vision comp. Zech. i. 9, 13, etc. Gabriel means "man of God." In Tobit iii. 17 Raphael is mentioned; in 2 Esdras v. 20, Uriel. This is the first mention of any angel's name. Michael is the highest archangel (Weber, System., 162 ff.), and in Jewish angelology Gabriel is identified with the Holy Spirit (Ruach Haqqodesh). As such he appears in the Qurân, ii. 91 (Behrmann).

556. Ben-Adam (Ezek. ii. 1).

557. Comp. Isa. xiv. 9: "All the great goats of the earth." A ram is a natural symbol for a chieftain.--Hom., Il., xiii. 491-493; Cic., De Div., i. 22; Plut., Sulla, c. 27; Jer. l. 8; Ezek. xxxiv. 17; Zech. x. 3, etc. See Vaux, Persia, p. 72.

558. "Strength of face" (LXX., anaides prosopo; Deut. xxviii. 50, etc.). "Understanding dark sentences" (Judg. xiv. 12; Ezek. xvii. 2: comp. v. 12).

559. The meaning is uncertain. It may mean (1) that he is only strong by God's permission; or (2) only by cunning, not by strength.

560. Comp. 2 Macc. iv. 9-15: "The priests had no courage to serve any more at the altar, but despising the Temple, and neglecting the sacrifices, hastened to be partakers of the unlawful allowance in the place of exercise ... not setting by the honours of their fathers, but liking the glory of the Grecians best of all."

561. Not merely the angelic prince of the host (Josh. v. 14), but God--"Lord of lords."

562. Comp. Esther i. 2. Though the vision took place under Babylon, the seer is strangely unconcerned with the present, or with the fate of the Babylonian Empire.

563. It is said to be the national emblem of Macedonia.

564. He is called "the King of Javan"--i.e., of the Ionians.

565. Isa. v. 26-29. Comp. 1 Macc. i. 3.

566. The fury of the he-goat represents the vengeance cherished by the Greeks against Persia since the old days of Marathon, Thermopylæ, Salamis, Platæa, and Mycale. Persia had invaded Greece under Mardonius (b.c. 492), under Datis and Artaphernes (b.c. 490), and under Xerxes (b.c. 480).

567. 1 Macc. vi. 1-16; 2 Macc. ix. 9; Job vii. 6; Prov. xxvi. 20.

568. So Diodorus Siculus (Exc. Vales., p. 293); Justin, xxxii. 2; Jer. in Dan., xi.; Strabo, xvi. 744.

569. Aurel. Vict., De Virr. Illustr., c. liv.

570. He conquered Egypt b.c. 170 (1 Macc. i. 17-20).

571. See 1 Macc. iii. 29-37.

572. Comp. Ezek. xx. 6, "which is the glory of all lands"; Psalm l. 2; Lam. ii. 15.

573. 1 Macc. i. 24-30. Dr. Pusey endeavours, without even the smallest success, to show that many things said of Antiochus in this book do not apply to him. The argument is based on the fact that the characteristics of Antiochus--who was a man of versatile impulses--are somewhat differently described by different authors; but here we have the aspect he presented to a few who regarded him as the deadliest of tyrants and persecutors.

574. See Hamburger, ii. 334 (s.v. "Haftara").

575. Comp. orge megale (1 Macc. i. 64; Isa. x. 5, 25, xxvi. 20; Jer. l. 5; Rom. ii. 5, etc.).

576. Comp. xi. 21.

577. Comp. ii. 34, xi. 45. Antiochus died of a long and terrible illness in Persia. Polybius (xxxi. 11) describes his sickness by the word daimonesas. Arrian (Syriaca, 66) says phthinon eteleutese. In 1 Macc. vi. 8-16 he dies confessing his sins against the Jews, but there is another story in 2 Macc. ix. 4-28.

578. Ver. 27, "I was gone" (or, "came to an end") "whole days." With this ekstasis comp. ii. 1, vii.

28; Exod. xxxiii. 20; Isa. vi. 5; Luke ix. 32; Acts ix. 4, etc. Comp. xii. 8; Jer. xxxii. 14, and (contra) Rev. xxii. 10.

579. In ver. 26 the R.V. renders "it belongeth to many days to come."

580. Comp. Gen. i. 5; 2 Cor. xi. 25. The word tamîd includes both the morning and evening sacrifice (Exod. xxix. 41). Pusey says (p. 220), "The shift of halving the days is one of those monsters which have disgraced scientific expositions 'of Hebrew.'" Yet this is the view of such scholars as Ewald, Hitzig, Kuenen, Cornill, Behrmann. The latter quotes a parallel: "vgl. im Hildebrandsliede sumaro ente wintro sehstie = 30 Jahr."

581. Matt. xxiv. 22.

582. "These five passages agree in making the final distress last during three years and a fraction: the only difference lies in the magnitude of the fraction" (Bevan, p. 127).

583. 1 Macc. iv. 41-56; 2 Macc. x. 1-5.

584. See on this period Diod. Sic., Fr., xxvi. 79; Liv., xlii. 29; Polyb., Legat., 71; Justin, xxxiv. 2; Jer., Comm. in Dan., xi. 22; Jahn, Hebr. Commonwealth, § xciv.; Prideaux, Connection, ii. 146.

585. Connection, ii. 188.

586. Gesch. d. V. Isr., i. 155.

587. Some of these dates are uncertain, and are variously given by different authorities.

# CHAPTER III - THE SEVENTY WEEKS

This chapter is occupied with the prayer of Daniel, and with the famous vision of the seventy weeks which has led to such interminable controversies, but of which the interpretation no longer admits of any certainty, because accurate data are not forthcoming.

The vision is dated in the first year of Darius, the son of Achashverosh, of the Median stock. [588] We have seen already that such a person is unknown to history. The date, however, accords well in this instance with the literary standpoint of the writer. The vision is sent as a consolation of perplexities suggested by the writer's study of the Scriptures; and nothing is more naturally imagined than the fact that the overthrow of the Babylonian Empire should have sent a Jewish exile to the study of the rolls of his holy prophets, to see what light they threw on the exile of his people.

He understood from "the books" the number of the years "whereof the word of the Lord came to Jeremiah the prophet for the accomplishing of the desolation of Jerusalem, even seventy years." [589] Such is the rendering of our Revisers, who here follow the A.V. ("I understood by books"), except that they rightly use the definite article (LXX., en tais bibloïs). Such too is the view of Hitzig. Mr. Bevan seems to have pointed out the real meaning of the passage, by referring not only to the Pentateuch generally, as helping to interpret the words of Jeremiah, but especially to Lev: xxvi. 18, 21, 24, 28. [590] It was there that the writer of Daniel discovered the method of interpreting the "seventy years" spoken of by Jeremiah. The Book of Leviticus had four times spoken of a sevenfold punishment--a punishment "seven times more" for the sins of Israel. Now this thought flashed upon the writer like a luminous principle. Daniel, in whose person he wrote, had arrived at the period at which the literal seventy years of Jeremiah were-- on some methods of computation--upon the eve of completion: the writer himself is living in the dreary times of Antiochus. Jeremiah had prophesied that the nations should serve the King of Babylon seventy years (Jer. xxv. 11), after which time God's vengeance should fall on Babylon; and again (Jer. xxix. 10, 11), that after seventy years the exiles should return to Palestine, since the thoughts of Jehovah towards them were thoughts of peace and not of evil, to give them a future and a hope.

The writer of Daniel saw, nearly four centuries later, that after all only a mere handful of the exiles, whom the Jews themselves compared to the chaff in comparison with the wheat, had returned from exile; that the years which followed had been cramped, dismal, and distressful; that the splendid hopes of the Messianic kingdom, which had glowed so brightly on the foreshortened horizon of Isaiah and so many of the prophets, had never yet been fulfilled; and that these anticipations never showed fewer signs of fulfilment than in the midst of the persecuting furies of Antiochus, supported by the widespread apostasies of the Hellenising Jews, and the vile ambition of such renegade high priests as Jason and Menelaus.

That the difficulty was felt is shown by the fact that the Epistle of Jeremy (ver. 2) extends the epoch of captivity to two hundred and ten years (7 × 30), whereas in Jer. xxix. 10 "seventy years" are distinctly mentioned. [591]

What was the explanation of this startling apparent discrepancy between "the sure word of prophecy" and the gloomy realities of history?

The writer saw it in a mystic or allegorical interpretation of Jeremiah's seventy years. The prophet could not (he thought) have meant seventy literal years. The number seven indeed played its usual mystic part in the epoch of punishment. Jerusalem had been taken b.c. 588; the first return of the exiles had been about b.c. 538. The Exile therefore had, from one point of view, lasted forty-nine years--i.e., 7 × 7. But even if seventy years were reckoned from the fourth year of Jehoiakim (b.c. 606?) to the decree of Cyrus (b.c. 536), and if these seventy years could be made out, still the hopes of the Jews were on the whole miserably frustrated. [592]

Surely then--so thought the writer--the real meaning of Jeremiah must have been misunderstood; or, at any rate, only partially understood. He must have meant, not "years," but weeks of years-- Sabbatical years. And that being so, the real Messianic fulfilments were not to come till four hundred and ninety years after the beginning of the Exile; and this clue he found in Leviticus. It was indeed a clue which lay ready to the hand of any one who was perplexed by Jeremiah's prophecy, for the word svv, hebdomas, means, not only the week, but also "seven," and the seventh year; [593] and the Chronicler had already declared that the reason why the land was to lie waste for seventy years was that "the land" was "to enjoy her Sabbaths"; in other words, that, as seventy Sabbatical years had been wholly neglected (and indeed unheard of) during the period of the monarchy--which he reckoned at four hundred and ninety years--therefore it was to enjoy those Sabbatical years continuously while there was no nation in Palestine to cultivate the soil. [594]

Another consideration may also have led the writer to his discovery. From the coronation of Saul to the captivity of Zachariah, reckoning the recorded length of each reign and giving seventeen years to Saul (since the "forty years" of Acts xiii. 21 is obviously untenable), gave four hundred and ninety years, or, as the Chronicler implies, seventy unkept Sabbatic years. The writer had no means for an accurate computation of the time which had elapsed since the destruction of the Temple. But as there were four hundred and eighty years and twelve high priests from Aaron to Ahimaaz, and four hundred and eighty years and twelve high priests from Azariah I. to Jozadak, who was priest at the beginning of the Captivity,--so there were twelve high priests from Jozadak to Onias III.; and this seemed to imply a lapse of some four hundred and ninety years in round numbers. [595]

The writer introduces what he thus regarded as a consoling and illuminating discovery in a striking manner. Daniel coming to understand for the first time the real meaning of Jeremiah's "seventy years," "set his face unto the Lord God, to seek prayer and supplication with fasting and sackcloth and ashes."[596]

His prayer is thus given:--

It falls into three strophes of equal length, and is "all alive and aglow with a pure fire of genuine repentance, humbly assured faith, and most intense petition." [597] At the same time it is the composition of a literary writer, for in phrase after phrase it recalls various passages of Scripture. [598] It closely resembles the prayers of Ezra and Nehemiah, and is so nearly parallel with the prayer of the apocryphal Baruch that Ewald regards it as an intentional abbreviation of Baruch ii. 1-iii. 39. Ezra, however, confesses the sins of his nation without asking for forgiveness; and Nehemiah likewise praises God for His mercies, but does not plead for pardon or deliverance; but Daniel entreats pardon for Israel and asks that his own prayer may be heard. The sins of Israel in vv. 5, 6, fall under the heads of wandering, lawlessness, rebellion, apostasy, and heedlessness. It is one of the marked tendencies of the later Jewish writings to degenerate into centos of phrases from the Law and the Prophets. It is noticeable that the name Jehovah occurs in this chapter of Daniel alone (in vv. 2, 4, 10, 13, 14, 20); and that he also addresses God as El, Elohim, and Adonai.

In the first division of the prayer (vv. 4-10) Daniel admits the faithfulness and mercy of God, and deplores the transgressions of his people from the highest to the lowest in all lands.

In the second part (vv. 11-14) he sees in these transgressions the fulfilment of "the curse and the oath" written in the Law of Moses, with special reference to Lev. xxvi. 14, 18, etc. In spite of all their sins and miseries they had not "stroked the face" of the Lord their God. [599]

The third section (vv. 15-19) appeals to God by His past mercies and deliverances to turn away His wrath and to pity the reproach of His people. Daniel entreats Jehovah to hear his prayer, to make His face shine on His desolated sanctuary, and to behold the horrible condition of His people and of His holy city. Not for their sakes is He asked to show His great compassion, but because His Name is called upon His city and His people. [600]

Such is the prayer; and while Daniel was still speaking, praying, confessing his own and Israel's sins, and interceding before Jehovah for the holy mountain--yea, even during the utterance of his prayer--the Gabriel of his former vision came speeding to him in full flight [601] at the time of the evening sacrifice. [602] The archangel tells him that no sooner had his supplication begun than he sped on his way, for Daniel is a dearly beloved one. [603] Therefore he bids him take heed to the word and to the vision:--

1. Seventy weeks are decreed upon thy people, and upon thy holy city [604] --
(a) to finish (or "restrain") the transgression;
(b) to make an end of (or "seal up," Theodot. sphragisai) sins; [605]
(g) to make reconciliation for (or "to purge away") iniquity;
(d) to bring in everlasting righteousness;
(e) to seal up vision and prophet (Heb., nabî; LXX., propheten); and
(z) to anoint the Most Holy (or "a Most Holy Place"; LXX., euphranai hagion hagion).

2. From the decree to restore Jerusalem unto the Anointed One (or "the Messiah"), the Prince, shall be seven weeks. For sixty-two weeks Jerusalem shall be built again with street and moat, though in troublous times. [606]

3. After these sixty-two weeks--
(a) an Anointed One shall be cut off, and shall have no help (?) (or "there shall be none belonging to him"); [607]
(b) the people of the prince that shall come shall destroy the city and the sanctuary;
(g) his end and the end shall be with a flood, and war, and desolation;
(d) for one week this alien prince shall make a covenant with many;
(e) for half of that week he shall cause the sacrifice and burnt offering to cease;
(z) and upon the wing of abominations [shall come] one that maketh desolate;
(e) and unto the destined consummation [wrath] shall be poured out upon a desolate one (?) (or

"the horrible one").

Much is uncertain in the text, and much in the translation; but the general outline of the declaration is clear in many of the chief particulars, so far as they are capable of historic verification. Instead of being a mystical prophecy which floated purely in the air, and in which a week stands (as Keil supposes) for unknown, heavenly, and symbolic periods--in which case no real information would have been vouchsafed--we are expressly told that it was intended to give the seer a definite, and even a minutely detailed, indication of the course of events.

Let us now take the revelation which is sent to the perplexed mourner step by step.

1. Seventy weeks are to elapse before any perfect deliverance is to come. We are nowhere expressly told that year-weeks are meant, but this is implied throughout, as the only possible means of explaining either the vision or the history. The conception, as we have seen, would come to readers quite naturally, since Shabbath meant in Hebrew, not only the seventh day of the week, but the seventh year in each week of years. Hence "seventy weeks" means four hundred and ninety years. [608] Not until the four hundred and ninety years--the seventy weeks of years--are ended will the time have come to complete the prophecy which only had a sort of initial and imperfect fulfilment in seventy actual years.

The precise meaning attached in the writer's mind to the events which are to mark the close of the four hundred and ninety years--namely, (a) the ending of transgression; (b) the sealing up of sins; (g) the atonement for iniquity; (d) the bringing in of everlasting righteousness; and (e) the sealing up of the vision and prophet (or prophecy [609])--cannot be further defined by us. It belongs to the Messianic hope. [610] It is the prophecy of a time which may have had some dim and partial analogies at the end of Jeremiah's seventy years, but which the writer thought would be more richly and finally fulfilled at the close of the Antiochian persecution. At the actual time of his writing that era of restitution had not yet begun.

But (z) another event, which would mark the close of the seventy year-weeks, was to be "the anointing of a Most Holy."

What does this mean?

Theodotion and the ancient translators render it "a Holy of Holies." But throughout the whole Old Testament "Holy of Holies" is never once used of a person, though it occurs forty-four times. [611] Keil and his school point to 1 Chron. xxiii. 13 as an exception; but "Nil agit exemptum quod litem lite resolvit."

In that verse some propose the rendering, "to sanctify, as most holy, Aaron and his sons for ever"; but both the A.V. and the R.V. render it, "Aaron was separated that he should sanctify the most holy things, he and his sons for ever." If there be a doubt as to the rendering, it is perverse to adopt the one which makes the usage differ from that of every other passage in Holy Writ.

Now the phrase "most holy" is most frequently applied to the great altar of sacrifice. [612] It is therefore natural to explain the present passage as a reference to the reanointing of the altar of sacrifice, primarily in the days of Zerubbabel, and secondarily by Judas Maccabæus after its profanation by Antiochus Epiphanes. [613]

2. But in the more detailed explanation which follows, the seventy year-weeks are divided into 7 + 62 + 1.

(a) At the end of the first seven week-years (after forty-nine years) Jerusalem should be restored, and there should be "an Anointed, a Prince." [614]

Some ancient Jewish commentators, followed by many eminent and learned moderns, [615] understand this Anointed One (Mashiach) and Prince (Nagîd) to be Cyrus; and that there can be no objection to conferring on him the exalted title of "Messiah" is amply proved by the fact that Isaiah himself bestows it upon him (Isa. xlv. 1).

Others, however, both ancient (like Eusebius) and modern (like Grätz), prefer to explain the term of the anointed Jewish high priest, Joshua, the son of Jozadak. For the term "Anointed" is given to the high priest in Lev. iv. 3, vi. 20; and Joshua's position among the exiles might well entitle him, as much as Zerubbabel himself, to the title of Nagîd or Prince. [616]

(b) After this restoration of Temple and priest, sixty-two weeks (i.e., four hundred and thirty-four years) are to elapse, during which Jerusalem is indeed to exist "with street and trench"--but in the straitness of the times. [617]

This, too, is clear and easy of comprehension. It exactly corresponds with the depressed condition of Jewish life during the Persian and early Grecian epochs, from the restoration of the Temple, b.c. 538, to b.c. 171, when the false high priest Menelaus robbed the Temple of its best treasures. This is indeed, so far as accurate chronology is concerned, an unverifiable period, for it only gives us three hundred and sixty-seven years instead of four hundred and thirty-four:--but of that I will speak later on. The punctuation of the original is disputed. Theodotion, the Vulgate, and our A.V. punctuate in ver. 25, "From the going forth of the commandment" ("decree" or "word") "that Jerusalem should be restored and rebuilt, unto an Anointed, a Prince, are seven weeks, and sixty-two weeks." Accepting this view, Von Lengerke and Hitzig make the seven weeks run parallel with the first seven in the sixty-two. This indeed makes the chronology a little more accurate, but introduces an unexplained and a fantastic element. Consequently most modern scholars, including even such writers as Keil, and our Revisers follow the Masoretic punctuation, and put the stop after the seven weeks, separating them entirely from the following sixty-two.

3. After the sixty-two weeks is to follow a series of events, and all these point quite distinctly to the epoch of Antiochus Epiphanes.

(a) Ver. 26.--An Anointed One [618] shall be cut off with all that belongs to him.

There can be no reasonable doubt that this is a reference to the deposition of the high priest Onias III., and his murder by Andronicus (b.c. 171). [619] This startling event is mentioned in 2 Macc. iv. 34, and by Josephus (Antt., XII. v. 1), and in Dan. xi. 22. It is added, "and no ... to him." [620] Perhaps the word "helper" (xi. 45) has fallen out of the text, as Grätz supposes; or the words may mean, "there is no [priest] for it [the people]." [621] The A.V. renders it, "but not for himself"; and in the margin, "and shall have nothing"; or, "and they [the Jews] shall be no more his people." The R.V. renders it, "and shall have nothing." I believe, with Dr. Joël, that in the Hebrew words veeyn lô there may be a sort of cryptographic allusion to the name Onias. [622]

(b) The people of the coming prince shall devastate the city and the sanctuary (translation uncertain).

This is an obvious allusion to the destruction and massacre inflicted on Jerusalem by Apollonius and the army of Antiochus Epiphanes (b.c. 167). Antiochus is called "the prince that shall come," because he was at Rome when Onias III. was murdered (b.c. 171). [623]

(g) "And until the end shall be a war, a sentence of desolation" (Hitzig, etc.); or, as Ewald renders it, "Until the end of the war is the decision concerning the horrible thing."

This alludes to the troubles of Jerusalem until the heaven-sent Nemesis fell on the profane enemy of the saints in the miserable death of Antiochus in Persia.

(d) But meanwhile he will have concluded a covenant with many for one week. [624]

In any case, whatever be the exact reading or rendering, this seems to be an allusion to the fact that Antiochus was confirmed in his perversity and led on to extremes in the enforcement of his attempt to Hellenise the Jews and to abolish their national religion by the existence of a large party of flagrant apostates. These were headed by their godless and usurping high priests, Jason and Menelaus. All this is strongly emphasised in the narrative of the Book of Maccabees. This attempted apostasy lasted for one week--i.e., for seven years; the years intended being probably the first seven of the reign of Antiochus, from b.c. 175 to b.c. 168. During this period he was aided by wicked men, who said, "Let us go and make a covenant with the heathen round about us; for since we departed from them we have had much sorrow." Antiochus "gave them licence to do after the ordinances of the heathen," so that they built a gymnasium at Jerusalem, obliterated the marks of circumcision, and were joined to the heathen (1 Macc. i. 10-15).

(e) For the half of this week (i.e., for three and a half years) the king abolished the sacrifice and the oblation or meat offering. [625]

This alludes to the suppression of the most distinctive ordinances of Jewish worship, and the general defilement of the Temple after the setting up of the heathen altar. The reckoning seems to be from the edict promulgated some months before December, 168, to December, 165, when Judas the Maccabee reconsecrated the Temple.

(z) The sentence which follows is surrounded with every kind of uncertainty.

The R.V. renders it, "And upon the wing [or, pinnacle] of abominations shall come [or, be] one that maketh desolate."

The A.V. has, "And for the overspreading of abominations" (or marg., "with the abominable armies") "he shall make it desolate." [626]

It is from the LXX. that we derive the famous expression, "abomination of desolation," referred to by St. Matthew (xxiv. 15: cf. Luke xxi. 20) in the last discourse of our Lord.

Other translations are as follows:--

Gesenius: "Desolation comes upon the horrible wing of a rebel's host."

Ewald: "And above will be the horrible wing of abominations."

Wieseler: "And a desolation shall arise against the wing of abominations."

Von Lengerke, Hengstenberg, Pusey: "And over the edge [or, pinnacle [627] ] of abominations [cometh] the desolator";--which they understand to mean that Antiochus will rule over the Temple defiled by heathen rites.

Kranichfeld and Keil: "And a destroyer comes on the wings of idolatrous abominations."

Kuenen, followed by others, boldly alters the text from ve'al k'naph, "and upon the wing," into ve'al kannô, "and instead thereof." [628]

"And instead thereof" (i.e., in the place of the sacrifice and meat offering) "there shall be abominations."

It is needless to weary the reader with further attempts at translation; but however uncertain may be the exact reading or rendering, few modern commentators doubt that the allusion is to the smaller heathen altar built by Antiochus above (i.e., on the summit) of the "Most Holy"--i.e., the great altar of burnt sacrifice--overshadowing it like "a wing" (kanaph), and causing desolations or abominations (shiqqootsîm). That this interpretation is the correct one can hardly be doubted in the light of the clearer references to "the abomination that maketh desolate" in xi. 31 and xii. 11. In favour of this we have the almost contemporary interpretation of the Book of Maccabees. The author of that history directly applies the phrase "the abomination of desolation" to the idol altar set up by Antiochus (1 Macc. i. 54, vi. 7).

(e) Lastly, the terrible drama shall end by an outpouring of wrath, and a sentence of judgment on "the desolation" (R.V.) or "the desolate" (A.V.).

This can only refer to the ultimate judgment with which Antiochus is menaced.

It will be seen then that, despite all uncertainties in the text, in the translation, and in the details, we have in these verses an unmistakably clear foreshadowing of the same persecuting king, and the same disastrous events, with which the mind of the writer is so predominantly haunted, and which are still more clearly indicated in the subsequent chapter.

Is it necessary, after an inquiry inevitably tedious, and of little or no apparently spiritual profit or significance, to enter further into the intolerably and interminably perplexed and voluminous discussions as to the beginning, the ending, and the exactitude of the seventy weeks? [629] Even St. Jerome gives, by way of specimen, nine different interpretations in his time, and comes to no decision of his own. After confessing that all the interpretations were individual guesswork, he leaves every reader to his own judgment, and adds: "Dicam quid unusquisque senserit, lectoris arbitrio derelinquens cujus expositionem sequi debeat."

I cannot think that the least advantage can be derived from doing so.

For scarcely any two leading commentators agree as to details;--or even as to any fixed principles by which they profess to determine the date at which the period of seventy weeks is to begin or is to end;--or whether they are to be reckoned continuously, or with arbitrary misplacements or discontinuations;--or even whether they are not purely symbolical, so as to have no reference to any chronological indications; [630] --or whether they are to be interpreted as referring to one special series of events, or to be regarded as having many fulfilments by "springing and germinal developments." The latter view is, however, distinctly tenable. It applies to all prophecies, inasmuch as history repeats itself; and our Lord referred to another "abomination of desolation" which in His days was yet to come. [631]

There is not even an initial agreement--or even the data as to an agreement--whether the "years" to be counted are solar years of three hundred and forty-three days, or lunar years, or "mystic" years, or Sabbath years of forty-nine years, or "indefinite" years; or where they are to begin and end, or in what fashion they are to be divided. All is chaos in the existing commentaries.

As for any received or authorised interpretation, there not only is none, but never has been. The Jewish interpreters differ from one another as widely as the Christian. Even in the days of the Fathers, the early exegetes were so hopelessly at sea in their methods of application that St. Jerome contents himself, just as I have done, with giving no opinion of his own. [632]

The attempt to refer the prophecy of the seventy weeks primarily or directly to the coming and death of Christ, or the desolation of the Temple by Titus, can only be supported by immense manipulations, and by hypotheses so crudely impossible that they would have made the prophecy practically meaningless both to Daniel and to any subsequent reader. The hopelessness of this attempt of the so-called "orthodox" interpreters is proved by their own fundamental disagreements. [633] It is finally discredited by the fact that neither our Lord, nor His Apostles, nor any of the earliest Christian writers once appealed to the evidence of this prophecy, which, on the principles of Hengstenberg and Dr. Pusey, would have been so decisive! If such a proof lay ready to their hand--a proof definite and chronological--why should they have deliberately passed it over, while they referred to other prophecies so much more general, and so much less precise in dates?

Of course it is open to any reader to adopt the view of Keil and others, that the prophecy is Messianic, but only typically and generally so.

On the other hand, it may be objected that the Antiochian hypothesis breaks down, because--though it does not pretend to resort to any of the wild, arbitrary, and I had almost said preposterous, hypotheses invented by those who approach the interpretation of the Book with a-priori and a-posteriori [634] assumptions--it still does not accurately correspond to ascertainable dates.

But to those who are guided in their exegesis, not by unnatural inventions, but by the great guiding principles of history and literature, this consideration presents no difficulty. Any exact accuracy of chronology would have been far more surprising in a writes of the Maccabean era than round numbers and vague computations. Precise computation is nowhere prevalent in the sacred books. The object of those books always is the conveyance of eternal, moral, and spiritual instruction. To such purely mundane and secondary matters as close reckoning of dates the Jewish writers show themselves manifestly indifferent. It is possible that, if we were able to ascertain the data which lay before the writer, his calculations might seem less divergent from exact numbers than they now appear. More than this we cannot affirm.

What was the date from which the writer calculated his seventy weeks? Was it from the date of Jeremiah's first prophecy (xxv. 12), b.c. 605? or his second prophecy (xxix. 10), eleven years later, b.c. 594? or from the destruction of the first Temple, b.c. 586? or, as some Jews thought, from the first year of "Darius the Mede"? or from the decree of Artaxerxes in Neh. ii. 1-9? or from the birth of Christ--the date assumed by Apollinaris? All these views have been adopted by various Rabbis and Fathers; but it is obvious that not one of them accords with the allusions of the narrative and prayer, except that which makes the destruction of the Temple the terminus a quo. In the confusion of historic reminiscences and the rarity of written documents, the writer may not have consciously distinguished this date (b.c. 588) from the date of Jeremiah's prophecy (b.c. 594). That there were differences of computation as regards Jeremiah's seventy years, even in the age of the Exile, is sufficiently shown by the different views as to their termination taken by the Chronicler (2 Chron. xxxvi. 22), who fixes it b.c. 536, and by Zechariah (Zech. i. 12), who fixes it about b.c. 519.

As to the terminus ad quem, it is open to any commentator to say that the prediction may point to many subsequent and analogous fulfilments; but no competent and serious reader who judges of these chapters by the chapters themselves and by their own repeated indications, can have one moment's hesitation in the conclusion that the writer is thinking mainly of the defilement of the Temple in the days of Antiochus Epiphanes, and its reconsecration (in round numbers) three and a half years later by Judas Maccabæus (December 25th, b.c. 164).

It is true that from b.c. 588 to b.c. 164 only gives us four hundred and twenty-four years, instead of four hundred and ninety years. How is this to be accounted for? Ewald supposes the loss of some passage in the text which would have explained the discrepancy; and that the text is in a somewhat chaotic condition is proved by its inherent philological difficulties, and by the appearance which it assumes in the Septuagint. The first seven weeks indeed, or forty-nine years, approximately correspond to the time between b.c. 588 (the destruction of the Temple) and b.c. 536 (the decree of Cyrus); but the following sixty-two weeks should give us four hundred and thirty-four years from the time of Cyrus to the cutting off of the Anointed One, by the murder of Onias III. in b.c. 171, whereas it only gives us three hundred and sixty-five. How are we to account for this miscalculation to the extent of at least sixty-five years?

Not one single suggestion has ever accounted for it, or has ever given exactitude to these computations on any tenable hypothesis. [635]

But Schürer has shown that exactly similar mistakes of reckoning are made even by so learned and industrious an historian as Josephus.

1. Thus in his Jewish War (VI. iv. 8) he says that there were six hundred and thirty-nine years between the second year of Cyrus and the destruction of the Temple by Titus (a.d. 70). Here is an error of more than thirty years.

2. In his Antiquities (XX. x.) he says that there were four hundred and thirty-four years between the Return from the Captivity (b.c. 536) and the reign of Antiochus Eupator (b.c. 164-162). Here is an error of more than sixty years.

3. In Antt., XIII. xi. 1, he reckons four hundred and eighty-one years between the Return from the Captivity and the time of Aristobulus (b.c. 105-104). Here is an error of some fifty years.

Again, the Jewish Hellenist Demetrius [636] reckons five hundred and seventy-three years from the Captivity of the Ten Tribes (b.c. 722) to the time of Ptolemy IV. (b.c. 222), which is seventy years too many. In other words, he makes as nearly as possible the same miscalculations as the writer of Daniel. This seems to show that there was some traditional error in the current chronology; and it cannot be overlooked that in ancient days the means for coming to accurate chronological conclusion were exceedingly imperfect. "Until the establishment of the Seleucid era (b.c. 312), the Jew had no fixed era whatsoever"; [637] and nothing is less astonishing than that an apocalyptic writer of the date of Epiphanes, basing his calculations on uncertain data to give an allegoric interpretation to an ancient prophecy, should have lacked the records which would alone have enabled him to calculate with exact precision. [638]

And, for the rest, we must say with Grotius, "Modicum nec prætor curat, nec propheta."

## Footnotes:

588. Achashverosh, Esther viii. 10; perhaps connected with Kshajârsha, "eye of the kingdom"

*The Expositor's Bible: The Book of Daniel*
(Corp. Inscr. Sem., ii. 125).

589. By "the books" is here probably meant the Thorah or Pentateuch, in which the writer discovered the key to the mystic meaning of the seventy years. It was not in the two sections of Jeremiah himself (called, according to Kimchi, Sepher Hamattanah and Sepher Hagalon) that he found this key. Jeremiah is here Yir'myah, as in Jer. xxvii.-xxix. See Jer. xxv. 11; Ezek. xxxvii. 21; Zech. i. 12. In the Epistle of Jeremy (ver. 2) the seventy years become seven generations (Chronos makros heos heppa geneon). See too Dillman's Enoch, p. 293.

590. Dan., p. 146. Comp. a similar usage in Aul. Gell., Noct. Att., iii. 10, "Se jam undecimam annorum hebdomadem ingressum esse"; and Arist., Polit., vii. 16.

591. See Fritzsche ad loc.; Ewald, Hist. of Isr., v. 140.

592. The writer of 2 Chron. xxxv. 17, 18, xxxvi. 21, 22, evidently supposed that seventy years had elapsed between the destruction of Jerusalem and the decree of Cyrus--which is only a period of fifty years. The Jewish writers were wholly without means for forming an accurate chronology. For instance, the Prophet Zechariah (i. 12), writing in the second year of Darius, son of Hystaspes (b.c. 520), thinks that the seventy years were only then concluding. In fact, the seventy years may be dated from b.c. 606 (fourth year of Jehoiakim); or b.c. 598 (Jehoiachin); or from the destruction of the Temple (b.c. 588); and may be supposed to end at the decree of Cyrus (b.c. 536); or the days of Zerubbabel (Ezra v. 1); or the decree of Darius (b.c. 518, Ezra vi. 1-12).

593. Lev. xxv. 2, 4.

594. 2 Chron. xxxvi. 21. See Bevan, p. 14.

595. See Cornill, Die Siebzig Jahrwochen Daniels, pp. 14-18.

596. The LXX. and Theodotion, with a later ritual bias, make the fasting a means towards the prayer: heurein proseuchen kai eleos en nesteiais.

597] Ewald, p. 278. The first part (vv. 4-14) is mainly occupied with confessions and acknowledgment of God's justice; the last part (vv. 15-19) with entreaty for pardon: confessio (vv. 4-14); consolatio (vv. 15-19) (Melancthon).

598. Besides the parallels which follow, it has phrases from Exod. xx. 6; Deut. vii. 21, x. 17; Jer. vii. 19; Psalm xliv. 16, cxxx. 4; 2 Chron. xxxvi. 15, 16. Mr. Deane (Bishop Ellicott's Commentary, p. 407) thus exhibits the details of special resemblances:-- Dan. ix. Ezra ix. Neh. ix. Baruch. Verse. Verse. Verse. 4 7 32 -- 5 7 33, 34 i. 11 6 7 32, 33 -- 7 6, 7 32, 33 i. 15-17 8 6, 7 33 -- 9 -- 17 -- 13 -- -- ii. 7 14 15 33 -- 15 -- 10 ii. 11 18 -- -- ii. 19 19 -- -- ii. 15

599. ix. 13 (Heb.). Comp. Exod. xxxii. 13; 1 Sam. xiii. 12; 1 Kings xiii. 6, etc.

600. Comp. Jer. xxxii. 17-23; Isa. lxiii. 11-16.

601. ix. 21. LXX., tachei pheromenos; Theodot., petomenos; Vulg., cito volans; A.V. and R.V., "being made to fly swiftly"; R.V. marg., "being sore wearied"; A.V. marg., "with weariness"; Von Lengerke, "being caused to hasten with haste." The verb elsewhere always connotes weariness. If that be the meaning here, it must refer to Daniel. If it here means "flying," it is the only passage in the Old Testament where angels fly; but see Isa. vi. 2; Psalm civ. 4, etc. The wings of angels are first mentioned in the Book of Enoch, lxi.; but see Rev. xiv. 6--cherubim and seraphim have wings.

602. In the time of the historic Daniel, as in the brief three and a half years of Antiochus, the tamîd had ceased.

603. ix. 23. Heb., eesh hamudôth; Vulg., vir desideriorum, "a man of desires"; Theodot., aner epithumion. Comp. x. 11, 19, and Jer. xxxi. 20, where "a pleasant child" is "a son of caresses"; and the "amor et deliciæ generis humani" applied to Titus; and the names David, Jedidiah, "beloved of Jehovah." The LXX. render the word eleeinos, "an object of pity."

604. Daniel used Shabuîm for weeks, not Shabuôth.

605. In ver. 24 the Q'rî and Kethîbh vary, as do also the versions.

606. For charoots, "moat" (Ewald), the A.V. has "wall," and in the marg. "breach" or "ditch." The word occurs for "ditches" in the Talmud. The text of the verse is uncertain.

607. Perhaps because neither Jason nor Menelaus (being apostate) were regarded as genuine successors of Onias III.

608. Numb. xiv. 34; Lev. xxvi. 34; Ezek. iv. 6.

609. Comp. Jer. xxxii. 11, 44.

610. See Isa. xlvi. 3, li. 5, liii. 11; Jer. xxiii. 6, etc.

611. For the anointing of the altar see Exod. xxix. 36, xl. 10; Lev. viii. 11; Numb. vii. 1. It would make no difference in the usus loquendi if neither Zerubbabel's nor Judas's altar was actually anointed.

612. It is only used thirteen times of the Debhîr, or Holiest Place.

613. 1 Macc. iv. 54.

614. Theodot., heos christou hegoumenou.

615. Saadia the Gaon, Rashi, Von Lengerke, Hitzig, Schürer, Cornill.

616. Hag. i. 1; Zech. iii. 1; Ezra iii. 2. Comp. Ecclus. xlv. 24; Jos., Antt., XII. iv. 2, prostates; and see Bevan, p. 156.

617. We see from Zech. i. 12, ii. 4, that even in the second year of Darius Hystaspis Jerusalem had neither walls nor gates; and even in the twentieth year of Artaxerxes the wall was still broken down and the gates burnt (Neh. i. 3).

618. LXX., apostathesetai chrisma kai ouk estai; Theodot., exolethreuthesetai chrisma kai ouk estin en auto; Aquil., ex. eleimmenos kai ouch huparxei auto.

619. See xi. 22. Von Lengerke, however, and others refer it to Seleucus Philopator, murdered by Heliodorus (b.c. 175).

620. Syr. Aquil., ouch huparxei auto; Theodot., kai ouk estin en auto; LXX., kai ouk estai; Vulg., "Et non erit ejus populus qui eum negaturus est." The A.V. "and not for himself" is untenable. It would have been vl' lv. See Pusey, p. 182, n.

621. Steudel, Hofmann. So too Cornill, p. 10: "Ein frommer Jude das Hoher Priesterthum mit Onias für erloschen ansah."

622. Comp. v'yn lv and chnyv (Joël, Notizen, p. 21).

623. Jos., Antt., XII. v. 4; 1 Macc. i. 29-40.

624. Here again the meaning is uncertain; and Grätz, altering the reading, thinks that it should be, "He shall abolish the covenant [with God] for the many"; or, "shall cause the many to transgress the covenant."

625. Dan. ix. 27. Heb., Zebach oo-minchah, "the bloody and unbloody offering."

626. The special allusion, whatever it may precisely mean, is found under three different designations: (i) In viii. 13 it is called happeshang shomeem; Gk., he hamartia eremoseos; Vulg., peccatum desolationis. (ii) In ix. 27 (comp. ix. 31) it is shiqqootsîm m'shomeem; Gk., bdelugma tes eremoseos; Vulg., abominatio desolationis. (iii) In xii. 11 it is shiqqoots shomeem; Gk., to bdelugma eremoseos; Vulg., abominatio in desolationem. Some traditional fact must (as Dr. Joël says) have underlain the rendering "of desolation" for "of the desolator." In xi. 31 Theodotion has ephanismenon, "of things done away with," for eremoseon. The expression with which the New Testament has made us so familiar is found also in 1 Macc. i. 51 (comp. 1 Macc. vi. 7): "they built the abomination of desolation upon the altar." There "the abomination" seems clearly to mean a smaller altar for heathen sacrifice to Zeus, built on the great altar of burnt offering. Perhaps the writer of Daniel took the word shomeem, "desolation," as a further definition of shiqqoots, "abomination," from popular speech; and it may have involved a reference to Lev. xxvi. 15-31: "If ye shall despise My statutes ... I will even appoint over you terror ... and I will make your cities waste, and appoint your sanctuaries unto desolation." The old Jewish exegetes referred the prophecy to Antiochus Epiphanes; Josephus and later writers applied it to the Romans. Old Christian expositors regarded it as Messianic; but even Jerome records nine different views of commentators, many of them involving the grossest historic errors and absurdities. Of Post-Reformation expositors down to the present century scarcely two agree in their interpretations. At the present day modern critics of any weight almost unanimously regard these chapters, in their primary significance, as vaticinia ex eventu, as some older Jewish and Christian exegetes had already done. Hitzig sarcastically says that the exegetes have here fallen into all sorts of shiqqootsîm themselves.

627. Comp. pterugion (Matt. iv. 5).

628. Kuenen, Hist. Crit. Onderzook., ii. 472.

629. Any one who thinks the inquiry likely to lead to any better results than those here indicated has only to wade through Zöckler's comment in Lange's Bibelwerk ("Ezekiel and Daniel," i. 186-221). It is hard to conceive any reading more intolerably wearisome; and at the close it leaves the reader in a state of more hopeless confusion than before. The discussion also occupies many pages of Pusey (pp. 162-231); but neither in his hypothesis nor any other are the dates exact. He can only say, "It were not of any account if we could not interpret these minor details. De minimis non curat lex." On the view that the seventy weeks were to end with the advent of Christ we ask: (1) Why do no two Christian interpreters agree about the interpretation? (2) Why did not the Apostles and Evangelists refer to so decisive an evidence?

630. On this, however, we may remark with Cornill, "Eine Apokalypse, deren apokalupseis unenthülbar sind, wäre ein nonsens, eine contradictio in adjecto" (Die Siebzig Jahrwochen, p. 3). The indication was obviously meant to be understood, and to the contemporaries of the writer, familiar with the minuter facts of the day, it probably was perfectly clear.

631. Luke ii. 25, 26, 38; Matt. xxiv. 15. Comp. 2 Thess. ii.; Jos., Antt., X. xxii. 7.

632. "Scio de hac quæstione ab eruditissimis viris varie disputatum et unumquemque pro captu ingenii sui dixisse quod senserat" (Jer. in Dan., ix.). In other words, there was not only no received interpretation in St. Jerome's day, but the comments of the Fathers were even then a chaos of arbitrary guesses.

633. Pusey makes out a table of the divergent interpretation of the commentators, whom, in his usual ecclesiastical fashion, he charitably classes together as "unbelievers," from Corrodi and Eichhorn down to Herzfeld. But quite as striking a table of divergencies might be drawn up of "orthodox"

commentators.

634. Thus Eusebius, without a shadow of any pretence at argument makes the last week mean seventy years! (Dem. Evan., viii.).

635. Jost (Gesch. d. Judenthums, i. 99) contents himself with speaking of "die Liebe zu prophetischer Auffassung der Vergangenheit, mit möglichst genauen Zahlenagaben, befriedigt, die uns leider nicht mehr verständlich erscheinen."

636. In Clem. Alex., Strom., i. 21.

637. Cornill, p. 14; Bevan, p. 54.

638. Schürer, Hist. of Jewish People, iii. 53, 54 (E. Tr.). This is also the view of Graf, Nöldeke, Cornill, and many others. In any case we must not be misled into an impossible style of exegesis of which Bleck says that "bei ihr alles möglich ist und alles für erlaubt gilt."

# CHAPTER IV - INTRODUCTION TO THE CONCLUDING VISION

The remaining section of the Book of Daniel forms but one vision, of which this chapter is the Introduction or Prologue.

Daniel is here spoken of in the third person.

It is dated in the third year of Cyrus (b.c. 535). [639] We have already been told that Daniel lived to see the first year of Cyrus (i. 21). This verse, if accepted historically, would show that at any rate Daniel did not return to Palestine with the exiles. Age, high rank, and opportunities of usefulness in the Persian Court may have combined to render his return undesirable for the interests of his people. The date--the last given in the life of the real or ideal Daniel--is perhaps here mentioned to account for the allusions which follow to the kingdom of Persia. But with the great and moving fortunes of the Jews after the accession of Cyrus, and even with the beginning of their new national life in Jerusalem, the author is scarcely at all concerned. He makes no mention of Zerubbabel the prince, nor of Joshua the priest, nor of the decree of Cyrus, nor of the rebuilding of the Temple; his whole concern is with the petty wars and diplomacy of the reign of Antiochus Epiphanes, of which an account is given, so minute as either to furnish us with historical materials unknown to any other historian, or else is difficult to reconcile with the history of that king's reign as it has been hitherto understood.

In this chapter, as in the two preceding, there are great difficulties and uncertainties about the exact significance of some of the verses, and textual emendations have been suggested. The readers of the Expositor's Bible would not, however, be interested in minute and dreary philological disquisitions, which have not the smallest moral significance, and lead to no certain result. The difficulties affect points of no doctrinal importance, and the greatest scholars have been unable to arrive at any agreement respecting them. Such difficulties will, therefore, merely be mentioned, and I shall content myself with furnishing what appears to be the best authenticated opinion.

The first and second verses are rendered partly by Ewald and partly by other scholars, "Truth is the revelation, and distress is great; [640] therefore understand thou the revelation, since there is understanding of it in the vision." The admonition calls attention to the importance of "the word," and the fact that reality lies beneath its enigmatic and apocalyptic form.

Daniel had been mourning for three full weeks, [641] during which he ate no dainty bread, [642] nor flesh, nor wine, nor did he anoint himself with oil. [643] But in the Passover month of Abib or Nisan, the first month of the year, and on the twenty-fourth day of that month, [644] he was seated on the bank of the great river, Hiddekel or Tigris, [645] when, lifting up his eyes, he saw a certain man clothed in fine linen like a Jewish priest, and his loins girded with gold of Uphaz. [646] His body was like chrysolite, [647] his face flashed like lightning, his eyes were like torches of fire, his arms and feet gleamed like polished brass, [648] and the sound of his words was as the sound of a deep murmur. [649] Daniel had companions with him; [650] they did not see the vision, but some supernatural terror fell upon them, and they fled to hide themselves. [651]

At this great spectacle his strength departed, and his brightness was changed to corruption; [652] and when the vision spoke he fell to the earth face downwards. A hand touched him, and partly raised him to the trembling support of his knees and the palms of his hands, [653] and a voice said to him, "Daniel, thou greatly beloved, [654] stand upright, and attend; for I am sent to thee." The seer was still trembling; but the voice bade him fear not, for his prayer had been heard, and for that reason this message had been sent to him. Gabriel's coming had, however, been delayed for three weeks, by his having to withstand for twenty days the prince of the kingdom of Persia. [655] The necessity of continuing the struggle was only removed by the arrival of Michael, one of the chief princes, [656] to help him, so that Gabriel was no longer needed [657] to resist the kings of Persia. [658] The vision was for many days, [659] and he had come to enable Daniel to understand it.

Once more Daniel was terrified, remained silent, and fixed his eyes on the ground, until one like the sons of men touched his lips, and then he spoke to apologise for his timidity and faintheartedness.

A third time the vision touched, strengthened, blessed him, and bade him be strong. "Knowest thou," the angel asked, "why I am come to thee? I must return to fight against the Prince of Persia, and while I am gone the Prince of Greece [Javan] will come. I will, however, tell thee what is announced in the writing of truth, the book of the decrees of heaven, though there is no one to help me against these hostile princes of Persia and Javan, except Michael your prince."

The difficulties of the chapter are, as we have said, of a kind that the expositor cannot easily remove. I have given what appears to be the general sense. The questions which the vision raises bear on matters of angelology, as to which all is purposely left vague and indeterminate, or which lie in a sphere wholly beyond our cognisance.

It may first be asked whether the splendid angel of the opening vision is also the being in the similitude of a man who thrice touches, encourages, and strengthens Daniel. It is perhaps simplest to suppose that this is the case, [660] and that the Great Prince tones down his overpowering glory to more familiar human semblance in order to dispel the terrors of the seer.

The general conception of the archangels as princes of the nations, and as contending with each other, belongs to the later developments of Hebrew opinion on such subjects. [661] Some have supposed that the "princes" of Persia and Javan to whom Gabriel and Michael are opposed are, not good angels, but demonic powers,--"the world-rulers of this darkness"--subordinate to the evil spirit whom St. Paul does not hesitate to call "the god of this world," and "the prince of the powers of the air." This is how they account for this "war in heaven," so that "the dragon and his angels" fight against "Michael and his angels." Be that as it may, this mode of presenting the guardians of the destinies of nations is one respecting which we have no further gleams of revelation to help us.

Ewald regards the two last verses of the chapter as a sort of soliloquy of the angel Gabriel with himself. He is pressed for time. His coming has already been delayed by the opposition of the guardian-power of the destinies of Persia. If Michael, the great archangel of the Hebrews, had not come to his aid, and (so to speak) for a time relieved guard, he would have been unable to come. But even the respite leaves him anxious. He seems to feel it almost necessary that he should at once return to contend against the Prince of Persia, and against a new adversary, the Prince of Javan, who is on his way to do mischief. Yet on the whole he will stay and enlighten Daniel before he takes his flight, although there is no one but Michael who aids him against these menacing princes. It is difficult to know whether this is meant to be ideal or real--whether it represents a struggle of angels against demons, or is merely meant for a sort of parable which represents the to-and-fro conflicting impulses which sway the destinies of earthly kingdoms. In any case the representation is too unique and too remote from earth to enable us to understand its spiritual meaning, beyond the bare indication that God sitteth above the water-floods and God remaineth a king for ever. It is another way of showing us that the heathen rage, and the people imagine a vain thing; that the kings of the earth set themselves and the rulers take counsel together; but that they can only accomplish what God's hand and God's counsel have predetermined to be done; and that when they attempt to overthrow the destinies which God has foreordained, "He that sitteth in the heavens shall laugh them to scorn, the Lord shall have them in derision." These, apart from all complications or developments of angelology or demonology, are the continuous lesson of the Word of God, and are confirmed by all that we decipher of His providence in His ways of dealing with nations and with men.

## *Footnotes:*

639. The LXX. date it in "the first year of Cyrus," perhaps an intentional alteration (i. 21). We see from Ezra, Nehemiah, and the latest of the Minor Prophets that there was scarcely even an attempt to restore the ruined walls of Jerusalem before b.c. 444.

640. Lit. "great warfare." It will be seen that the A.V. and R.V. and other renderings vary widely from this; but nothing very important depends on the variations. Instead of taking the verbs as imperatives addressed to the reader, Hitzig renders, "He heeded the word, and gave heed to the vision."

641. Lit. "weeks of days" (Gen. xli. 1; Deut. xxi. 13: "years of days").

642. "Bread of desires" is the opposite of "bread of affliction" in Deut. xvi. 3. Comp. Gen. xxvii. 25; Isa. xxii. 13, etc.

643. Comp. Amos vi. 6; Ruth iii. 3; 2 Sam. xii. 20, xiv. 2.

644. He fasted from Abib 3 to 24. The festival of the New Moon might prevent him from fasting on Abib 1, 2.

645. Hiddekel ("the rushing") occurs only in Gen. ii. 14. It is the Assyrian idiglat.

646. For the girdle see Ezek. xxiii. 15. Ewald (with the Vulg., Chald., and Syriac) regards Uphaz as a clerical error for Ophir (Psalm xlv. 9). LXX., Mophaz (Jer. x. 9, where alone it occurs). The LXX. omit it here. Vulg., Auro obrizo.

647. Heb., eben tarshish (Exod. xxviii. 2); Vulg., crysolithus; R.V. and A.V., "beryl" (Ezek. i. 16). Comp. Skr., tarisha, "the sea."

648. Theodot., ta skele; LXX., hoi podes (Rev. i. 15)--lit. "foot-hold"; Vulg., quæ deorsum sunt usque ad pedes.

649. This description of the vision follows Ezek. i. 16-24, ix. 2, and is followed in Rev. i. 13-15. The "deep murmur" is referred to the sound of the sea by St. John; A.V., "the voice of a multitude"; LXX., thorubos. Comp. Isa. xiii. 4; Ezek. xliii. 2.

650. Rashi guesses that they were Haggai, Zechariah, and Malachi.

651. Comp. Acts ix. 7, xxii. 11.

652. Comp. Hab. iii. 16; Dan. viii. 18.

653. Lit. "shook" or "caused me to tremble upon my knees and the palms of my hand."

654. x. 11. LXX., anthropos eleeinos ei; Tert., De Jejun., 7, "homo es miserabilis" (sc., "jejunando").

655. The protecting genius of Persia (Isa. xxiv. 21; Psalm lxxxii.; Ecclus. xvii. 17).

656. Michael, "who is like God" (Jude 9; Rev. xii. 7).

657. Heb., nôthartî. "I came off victorious," or "obtained the precedence" (Luther, Gesenius, etc.); "I was delayed" (Hitzig); "I was superfluous" (Ewald); "Was left over" (Zöckler); "I remained" (A.V.); "Was not needed" (R.V. marg.). The LXX. and Theodoret seem to follow another text.

658. LXX., "with the army of the king of the Persians."

659. Again the text and rendering are uncertain.

660. So Hitzig and Ewald. The view that they are distinct persons is taken by Zöckler, Von Lengerke, etc. Other guesses are that the "man clothed in linen" is the angel who called Gabriel (viii. 16); or Michael; or "the angel of the Covenant" (Vitringa); or Christ; or "he who letteth" (ho katechon, 2 Thess. ii. 7), whom Zöckler takes to be "the good principle of the world-power."

661. Thus in the LXX. (Dent, xxxii. 8) we read of angels of the nations. See too Isa. xlvi. 2; Jer. xlvi. 25. Comp. Baruch iv. 7; Ecclus. xvii. 17; Frankel, Vorstudien, p. 66.

# CHAPTER V - AN ENIGMATIC PROPHECY PASSING INTO DETAILS OF THE REIGN OF ANTIOCHUS EPIPHANES

*"Pone hæc dici de Antiocho, quid nocet religioni nostræ?"*--Hieron. ed. Vallars, v. 722.

If this chapter were indeed the utterance of a prophet in the Babylonian Exile, nearly four hundred years before the events--events of which many are of small comparative importance in the world's history--which are here so enigmatically and yet so minutely depicted, the revelation would be the most unique and perplexing in the whole Scriptures. It would represent a sudden and total departure from every method of God's providence and of God's manifestation of His will to the minds of the prophets. It would stand absolutely and abnormally alone as an abandonment of the limitations of all else which has ever been foretold. And it would then be still more surprising that such a reversal of the entire economy of prophecy should not only be so widely separated in tone from the high moral and spiritual lessons which it was the special glory of prophecy to inculcate, but should come to us entirely devoid of those decisive credentials which could alone suffice to command our conviction of its genuineness and authenticity. "We find in this chapter," says Mr. Bevan, "a complete survey of the history from the beginning of the Persian period down to the time of the author. Here, even more than in the earlier vision, we are able to perceive how the account gradually becomes more definite as it approaches the latter part of the reign of Antiochus Epiphanes, and how it then passes suddenly from the domain of historical facts to that of ideal expectations." [662] In recent days, when the force of truth has compelled so many earnest and honest thinkers to the acceptance of historic and literary criticism, the few scholars who are still able to maintain the traditional views about the Book of Daniel find themselves driven, like Zöckler and others, to admit that even if the Book of Daniel as a whole can be regarded as the production of the exiled seer five and a half centuries before Christ, yet in this chapter at any rate there must be large interpolations. [663]

There is here an unfortunate division of the chapters. The first verse of chap. xi. clearly belongs to the last verses of chap. x. It seems to furnish the reason why Gabriel could rely on the help of Michael, and therefore may delay for a few moments his return to the scene of conflict with the Prince of Persia and the coming King of Javan. Michael will for that brief period undertake the sole responsibility of maintaining the struggle, because Gabriel has put him under a direct obligation by special assistance which he rendered to him only a little while previously in the first year of the Median Darius. [664] Now, therefore, Gabriel, though in haste, will announce to Daniel the truth.

The announcement occupies five sections.

First Section (xi. 2-9).--Events from the rise of Alexander the Great (b.c. 336) to the death of Seleucus Nicator (b.c. 280). There are to be three kings of Persia after Cyrus (who is then reigning), of whom the third is to be the richest; [665] and "when he is waxed strong through his riches, he shall stir up the all [666] against the realm of Javan."

There were of course many more than four kings of Persia [667] : viz.--

b.c. Cyrus 536 Cambyses 529 Pseudo-Smerdis 522 Darius Hystaspis
521 Xerxes I.485 Artaxerxes I. (Longimanus) 464 Xerxes II.
425 Sogdianus425 Darius Nothus
424 Artaxerxes II. (Mnemon) 405 Artaxerxes III.359 Darius Codomannus 336

But probably the writer had no historic sources to which to refer, and only four Persian kings are prominent in Scripture--Cyrus, Darius, Xerxes, and Artaxerxes. Darius Codomannus is indeed mentioned in Neh. xii. 22, but might have easily been overlooked, and even confounded with another Darius in uncritical and unhistorical times. The rich fourth king who "stirs up the all against the realm of Grecia" might be meant for Artaxerxes I., but more probably refers to Xerxes (Achashverosh, or Ahasuerus), and his immense and ostentatious invasion of Greece (b.c. 480). His enormous wealth is dwelt upon by Herodotus. [668]

Ver. 3 (b.c. 336-323).--Then shall rise a mighty king (Alexander the Great), and shall rule with great dominion, and do according to his will. "Fortunam solus omnium mortalium in potestate habuit," says his historian, Quintus Curtius. [669]

Ver. 4 (b.c. 323).--But when he is at the apparent zenith of his strength his kingdom shall be broken, and shall not descend to any of his posterity, [670] but (b.c. 323-301) shall be for others, and shall ultimately (after the Battle of Ipsus, b.c. 301) be divided towards the four winds of heaven, into the kingdoms of Cassander (Greece and Macedonia), Ptolemy (Egypt, Coele-Syria, and Palestine), Lysimachus (Asia Minor), and Seleucus (Upper Asia).

Ver. 5.--Of these four kingdoms and their kings the vision is only concerned with two--the kings of the South [671] (i.e., the Lagidæ, or Egyptian Ptolemies, who sprang from Ptolemy Lagos), and the kings of the North (i.e., the Antiochian Seleucidæ). They alone are singled out because the Holy Land became a sphere of contentions between these rival dynasties. [672]

b.c. 306.--The King of the South (Ptolemy Soter, son of Lagos) shall be strong, and shall ultimately assume the title of Ptolemy I., King of Egypt.

But one of his princes or generals (Seleucus Nicator) shall be stronger, [673] and, asserting his independence, shall establish a great dominion over Northern Syria and Babylonia.

Ver. 6 (b.c. 250).--The vision then passes over the reign of Antiochus II. (Soter), and proceeds to say that "at the end of years" (i.e., some half-century later, b.c. 250) the kings of the North and South should form a matrimonial alliance. The daughter of the King of the South--the Egyptian Princess Berenice, daughter of Ptolemy II. (Philadelphus), should come to the King of the North (Antiochus Theos) to make an agreement. This agreement (marg., "equitable conditions") was that Antiochus Theos should divorce his wife and half-sister Laodice, and disinherit her children, and bequeath the throne to any future child of Berenice, who would thus unite the empires of the Ptolemies and the Seleucidæ. [674] Berenice took with her so vast a dowry that she was called "the dowry-bringer" (phernophoros). [675] Antiochus himself accompanied her as far as Pelusium (b.c. 247). But the compact ended in nothing but calamity. For, two years after, Ptolemy II. died, leaving an infant child by Berenice. But Berenice did "not retain the strength of her arm," [676] since the military force which accompanied her proved powerless for her protection; nor did Ptolemy II. abide, nor any support which he could render. On the contrary, there was overwhelming disaster. Berenice's escort, her father, her husband, all perished, and she herself and her infant child were murdered by her rival, Laodice (b.c. 246), in the sanctuary of Daphne, whither she had fled for refuge.

Ver. 7 (b.c. 285-247).--But the murder of Berenice shall be well avenged. For "out of a shoot from her roots" stood up one in his office, even her brother Ptolemy III. (Euergetes), who, unlike the effeminate Ptolemy II., did not entrust his wars to his generals, but came himself to his army. He shall completely conquer the King of the North (Seleucus II., Kallinikos, son of Antiochus Theos and Laodice), shall seize his fortress (Seleucia, the port of Antioch). [677]

Ver. 8 (b.c. 247).--In this campaign Ptolemy Euergetes, who earned the title of "Benefactor" by this vigorous invasion, shall not only win immense booty--four thousand talents of gold and many jewels, and forty thousand talents of silver--but shall also carry back with him to Egypt the two thousand five hundred molten images, [678] and idolatrous vessels, which, two hundred and eighty years before (b.c. 527), Cambyses had carried away from Egypt. [679]

After this success he will, for some years, refrain from attacking the Seleucid kings. [680]

Ver. 9 (b.c. 240).--Seleucus Kallinikos makes an attempt to avenge the shame and loss of the invasion of Syria by invading Egypt, but he returns to his own land totally foiled and defeated, for his fleet was destroyed by a storm. [681]

Second Section (vv. 10-19).--Events from the death of Ptolemy Euergetes (b.c. 247) to the death of Antiochus III. (the Great, b.c. 175). In the following verses, as Behrmann observes, there is a sort of dance of shadows, only fully intelligible to the initiated.

Ver. 10.--The sons of Seleucus Kallinikos were Seleucus III. (Keraunos, b.c. 227-224) and Antiochus the Great (b.c. 224-187). Keraunos only reigned two years, and in b.c. 224 his brother Antiochus III. succeeded him. Both kings assembled immense forces to avenge the insult of the Egyptian invasion, the defeat of their father, and the retention of their port and fortress of Seleucia. It was only sixteen miles from Antioch, and being still garrisoned by Egyptians, constituted a standing danger and insult to their capital city.

Ver. 11.--After twenty-seven years the port of Seleucia is wrested from the Egyptians by Antiochus the Great, and he so completely reverses the former successes of the King of the South as to conquer Syria as far as Gaza.

Ver. 12 (b.c. 217).--But at last the young Egyptian King, Ptolemy IV. (Philopator), is roused from his dissipation and effeminacy, advances to Raphia (southwest of Gaza) with a great army of twenty thousand foot, five thousand horse, and seventy-three elephants, and there, to his own immense self-exaltation, he inflicts a severe defeat on Antiochus, and "casts down tens of thousands." [682] Yet the victory is illusive, although it enables Ptolemy to annex Palestine to Egypt. For Ptolemy "shall not show himself strong," but shall, by his supineness, and by making a speedy peace, throw away all the fruits of his victory, while he returns to his past dissipation (b.c. 217-204). [683]

Ver. 13.--Twelve years later (b.c. 205) Ptolemy Philopator died, leaving an infant son, Ptolemy

Epiphanes. Antiochus, smarting from his defeat at Raphia, again assembled an army which was still greater than before (b.c. 203), and much war-material. In the intervening years he had won great victories in the East as far as India.

Ver. 14.--Antiochus shall be aided by the fact that many--including his ally Philip, King of Macedon, and various rebel-subjects of Ptolemy Epiphanes--stood up against the King of Egypt and wrested Phoenicia and Southern Syria from him. The Syrians were further strengthened by the assistance of the "children of the violent" among the Jews, "who shall lift themselves up to fulfil the vision of the oracle; [684] but they shall fall." We read in Josephus that many of the Jews helped Antiochus; [685] but the allusion to "the vision" is entirely obscure. Ewald supposes a reference to some prophecy no longer extant. Dr. Joël thinks that the Hellenising Jews may have referred to Isa. xix. in favour of the plans of Antiochus against Egypt.

Vv. 15, 16.--But however much any of the Jews may have helped Antiochus under the hope of ultimately regaining their independence, their hopes were frustrated. The Syrian King came, besieged, and took a well-fenced city--perhaps an allusion to the fact that he wrested Sidon from the Egyptians. After his great victory over the Egyptian general Scopas at Mount Panium (b.c. 198), the routed Egyptian forces, to the number of ten thousand, flung themselves into that city. [686] This campaign ruined the interests of Egypt in Palestine, "the glorious land." [687] Palestine now passed to Antiochus, who took possession "with destruction in his hand."

Ver. 17 (b.c. 198-195).--After this there shall again be an attempt at "equitable negotiations"; by which, however, Antiochus hoped to get final possession of Egypt and destroy it. He arranged a marriage between "a daughter of women"--his daughter Cleopatra--and Ptolemy Epiphanes. But this attempt also entirely failed.

Ver. 18 (b.c. 190).--Antiochus therefore "sets his face in another direction," and tries to conquer the islands and coasts of Asia Minor. But a captain--the Roman general, Lucius Cornelius Scipio Asiaticus--puts an end to the insolent scorn with which he had spoken of the Romans, and pays him back with equal scorn, [688] utterly defeating him in the great Battle of Magnesia (b.c. 190), and forcing him to ignominious terms.

Ver. 19 (b.c. 175).--Antiochus next turns his attention ("sets his face") to strengthen the fortresses of his own land in the east and west; but making an attempt to recruit his dissipated wealth by the plunder of the Temple of Belus in Elymais, "stumbles and falls, and is not found."

Third Section (vv. 20-27).--Events under Seleucus Philopator down to the first attempts of Antiochus Epiphanes against Egypt (b.c. 170).

Ver. 20.--Seleucus Philopator (b.c. 187-176) had a character the reverse of his father's. He was no restless seeker for glory, but desired wealth and quietness. [689] Among the Jews, however, he had a very evil reputation, for he sent a mere tax-collector, Heliodorus--"to pass through the glory of the kingdom." [690] He only reigned twelve years, and then was "broken"--i.e., murdered by Heliodorus, neither in anger nor in battle, but by poison administered by this "tax-collector." The versions all vary, but I feel little doubt that Dr. Joël is right when he sees in the curious phrase nogesh heder malkooth, "one that shall cause a raiser of taxes to pass over the kingdom"--of which neither Theodotion nor the Vulgate can make anything--a cryptographic allusion to the name Heliodorus; [691] and possibly the predicted fate may (by a change of subject) also refer to the fact that Heliodorus was checked, not by force, but by the vision in the Temple (2 Macc. v. 18, iii. 24-29). We find from 2 Macc. iv. 1 that Simeon, the governor of the Temple, charged Onias with a trick to terrify Heliodorus. This is a very probable view of what occurred. [692]

Ver. 21.--Seleucus Philopator died b.c. 175 without an heir. This made room for a contemptible person, a reprobate, who had no real claim to royal dignity, [693] being only a younger son of Antiochus the Great. He came by surprise, "in time of security," and obtained the kingdom by flatteries. [694]

Ver. 22.--Yet "the overflowing wings of Egypt" (or "the arms of a flood") "were swept away before him and broken; yea, and even a covenanted or allied prince." Some explain this of his nephew Ptolemy Philometor, others of Onias III., "the prince of the covenant"--i.e., the princely high priest, whom Antiochus displaced in favour of his brother, the apostate Joshua, who Græcised his name into Jason, as his brother Onias did in calling himself Menelaus. [695]

Ver. 23.--This mean king should prosper by deceit which he practised on all connected with him; [696] and though at first he had but few adherents, he should creep into power.

Ver. 24.--"In time of security shall he come, even upon the fattest places of the province." By this may be meant his invasions of Galilee and Lower Egypt. Acting unlike any of his royal predecessors, he shall lavishly scatter his gains and his booty among needy followers, [697] and shall plot to seize Pelusium, Naucratis, Alexandria, and other strongholds of Egypt for a time.

Ver. 25.--After this (b.c. 171) he shall, with a "great army," seriously undertake his first invasion of Egypt, and shall be met by his nephew Ptolemy Philometor with another immense army. In spite of this, the young Egyptian King shall fail through the treachery of his own courtiers. He shall be outwitted and treacherously undermined by his uncle Antiochus. Yes! even while his army is fighting, and many are being slain, the very men who "eat of his dainties," even his favourite and trusted courtiers Eulæus and Lenæus, will be devising his ruin, and his army shall be swept away.

Vv. 26, 27 (b.c. 174).--The Syrians and the Egyptian King, nephew and uncle, shall in nominal amity sit at one banquet, eating from one table; [698] but all the while they will be distrustfully plotting against each other and "speaking lies" to each other. Antiochus will pretend to ally himself with the young Philometor against his brother Ptolemy Euergetes II.--generally known by his derisive nickname as Ptolemy Physkon [699] --whom after eleven months the Alexandrians had proclaimed king. But all these plots and counter-plots should be of none effect, for the end was not yet.

Fourth Section (vv. 28-35).--Events between the first attack of Antiochus on Jerusalem (b.c. 170) and his plunder of the Temple to the first revolt of the Maccabees (b.c. 167).

Ver. 28 (b.c. 168).--Returning from Egypt with great plunder, Antiochus shall set himself against the Holy Covenant. He put down the usurping high priest Jason, who, with much slaughter, had driven out his rival usurper and brother, Menelaus. He massacred many Jews, and returned to Antioch enriched with golden vessels seized from the Temple. [700]

Ver. 29.--In b.c. 168 Antiochus again invaded Egypt, but with none of the former splendid results. For Ptolemy Philometor and Physkon had joined in sending an embassy to Rome to ask for help and protection. In consequence of this, "ships from Kittim" [701] --namely, the Roman fleet--came against him, bringing the Roman commissioner, Gaius Popilius Lænas. When Popilius met Antiochus, the king put out his hand to embrace him; but the Roman merely held out his tablets, and bade Antiochus read the Roman demand that he and his army should at once evacuate Egypt. "I will consult my friends on the subject," said Antiochus. Popilius, with infinite haughtiness and audacity, simply drew a circle in the sand with his vine-stick round the spot on which the king stood, and said, "You must decide before you step out of that circle." Antiochus stood amazed and humiliated; but seeing that there was no help for it, promised in despair to do all that the Romans demanded. [702]

Ver. 30.--Returning from Egypt in an indignant frame of mind, he turned his exasperation against the Jews and the Holy Covenant, especially extending his approval to those who apostatised from it.

Ver. 31.--Then (b.c. 168) shall come the climax of horror. Antiochus shall send troops to the Holy Land, who shall desecrate the sanctuary and fortress of the Temple, and abolish the daily sacrifice (Kisleu 15), and set up the abomination that maketh desolate. [703]

Ver. 32.--To carry out these ends the better, and with the express purpose of putting an end to the Jewish religion, he shall pervert or "make profane" by flatteries the renegades who are ready to apostatise from the faith of their fathers. But there shall be a faithful remnant who will bravely resist him to the uttermost. "The people who know their God will be valiant, and do great deeds."

Ver. 33.--To keep alive the national faith "wise teachers of the people shall instruct many," and will draw upon their own heads the fury of persecution, so that many shall fall by sword, and by flame, and by captivity, and by spoliation for many days.

Ver. 34.--But in the midst of this fierce onslaught of cruelty they shall be "holpen with a little help." There shall arise the sect of the Chasidîm, or "the Pious," bound together by Tugendbund to maintain the Laws which Israel received from Moses of old. [704] These good and faithful champions of a righteous cause will indeed be weakened by the false adherence of waverers and flatterers.

Ver. 35.--To purge the party from such spies and Laodiceans, the teachers, like the aged priest Mattathias at Modin, and the aged scribe Eleazar, will have to brave even martyrdom itself till the time of the end.

Fifth Section (vv. 36-45, b.c. 147-164).--Events from the beginning of the Maccabean rising to the death of Antiochus Epiphanes.

Ver. 36.--Antiochus will grow more arbitrary, more insolent, more blasphemous, from day to day, calling himself "God" (Theos) on his coins, and requiring all his subjects to be of his religion, [705] and so even more kindling against himself the wrath of the God of gods by his monstrous utterances, until the final doom has fallen.

Ver. 37.--He will, in fact, make himself his own god, paying no regard (by comparison) to his national or local god, the Olympian Zeus, nor to the Syrian deity, Tammuz-Adonis, "the desire of women." [706]

> "Tammuz came next behind,
> Whose yearly wound in Lebanon allured
> The Syrian damsels to lament his fate
> In amorous ditties all a summer day.
> While smooth Adonis from his native rock
> Ran purple to the sea--supposed with blood
> Of Tammuz yearly wounded. The love tale
> Infected Zion's daughters with like heat."

Ver. 38.--The only God to whom he shall pay marked respect shall be the Roman Jupiter, the god of the Capitol. To this god, to Jupiter Capitolinus, not to his own Zeus Olympios, the god of his Greek fathers, he shall erect a temple in his capital city of Antioch, and adorn it with gold and silver and precious stones. [707]

Ver. 39.--"And he shall deal with the strongest fortresses by the help of a strange god" [708] -- namely, the Capitoline Jupiter (Zeus Polieus)--and shall crowd the strongholds of Judæa with heathen colonists who worship the Tyrian Hercules (Melkart) and other idols; and to these heathen he shall give wealth and power.

Ver. 40.--But his evil career shall be cut short. Egypt, under the now-allied brothers Philometor and Physkon, shall unite to thrust at him. Antiochus will advance against them like a whirlwind, with many chariots and horsemen, and with the aid of a fleet.

Vv. 41-45.--In the course of his march he shall pass through Palestine, "the glorious land," [709] with disastrous injury; but Edom, Moab, and the bloom of the kingdom of Ammon shall escape his hand. Egypt, however, shall not escape. By the aid of the Libyans and Ethiopians who are in his train he shall plunder Egypt of its treasures. [710]

How far these events correspond to historic realities is uncertain. Jerome says that Antiochus invaded Egypt a third time in b.c. 165, the eleventh year of his reign; but there are no historic traces of such an invasion, and most certainly Antiochus towards the close of his reign, instead of being enriched with vast Egyptian spoils, was struggling with chronic lack of means. Some therefore suppose that the writer composed and published his enigmatic sketch of these events before the close of the reign of Antiochus, and that he is here passing from contemporary fact into a region of ideal anticipations which were never actually fulfilled.

Ver. 43 (b.c. 165).--In the midst of this devastating invasion of Egypt, Antiochus shall be troubled with disquieting rumours of troubles in Palestine and other realms of his kingdom. He will set out with utter fury to subjugate and to destroy, determining above all to suppress the heroic Maccabean revolt which had inflicted such humiliating disasters upon his generals, Seron, Apollonius, and Lysias. [711]

Ver. 45 (b.c. 164).--He shall indeed advance so far as to pitch his palatial tent [712] "between the sea and the mountain of the High Glory"; but he will come to a disastrous and an unassisted end. [713]

These latter events either do not correspond with the actual history, or cannot be verified. So far as we know Antiochus did not invade Egypt at all after b.c. 168. Still less did he advance from Egypt, or pitch his tent anywhere near Mount Zion. Nor did he die in Palestine, but in Persia (b.c. 165). The writer, indeed, strong in faith, anticipated, and rightly, that Antiochus would come to an ignominious and a sudden end--God shooting at him with a swift arrow, so that he should be wounded. But all accurate details seem suddenly to stop short with the doings in the fourth section, which may refer to the strange conduct of Antiochus in his great festival in honour of Jupiter at Daphne. Had the writer published his book after this date, he could not surely have failed to speak with triumphant gratitude and exultation of the heroic stand made by Judas Maccabæus and the splendid victories which restored hope and glory to the Holy Land. I therefore regard these verses as a description rather of ideal expectation than of historic facts.

We find notices of Antiochus in the Books of Maccabees, in Josephus, in St. Jerome's Commentary on Daniel, and in Appian's Syriaca. We should know more of him and be better able to explain some of the allusions in this chapter if the writings of the secular historians had not come down to us in so fragmentary a condition. The relevant portions of Callinicus Sutoricus, Diodorus Siculus, Polybius, Posidonius, Claudius, Theon, Andronicus, Alypius, and others are all lost--except a few fragments which we have at second or third hand. Porphyry introduced quotations from these authors into the twelfth book of his Arguments against the Christians; but we only know his book from Jerome's ex-parte quotations. Other Christian treatises, written in answer to Porphyry by Apollinaris, Eusebius, and Methodius, are only preserved in a few sentences by Nicetas and John of Damascus. The loss of Porphyry and Apollinarius is especially to be regretted. Jerome says that it was the extraordinarily minute correspondence of this chapter of Daniel with the history of Antiochus Epiphanes that led Porphyry to the conviction that it only contained vaticinia ex eventu. [714]

Antiochus died at Tabæ in Paratacæne on the frontiers of Persia and Babylonia about b.c. 163. The Jewish account of his remorseful deathbed may be read in 1 Macc. vi. 1-16: "He laid him down upon his bed, and fell sick for grief; and there he continued many days, for his grief was ever more and more; and he made account that he should die." He left a son, Antiochus Eupator, aged nine, under the charge of his flatterer and foster-brother Philip. [715] Recalling the wrongs he had inflicted on Judæa and Jerusalem, he said: "I perceive, therefore, that for this cause these troubles are come upon me; and, behold, I perish through great grief in a strange land."

## Footnotes:

662. Daniel, p. 162.
663. On this chapter see Smend, Zeitschr. für Alttest. Wissenschaft, v. 241.
664. Ewald, Prophets, v. 293 (E. Tr.).
665. Doubtless the three mentioned in Ezra iv. 5-7: Ahasuerus (Xerxes), Artaxerxes, and Darius.
666. Heb., Hakkôl--lit. "the all." There were probably Jews in his army (Jos. c. Ap., I. 22: comp. Herod., vii. 89).
667. Zöckler met the difficulty by calling the number four "symbolic," a method as easy as it is profoundly unsatisfactory.
668. Herod., iii. 96, iv. 27-29.
669. Q. Curt., X. v. 35.
670. See Grote, xii. 133. Alexander had a natural son, Herakles, and a posthumous son, Alexander, by Roxana. Both were murdered--the former by Polysperchon. See Diod. Sic., xix. 105, xx. 28; Pausan., ix. 7; Justin, xv. 2; Appian, Syr., c. 51.
671. The King of the Negeb (comp. Isa. xxx. 6, 7). LXX., Egypt. Ptolemy assumed the crown about b.c. 304.
672. See Stade, Gesch., ii. 276. Seleucus Nicator was deemed so important as to give his name to the Seleucid æra (1 Macc. i. 10, ete basileias Hellenon).
673. Diod. Sic., xix. 55-58; Appian, Syr., c. 52. He ruled from Phrygia to the Indus, and was the most powerful of the Diadochi. The word one is not expressed in the Hebrew: "but as for one of his captains." There may be some corruption of the text. Seleucus can scarcely be regarded as a vassal of Ptolemy, but of Alexander.
674. Appian, Syr., c. 55; Polyænus, viii. 50; Justin, xxvii. 1. See Herzberg, Gesch. v. Hellas u. Rom., i. 576. Dates are not certain.
675. Jer., ad loc. (Dan. xi. 6).
676. The rendering is much disputed, and some versions, punctuating differently, have, "his seed [i.e., his daughter] shall not stand." Every clause of the passage has received varying interpretations.
677. Polyb., v. 58.
678. Heb., nasîkîm; LXX., ta choneuta; Vulg., sculptilia.
679. Herodotus (iii. 47) says that he ordered the images to be burnt. On the Marmor Adulitanum, Ptolemy Euergetes boasted that he had united Mesopotamia, Babylonia, Persia, Susiana, Media, and all countries as far as Bactria under his rule. The inscription was seen at Adules by Cosmas Indicopleustes, and recorded by him (Wolf u. Buttmann, Museum, ii. 162).
680. R.V. marg., "He shall continue more years than the King of the North." Ptolemy Euergetes died b.c. 247; Seleucus Kallinikos, b.c. 225. It must be borne in mind that in almost every clause the readings, renderings, and interpolations vary. I give what seem to be the best attested and the most probable.
681. Justin, xxvii. 2.
682. See 3 Macc. i. 2-8; Jos., B. J., IV. xi. 5. The Seleucid army lost ten thousand foot, three hundred horse, five elephants, and more than four thousand prisoners (Polyb., v. 86).
683. Justin says (xxx. i): "Spoliasset regem Antiochum si fortunam virtute juvisset."
684. Chazôn, "the vision." Grätz renders it, "to cause the Law to totter"; but this cannot be right.
685. E.g., Joseph, and his son Hyrcanus.
686. Polyb., xxviii. 1; Liv., xxxiii. 19; Jos., Antt., XII. iii. 4. See St. Jerome, ad loc.
687. Vulg., terra inclyta; but in viii. 9, fortitudo.
688. In the choice of the Hebrew words qatsîn cher'patho lo, Dr. Joël suspects a sort of anagram of Cornelius Scipio, like the apo melitos for Ptolemy, and the hion Heras for Arsione in Lycophron; but the real meaning and rendering of the verse are highly uncertain.
689. Liv., xii. 19: "Otiosum, nullisque admodum rebus gestis nobilitatum."
690. 2 Macc. iii. 7 ff. The reading and rendering are very uncertain.
691. Joël, Notizen, p. 16.
692. See Jost, i. 110.
693. Vulg., vilissimus et indignus decore regio; R.V., "to whom they had not given the honour of a kingdom"; Ewald, "upon him shall not be set the splendour of a kingdom." Dr. Joël sees in nibzeh a contemptuous paronomasia on "Epiphanes" (Notizen, p. 17).
694. Dan. viii. 22; 2 Macc. v. 25.
695. Jos., Antt., XII. v. 1.
696. Jerome, amicitias simulans.
697. See 1 Macc. iii. 30; 1 Macc. i. 19; Polyb., xxvii. 17; Diod. Sic., xxx. 22. What his unkingly stratagems were we do not know.
698. Liv., xliv. 19: "Antiochus per honestam speciem majoris Ptolemæi reducendi in regnum," etc.
699. Or "Paunch." He was so called from his corpulence. Comp. the name Mirabeau, Tonneau.

*The Expositor's Bible: The Book of Daniel*

700. 2 Macc. v. 5-21; 1 Macc. i. 20-24.

701. The LXX. render this hexousi Rhomaioi. Comp. Numb. xxiv. 24; Jerome, Trieres et Romani. On "Chittim" (Gen. x. 4) see Jos., Antt., I. vi. 1.

702. Polyb., xxix. 11; Appian, Syr., 66; Liv., xlv. 12; Vell. Paterc., i. 10. According to Polybius (xxxi. 5), Epiphanes, by his crafty dissimulation, afterwards completely hoodwinked the ambassador Tiberius Gracchus.

703. 2 Macc. vi. 2. Our best available historical comments on this chapter are to be found in the two books of Maccabees.

704. 1 Macc. ii. 42, iii. 11, iv. 14, vii. 13; 2 Macc. xiv. 6.

705. Diod. Sic, xxxi. 1; 1 Macc. i. 43. Polybius (xxxi. 4) says "he committed sacrilege in most of the temples" (ta pleista ton hieron).

706. Jahn (Heb. Com., § xcii.) sees in the words "neither shall he regard the desire of women" an allusion to his exclusion of women from the festival at Daphne. Some explain the passage by his robbery of the Temple of Artemis or Aphrodite in Elymais (Polyb., xxxi. 11; Appian, Syr., 66; 1 Macc. vi. 1-4; 2 Macc. ix. 2). All is vague and uncertain.

707. Polyb., xxvi. 10; 2 Macc. vi. 2; Liv., xii. 20. The Hebrew Eloah Mauzzîm is understood by the LXX., Theodotion, the Vulgate, and Luther to be a god called Mauzzim (Maozeim). See Herzog, Real-Encycl., s.v. "Meussin." Cicero (c. Verr., vii. 72) calls the Capitol arx omnium nationum. The reader must judge for himself as to the validity of the remark of Pusey (p. 92), that "all this is alien from the character of Antiochus."

708. R.V. The translation is difficult and uncertain.

709. The LXX. here render this expression (which puzzled them, and which they omit in vv. 16, 41) by thelesis. Theodot., ten gen tou Sabaeim.

710. Ewald takes these for metaphoric designations of the Hellenising Jews. Some (e.g., Zöckler) understand these verses as a recapitulation of the exploits of Antiochus. The whole clause is surrounded by historic uncertainties.

711. The origin of the name Maccabee still remains uncertain. Some make it stand for the initials of the Hebrew words, "Who among the gods is like Jehovah?" in Exod. xv. 11; or of Mattathias Kohen (priest), Ben-Johanan (Biesenthal). Others make it mean "the Hammerer" (comp. Charles Martel). See Jost, i. 116; Prideaux, ii. 199 (so Grotius, and Buxtorf, De Abbreviaturis).

712. Vulg., Aphadno. The LXX. omit it. Theodot., Apadano; Symm., "his stable."

713. Porphyry says that "he pitched his tent in a place called Apedno, between the Tigris and Euphrates"; but even if these rivers should be called seas, they have nothing to do with the Holy Mountain. Apedno seems to be a mere guess from the word 'phdn, "palace" or "tent," in this verse. See Jer. xliii. 10 (Targum). Roland, however, quotes Procopius (De ædif. Justiniani, ii. 4) as authority for a place called Apadnas, near Amida, on the Tigris. See Pusey, p. 39.

714. Jahn, § xcv.

715. 2 Macc. ix.; Jos., Antt., XII. ix. 1, 2; Milman, Hist. of the Jews, ii. 9. Appian describes his lingering and wasting illness by the word phthinon (Syriaca, 66).

*Frederic William Farrar*

# CHAPTER VI - THE EPILOGUE

The twelfth chapter of the Book of Daniel serves as a general epilogue to the Book, and is as little free from difficulties in the interpretation of the details as are the other apocalyptic chapters.

The keynote, however, to their right understanding must be given in the words "At that time," with which the first verse opens. The words can only mean "the time" spoken of at the end of the last chapter, the days of that final effort of Antiochus against the holy people which ended in his miserable death.

"At that time," then--i.e., about the year b.c. 163--the guardian archangel of Israel, "Michael, the great prince which standeth for the children of thy people," shall stand up for their deliverance.

But this deliverance should resemble many similar crises in its general characteristics. It should not be immediate. On the contrary, it should be preceded by days of unparalleled disorder and catastrophe--"a time of trouble, such as never was since there was a nation even to that same time." We may, for instance, compare with this the similar prophecy of Jeremiah (xxx. 4-11): "And these are the words which the Lord spake concerning Israel and concerning Judah. For thus saith the Lord; We have heard a voice of trembling, of fear, and not of peace.... Alas! for that day is great, so that none is like it: it is even the time of Jacob's trouble; but he shall be saved out of it. And it shall come to pass in that day, saith the Lord, that I will burst thy bonds.... Therefore fear thou not, O Jacob, My servant, saith the Lord; neither be dismayed, O Israel.... For I am with thee, saith the Lord, to save thee. For I will make a full end of all the nations whither I have scattered thee, but I will not make a full end of thee: but I will correct thee with judgment, and will in nowise leave thee unpunished." [716]

The general conception is so common as even to have found expression in proverbs,--such as, "The night is darkest just before the dawn"; and, "When the tale of bricks is doubled, Moses comes." Some shadow of similar individual and historic experiences is found also among the Greeks and Romans. It lies in the expression theos apo mechanes, and also in the lines of Horace,--

"Nec Deus intersit nisi dignus vindice nodus
Intersit."

We find the same expectation in the apocryphal Book of Enoch, [717] and we find it reflected in the Revelation of St. John, [718] where he describes the devil as let loose and the powers of evil as gathering themselves together for the great final battle of Armageddon before the eternal triumph of the Lamb and of His saints. In Rabbinic literature there was a fixed anticipation that the coming of the Messiah must inevitably be preceded by "pangs" or "birth-throes," of which they spoke as the vly msych. [719] These views may partly have been founded on individual and national experience, but they were doubtless deepened by the vision of Zechariah (xii.).

"Behold, a day of the Lord cometh, when thy spoil shall be divided in the midst of thee. For I will gather all nations against Jerusalem to battle; and the city shall be taken, and the houses rifled, and the women ravished; and half of the people shall go forth into captivity, and the residue of the people shall not be cut off from the city. Then shall the Lord go forth, and fight against those nations, as when He fought in the day of battle. And His feet shall stand in that day upon the Mount of Olives.... And it shall come to pass in that day, that the light shall not be light, but cold and ice: [720] but it shall be one day that is known unto the Lord, not day and not night: but it shall come to pass that at evening time there shall be light." [721]

The anticipation of the saintly writer in the days of the early Maccabean uprising, while all the visible issues were still uncertain, and hopes as yet unaccomplished could only be read by the eyes of faith, were doubtless of a similar character. When he wrote Antiochus was already concentrating his powers to advance with the utmost wrath and fury against the Holy City. Humanly speaking, it was certain that the holy people could oppose no adequate resistance to his overwhelming forces, in which he would doubtless be able to enlist contingents from many allied nations. What could ensue but immeasurable calamity to the great majority? Michael indeed, their prince, should do his utmost for them; but it would not be in his power to avert the misery which should fall on the nation generally.

Nevertheless, they should not be given up to utter or to final destruction. As in the days of the Assyrians the name Shear-jashub, which Isaiah gave to one of his young sons, was a sign that "a remnant should be left," so now the seer is assured that "thy people shall be delivered"--at any rate "every one that shall be found written in the book."

"Written in the book"--for all true Israelites had ever believed that a book of record, a book of remembrance, lies ever open before the throne of God, in which are inscribed the names of God's faithful ones; as well as that awful book in which are written the evil deeds of men. [722] Thus in Exodus (xxxii. 33) we read, "Whosoever hath sinned against Me, him will I blot out of My book," which tells us of the records against the guilty. In Psalm lxix. 28 we read, "Let them be blotted out of the book of life, and not be written with the righteous." That book of the righteous is specially mentioned by Malachi: "Then they that feared the Lord spake one with another: and the Lord hearkened and heard, and a book of remembrance was written before him for them that feared the Lord and called upon His Name." [723] And St. John refers to these books at the close of the Apocalypse: "And I saw the dead, the great and the small, standing before the throne; and books were opened: and another book was opened, which is the book of life: and the dead were judged out of the things which were written in the books, according to their works.... And if any one was not found written in the book of life, he was cast in the lake of fire." [724]

In the next verse the seer is told that "many of them that sleep in the dust of the earth shall awake, some to everlasting life, and some to shame and everlasting abhorrence." [725]

It is easy to glide with insincere confidence over the difficulties of this verse, but they are many.

We should naturally connect it with what goes before as a reference to "that time"; and if so, it would seem as though--perhaps with reminiscences of the concluding prophecy of Isaiah [726] --the writer contemplated the end of all things and the final resurrection. [727] If so, we have here another instance to be added to the many in which this prophetic vision of the future passed from an immediate horizon to another infinitely distant. And if that be the correct interpretation, this is the earliest trace in Scripture of the doctrine of individual immortality. Of that doctrine there was no full knowledge--there were only dim prognostications or splendid hopes [728] --until in the fulness of the times Christ brought life and immortality to light. For instance, the passage here seems to be doubly limited. It does not refer to mankind in general, but only to members of the chosen people; and it is not said that all men shall rise again and receive according to their works, but only that "many" shall rise to receive the reward of true life, [729] while others shall live indeed, but only in everlasting shame.

To them that be wise--to "the teacher," [730] and to those that turn the many to "righteousness"--there is a further promise of glory. They "shall shine as the brightness of the firmament, and as the stars for ever and ever." There is here, perhaps, a reminiscence of Prov. iv. 18, 19, which tells us that the way of the wicked is as darkness, whereas the path of the just is as the shining light that shineth more and more unto the perfect day. Our Lord uses a similar metaphor in his explanation of the Parable of the Tares: "Then shall the righteous shine forth as the sun in the kingdom of their Father." [731] We find it once again in the last verse of the Epistle of St. James: "Let him know, that he who hath converted a sinner from the error of his way shall save a soul from death, and shall hide a multitude of sins."

But there is a further indication that the writer expected this final consummation to take place immediately after the troubles of the Antiochian assault; for he describes the angel Gabriel as bidding Daniel "to seal the Book even to the time of the end." Now as it is clear that the Book was, on any hypothesis, meant for the special consolation of the persecuted Jews under the cruel sway of the Seleucid King, and that then first could the Book be understood, the writer evidently looked for the fulfilment of his last prophecies at the termination of these troubles. This meaning is a little obscured by the rendering, "many shall run to and fro, and knowledge shall be increased." Ewald, Maurer, and Hitzig take the verse, which literally implies movement hither and thither, in the sense, "many shall peruse the Book." [732] Mr. Bevan, however, from a consideration of the Septuagint Version of the words, "and knowledge shall be increased"--for which they read, "and the land be filled with injustice"--thinks that the original rendering would be represented by, "many shall rush hither and thither, and many shall be the calamities." In other words, "the revelation must remain concealed, because there is to ensue a long period of commotion and distress." [733] If we have been convinced by the concurrence of many irresistible arguments that the Book of Daniel is the product of the epoch which it most minutely describes, we can only see in this verse a part of the literary form which the Book necessarily assumed as the vehicle for its lofty and encouraging messages.

The angel here ceases to speak, and Daniel, looking round him, becomes aware of the presence of two other celestial beings, one of whom stood on either bank of the river. [734] "And one said to the man clothed in linen, which was above the waters of the river, How long to the end of these wonders?" [735] There is a certain grandeur in the vagueness of description, but the speaker seems to be one of the two angels standing on either "lip" of the Tigris. "The man clothed in linen," who is hovering in the air above the waters of the river, is the same being who in viii. 16 wears "the appearance of a man," and calls "from between the banks of Ulai" to Gabriel that he is to make Daniel understand the vision. He is also, doubtless, the "one man clothed in linen, whose loins were girded with fine gold of Uphaz, his body like the beryl, his face as flashing lightning, his eyes as burning torches, and his voice like the deep murmur of a multitude," who strikes such terror into Daniel and his comrades in the vision of chap. x. 5, 6;--and though all is left uncertain, "the great prince Michael" may perhaps be intended.

The question how long these marvels were to last, and at what period the promised deliverance should be accomplished, was one which would naturally have the intensest interest to those Jews who--

in the agonies of the Antiochian persecution and at the beginning of the "little help" caused by the Maccabean uprising--read for the first time the fearful yet consolatory and inspiring pages of this new apocalypse. The answer is uttered with the most solemn emphasis. The Vision of the priest-like and gold-girded angel, as he hovers above the river-flood, "held up both his hands to heaven," and swears by Him that liveth for ever and ever that the continuance of the affliction shall be "for a time, times, and a half." So Abraham, to emphasise his refusal of any gain from the King of Sodom, says that he has "lifted up his hand unto the Lord, the Most High God, that he would not take from a thread to a shoe-latchet." And in Exod. vi. 8, when Jehovah says "I did swear," the expression means literally, "I lifted up My hand." [736] It is the natural attitude of calling God to witness; and in Rev. x. 5, 6, with a reminiscence of this passage, the angel is described as standing on the sea, and lifting his right hand to heaven to swear a mighty oath that there should be no longer delay.

The "time, two times, and half a time" of course means three years and a half, as in vii. 25. There can be little doubt that their commencement is the terminus a quo which is expressly mentioned in ver. 11: "the time that the daily sacrifice shall be taken away." We have already had occasion to see that three years, with a margin which seems to have been variously computed, does roughly correspond to the continuance of that total desecration of the Temple, and extinction of the most characteristic rites of Judaism, which preceded the death of Antiochus and the triumph of the national cause.

Unhappily the reading, rendering, and interpretation of the next clause of the angel's oath are obscure and uncertain. It is rendered in the R.V., "and when they have made an end of breaking in pieces the power of the holy people, all these things shall be finished." As to the exact translation many scholars differ. Von Lengerke translates it, "and when the scattering of a part of the holy people should come to an end, all this should be ended." The Septuagint Version is wholly unintelligible. Mr. Bevan suggests an alteration of the text which would imply that, "when the power of the shatterer of the holy people [i.e., Antiochus] should come to an end, all these things should be ended." This no doubt would not only give a very clear sense, but also one which would be identical with the prophecy of vii. 25, that "they [the times and the law] shall be given unto his hand until a time and times and half a time." [737] But if we stop short at the desperate and uncertain expedient of correcting the original Hebrew, we can only regard the words as implying (in the rendering of our A.V. and R.V.) that the persecution and suppression of Israel should proceed to their extremest limit, before the woe was ended; and of this we have already been assured. [738]

The writer, in the person of Daniel, is perplexed by the angel's oath, and yearns for further enlightenment and certitude. He makes an appeal to the vision with the question, "O my lord, what shall be the issue [or, latter end] of these things?" In answer he is simply bidden to go his way--i.e., to be at peace, and leave all these events to God, [739] since the words are shut up and sealed till the time of the end. In other words, the Daniel of the Persian Court could not possibly have attached any sort of definite meaning to minutely detailed predictions affecting the existence of empires which would not so much as emerge on the horizon till centuries after his death. These later visions could only be apprehended by the contemporaries of the events which they shadowed forth.

"Many," continued the angel, "shall purify themselves, and make themselves white, and be refined; but the wicked shall do wickedly: and none of the wicked shall understand; the teachers shall understand." [740]

The verse describes the deep divisions which should be cleft among the Jews by the intrigues and persecutions of Antiochus. Many would cling to their ancient and sacred institutions, and purified by pain, purged from all dross of worldliness and hypocrisy in the fires of affliction, like gold in the furnace, would form the new parties of the Chasidîm and the Anavîm, "the pious" and "the poor." They would be such men as the good high priest Onias, Mattathias of Modin and his glorious sons, the scribe Eleazar, and the seven dauntless martyrs, sons of the holy woman who unflinchingly watched their agonies and encouraged them to die rather than to apostatise. But the wicked would continue to be void of all understanding, and would go on still in their wickedness, like Jason and Menelaus, the renegade usurpers of the high-priesthood. These and the whole Hellenising party among the Jews, for the sake of gain, plunged into heathen practices, made abominable offerings to gods which were no gods, and in order to take part in the naked contests of the Greek gymnasium which they had set up in Jerusalem, deliberately attempted to obliterate the seal of circumcision which was the covenant pledge of their national consecration to the Jehovah of their fathers.

"And from the time that the continual burnt offering shall be taken away, and the abomination that maketh desolate set up, there shall be a thousand two hundred and ninety days."

If we suppose the year to consist of twelve months of thirty days, then (with the insertion of one intercalary month of thirty days) twelve hundred and ninety days is exactly three and a half years. We are, however, faced by the difficulty that the time from the desecration of the Temple till its reconsecration by Judas Maccabæus seems to have been exactly three years; [741] and if that view be founded on correct chronology, we can give no exact interpretation of the very specific date here furnished.

Our difficulties are increased by the next clause: "Blessed is he that waiteth, and cometh to the thousand three hundred and five and thirty days."

All that we can conjecture from this is that, at the close of twelve hundred and ninety days, by the writer's reckoning from the cessation of the daily burnt offering, and the erection of the heathen abomination which drove all faithful Jews from the Temple, up to the date of some marked deliverance, would be three and a half years, but that this deliverance would be less complete and beatific than another and later deliverance which would not occur till forty-five days later. [742]

Reams of conjecture and dubious history and imaginative chronology have been expended upon the effort to give any interpretation of these precise data which can pretend to the dignity of firm or scientific exegesis. Some, for instance, like Keil, regard the numbers as symbolical, which is equivalent to the admission that they have little or no bearing on literal history; others suppose that they are conjectural, having been penned before the actual termination of the Seleucid troubles. Others regard them as only intended to represent round numbers. Others again attempt to give them historic accuracy by various manipulations of the dates and events in and after the reign of Antiochus. Others relegate the entire vision to periods separated from the Maccabean age by hundreds of years, or even into the remotest future. And none of these commentators, by their researches and combinations, have succeeded in establishing the smallest approach to conviction in the minds of those who take the other views. There can be little doubt that to the writer and his readers the passage pointed either to very confident expectations or very well-understood realities; but for us the exact clue to the meaning is lost. All that can be said is that we should probably understand the dates better if our knowledge of the history of b.c. 165-164 was more complete. We are forced to content ourselves with their general significance. It is easy to record and to multiply elaborate guesses, and to deceive ourselves with the merest pretence and semblance of certainty. For reverent and severely honest inquiries it seems safer and wiser to study and profit by the great lessons and examples clearly set before us in the Book of Daniel, but, as regards many of its unsolved difficulties, to obey the wise exhortation of the Rabbis,--

"Learn to say, 'I do not know.'"

## *Footnotes:*

716. See too Joel ii. 2.
717. Enoch xc. 16.
718. Rev. xvi. 14, xix. 19.
719. Comp. Matt. xxiv. 6, 7, 21, 22.
720. Such is the reading of the LXX., Vulgate, Peshitta, Symmachus, etc.
721. Zech. xiv. 1-7.
722. Comp. vii. 10: "And the books were opened."
723. Mal. iii. 16.
724. Rev. xx. 12-15. Compare too Phil. iv. 3: "With Clement also, and the rest of my fellow-workers, whose names are in the book of life."
725. "Many sleepers in the land of dust" seems to mean the dead. Comp. Jer. li. 39; Psalm xxii. 29; 1 Thess. iv. 14; Acts vii. 60. For "shame" see Jer. xxiii. 40. The word for "abhorrence" only occurs in Isa. lxvi. 24. The allusion seems to be to the anastasis kriseos (John v. 29), the deuteros thanatos of Rev. xx. 14. Comp. Enoch xxii.
726. Isa. lxvi. 24.
727. It is certain that the doctrine of the Resurrection acquired more clearness in the minds of the Jews at and after the period of the Exile; nor is there anything derogatory to the workings of the Spirit of God which lighteth every man, in the view which supposes that they may have learnt something on this subject from the Babylonians and Assyrians. See the testimonies of St. Peter and St. Paul as to some degree of Ethnic inspiration in Acts x. 34, 35, xvii. 25-31.
728. See Ezek. xxxvii. 1-4.
729. Theodoret says that "many" means "all," as in Rom. v. 15; but there it is "the many," and the parallel is altogether defective. Hofmann gets over the difficulty by rendering it, "And in multitudes shall they arise." Many commentators explain it not of the final but of some partial resurrection. Few will now be content with such autocratic remarks as that of Calvin: "Multos hic ponit pro omnibus ut certum est."
730. Lit. "those that justify the multitude." Comp. Isa. liii. 11, and see Dan. xi. 33-35.
731. Matt. xiii. 43; 1 Cor. xv. 41; Rev. ii. 28.
732. Comp. Zech. iv. 10. This sense cannot be rigidly established.
733. He refers to 1 Macc. i. 9, which says of the successors of Alexander, kai eplethunan kaka en te ge.
734. Jerome guesses that they are the angels of Persia and Greece. The word hy'r lit. "the canal," is often used of the Nile.
735. The LXX. reads kai heipa, "and I said," making Daniel the speaker (so too the Vulgate); but

the form of the passage is so closely analogous to viii. 13, as to leave no doubt that here too "one saint is speaking to another saint."

736. Comp. Gen. xiv. 22; Deut. xxxii. 40, "For I lift up My hand unto heaven, and say, I live for ever"; Ezek. xx. 5, 6, etc.

737. Those who can rest content with such exegesis may explain this to imply that "the reign of antichrist will be divided into three periods--the first long, the second longer, the third shortest of all," just as the seventy weeks of chap. ix. are composed of $7 \times 62 \times 1$.

738. By way of comment see 1 Macc. v.; 2 Macc. viii.

739. Ik is encouraging, as in ver. 13.

740. Comp. Rev. xxii. 11.

741. The small heathen altar to Zeus was built by Antiochus upon the great altar of burnt offering on Kisleu 15, b.c. 168. The revolt of Mattathias and his seven sons began b.c. 167. Judas the Maccabee defeated the Syrian generals Apollonius, Seron, and Gorgias b.c. 166, and Lysias at Beth-sur in b.c. 165. He cleansed and rededicated the Temple on Kisleu 25, b.c. 165.

742. The "time, times, and a half." The 1,290 days, 1,335 days and the 1,150 days, and the 2,300 days of viii. 14 all agree in indicating three years with a shorter or longer fraction. It will be observed that in each case there is a certain reticence or vagueness as to the terminus ad quem. It is interesting to note that in Rev. xi. 2, 3, the period of 42 months = 1,260 days = $3\frac{1}{2}$ years of months of 30 days with no intercalary month.

www.ingramcontent.com/pod-product-compliance
Lightning Source LLC
Chambersburg PA
CBHW022107160426
43198CB00008B/380